REMAINDERS
OF THE DAY

REMAINDERS OF THE DAY

More Diaries from The Bookshop, Wigtown

SHAUN BYTHELL

PROFILE BOOKS

This paperback edition first published in 2023

First published in Great Britain in 2022 by
Profile Books Ltd
29 Cloth Fair
London
ECIA 7JQ
www.profilebooks.com

10 9 8 7 6 5 4 3 2 1

Typeset in Granjon by MacGuru Ltd
Printed and bound in Great Britain by
CPI Group (UK) Ltd, Croydon CRO 4YY

The moral right of the author has been asserted.

A CIP catalogue record for this book is available from the British Library.

ISBN 978 1 80081 243 7
eISBN 978 1 80081 244 4

FEBRUARY

Booksellers are constantly giving their patrons extraordinary
bargains. In London recently a copy of an early edition of Keats'
Poems, originally bought from a dealer for 2s was sold for £140,
and a first edition of Burns' Poems bought in Edinburgh for 1s 6d
brought £350.

R. M. Williamson, Bits from an Old Bookshop (John Menzies,
Edinburgh, 1904)

Williamson may well have been in a position to afford the luxury of
giving his patrons extraordinary bargains. Not all of us are. In part,
what he says remains true, though; provided you sell a book for
more than you've paid for it, what happens to it after that is largely
in the hands of fate. Buying and selling books prior to the advent
of the internet was a matter of judgement based on experience and
a pile of old auction catalogues and records. Now – if anything out
of the ordinary falls into my hands – I tend to go straight online to
see what other people are selling it for and base my price on that.

   When I discovered Williamson's beautifully produced book in
a box that I'd bought from a house in Edinburgh in the embers
of last year, I couldn't resist dipping into it straight away. My
first instinct was that he was so generous about his customers, so
passionate about his trade and so unfeasibly knowledgeable that
he must have been a fictional creation, but last year a customer
brought in a four-volume set of *The Works of Robert Burns*, calf-
bound and published in 1823. Slipped between the endpapers of
the first volume was a letter, in the original envelope, stamped and
dated Saturday 9 February 1929. It was a handwritten response
to an M. Maclean Esq., and in beautiful cursive handwriting it
explained that 'In reply to you, I can't think that your friend's
edition of Burns is of high value. If, however, he is in any doubt
he should write to Maggs Bros, Booksellers, London. Yours,

R. M. Williamson.' Williamson's astonishment that a Kilmarnock edition of Burns could have made £350 in the early twentieth century would doubtless have been surpassed had he known that a copy sold for £40,000 in 2012 through the Edinburgh saleroom Lyon & Turnbull.

Williamson's business no longer exists, but Maggs – to whom he commended Mr Maclean for further advice – is still a distinguished force in the world of rare and antiquarian bookselling; in 1932 they pulled off the bookseller's dream of buying (from the recently Soviet Russia) a Gutenberg Bible and a Codex Sinaiticus, or 'Sinai Bible' – a handwritten copy of one of only four texts of a Christian Bible in ancient Greek, written in the fifth century. Sixteen years prior, though, and among their most famous and unlikely acquisitions, was the purchase of Napoleon Bonaparte's penis, which they bought in 1916 from a source with highly credible provenance: direct descendants of Francesco Antommarchi, who conducted the autopsy on Napoleon's body. He had been bribed (it appears) by the emperor's chaplain to remove the member in a posthumous act of revenge for Napoleon's repeated mockery of his chaplain for impotence. I'm not entirely sure that it's possible to emasculate a corpse.

Maggs sold the dismembered member to an American antiquarian bookseller in 1924 for £400. According to that most reliable of sources, Wikipedia: 'A documentary that aired on Channel 4, *Dead Famous DNA*, described it as "very small" and measured it to be 1.5 inches (3.8 cm). It is not known what size it was during Napoleon's lifetime.' The item's current owner has allowed only ten people to see it, and has apparently been offered over $100,000 for it.

Shortly after I bought the shop in November 2001, a customer asked if I could help him sell a document which he claimed contained irrefutable evidence that Napoleon had been poisoned, and had not – as history records – died of stomach cancer while exiled in Saint Helena. There was a whiff of the mysterious, bordering on questionable, and possibly with a foot in the illegal, about how this man had come to be in possession of the document, so, following repeated requests from him for help in selling the letter, I made a series of unconvincing excuses explaining why I was unable to assist in the sale of something that he could very easily have consigned to an auction himself. This document must – if it was genuine – have been written by the same penectomist who removed Napoleon's manhood. I have no idea what happened to the letter; it may well be languishing in a box somewhere, hopefully to be discovered in time – like a lost Caravaggio or Leonardo – and possibly to change our interpretation of history.

Such are the potential treasures that you invite into your bookshop when you throw open the doors every morning.

Not tonight, Josephine.

FRIDAY, 5 FEBRUARY

Online orders: 4
Books found: 4

At 9.45 a.m. a pink-haired woman appeared in the shop, strode through the front room and up the stairs, clearly for Petra's belly-dancing class. Petra turned up ten minutes later, and the usual banging and thumping distracted the only customer to grace the shop all day. Petra – for the uninitiated – is an Austrian woman who is about my age (forty-six at the time of writing), with twin daughters, who decided to move to Galloway a few years ago. She's charming, leans heavily towards conspiracy theories and is convinced that she can make a living in this impoverished corner of Scotland by teaching belly-dancing, which she does in the drawing room above my shop. Every Friday she turns up, convinced that crowds will appear, only to discover that one or possibly two people have either the time or the inclination to attend. It never dampens her spirit, though, and she keeps at it, week after week.

My father dropped in at 11 a.m. with the curtains for the bothy, which mother had shortened. The bothy is the old garden-er's cottage behind the shop, which I've turned back into a small house, recently occupied by my good friend Carol-Ann. My father was en route to a funeral: that of Michael Dunlop, a local farmer. I hadn't heard that he'd died. As he was about to leave, Ben and

Katie (who are taking over The Ploughman, the local pub) called in to discuss advertising in the Spring Festival programme. I introduced them to my father, who told them that he'd heard about their enterprise and was looking forward to seeing what they're doing to the place. He asked them what sort of food they're going to have on the menu (my father is particularly old-fashioned in his tastes). Ben replied, 'Thirteen types of burger.' To which my father replied: 'I don't like burgers. What will there be for me to eat?' Ben, in his stereotypically French way, shrugged his shoulders and grunted. I suspect that this is not the last time he's going to have a conversation of this kind. Katie, Ben's German partner, clearly saw a potentially lost customer and chipped in with, 'We'll have chicken wings and other things for people who don't eat burgers,' which vaguely seemed to appease my father.

Caroline McQuistin, a young local woman who is training to be a photographer, arrived with her camera kit at about noon and spent the next three hours taking photographs for her university project. While she was here, a woman – well wrapped against the weather – appeared. I mistook her for Colette (who's running The Open Book – an Airbnb which gives people the opportunity to run a bookshop in Wigtown – this week) and began introducing her to Caroline. It turned out that it wasn't Colette at all. It was Jane from the festival office, who is married to Caroline's father's cousin, and who knows her very well. All rather embarrassing.

Courier collected twelve boxes of books to be taken to the Amazon warehouse in Dunfermline for sale through their Fulfilled By Amazon system at 4 p.m. FBA is another of Amazon's invidious schemes to lure booksellers into its dark world. Most of us struggle with storage space, so Amazon has created a system by which we – as booksellers – list and box our online stock, then ship it to one of their warehouses, from which they are sent to customers. There are (unsurprisingly) numerous charges, but at the moment it seems like it's almost worth doing. No doubt that will change as the charges and commissions creep up, as they always do.

Petra called at six o'clock and asked if I wanted a lift to the pub. The Ploughman – the pub in Wigtown – is closed, so we have to make the epic trek to Bladnoch (one mile) for the Friday night pub expedition. Picked up Colette from The Open Book en route. Colette is a woman who I would guess is a few years younger than I am. She has fitted into Wigtown as though she belongs here, and everyone seems to have embraced her. Callum, Tom and Willeke turned up at 7.30 p.m. Home at midnight, fell asleep on the sofa.

Till total £7
1 customer

SATURDAY, 6 FEBRUARY

Online orders: 3
Books found: 2

Colette came round to say goodbye at 11.30 a.m. Her week at The Open Book has ended. I have no idea if she had any customers, but she seems to have enjoyed herself; possibly because she didn't have any customers. I hope she'll return. She fitted into Wigtown like part of a jigsaw.

Telephone call at 11 a.m. from a woman in Maybole who has books to sell. I've arranged to meet her there next Thursday.

Message from Floraidh:

> Biffs. How's it going? I'm trying to get a flat for second year and I need a reference from an employer. Think you can string a few words together?

Floraidh worked in the shop one summer when she was a student. She was idle, obstreperous and treated the shop as her own empire. She was in many ways the perfect employee.

Peter and Heather Bestel arrived at noon to borrow the van. Peter's our local computer expert and can fix pretty much everything. Heather is more spiritual than practical, and their daughter Zoë is a superb musician who seems to have bridged her parents' two worlds.

Roseanne and Ian (dairy farmers from nearby Newton

Stewart) dropped in at lunchtime. Ian spotted a booklet about growing tobacco in Scotland which I'd recently bought and told a story about a local farmer who used to grow the stuff in his greenhouse thirty years ago. When the National Farmers' Union have their annual general meetings, they pick a different county every year and the local farmers supply produce for the dinner. When the AGM was in Wigtownshire three decades ago, the delegates were treated to cigars rolled from the locally produced tobacco. Ian bought the booklet.

At 4 p.m. a woman found a boxed set of Sue Grafton novels and asked if I'd break the set as she only wanted one of the books. I said no. She was furious.

Till total £49
5 customers

MONDAY, 8 FEBRUARY

Online orders: 6
Books found: 5

I came downstairs at 8 a.m. to what sounded like a child crying. I followed the sound into the Scottish room to find two cats fighting, locked tooth and claw together, hissing. I shouted at them but to no avail, so eventually I kicked them and they shot out of the cat flap in close succession, leaving clumps of fur all over the floor.

At 10 a.m. a tall man brought in a box of books of military history which he exchanged for a single book, a regimental history of the Gordon Highlanders priced at £12.50. As he left, a man who looked remarkably like the journalist John Sergeant brought in an overnight case full of books on racing cars, mostly rubbish. I gave him £5 for a few of them.

Shortly before lunchtime a short, squat man came in with an equally short, squat dog on a lead. Captain (the shop's cat) has worked out that he's fairly safe from dogs on leads, and has taken to taunting them by sitting – usually on the stairs – just out of range. He was almost caught out this morning, though, when the dog spotted him and went for him, dragging his owner with him. Captain was off like a shot, and the customer ended up flat on his back at the bottom of the stairs.

I've taken to writing a daily thought on a blackboard which I put outside the shop in the morning. This was today's:

Some people (so we're told) don't read. What unfulfilling lives they lead.

Peter and Heather returned the van in the evening. They're off to the south of England next week, taking Zoë on tour. Apparently she has about a dozen gigs lined up.

Telephone call from Emanuela telling me that she's coming to visit. I have to pick her up from Lockerbie on Wednesday at 5.20 p.m. Emanuela worked in the shop last year. She's Italian – Genovese – and was remarkably industrious, and equally eccentric.

Till total £134
4 customers

TUESDAY, 9 FEBRUARY

Online orders: 3
Books found: 3

Shortly after I opened the shop, I checked the Facebook page to discover that we're being followed by Tom Morton, doyen of BBC Radio Scotland.

Letter in today's post addressed to 'The Book Shop (The best in Scotland)'. No great surprise to discover that it was from a self-published author who wanted me to stock his book containing his ruminations on the Resurrection.

Sandy the tattooed pagan appeared at 11 a.m. He brought in a box of books. I gave him credit of £25. We discussed love and loss, subjects on which he is remarkably profound. Sandy is one of my few regular customers; he's covered in tattoos, and claims to be the most tattooed man in Scotland. I hate to write this for fear of him reading it, but he is charming, witty, intelligent and a captivating storyteller. I often wander through the shop to put books on shelves and find him surrounded by customers who are entranced by his stories.

An elderly couple brought in two boxes of books at lunchtime. The husband pointed at the smaller box and told me, conspiratorially, 'That's the good stuff', as though we were involved in some sort of narcotics exchange. As it turned out, they were nearly all unsellable, but I gave them £15 for the few that were reasonable.

Two Spanish women came in at 11.30 a.m. They're running The Open Book for two weeks.

Willeke came in to tell me that I'm invited to Margi's for supper tomorrow night. She and Sandy recognised one another from Andrew's SNP Burns Night supper, at which they'd been sitting beside each other and had a lengthy chat during which Sandy flirted quite expansively. Margi is a Dutch woman who moved to Wigtown a few years ago, and is a breath of fresh air – she's a retired Cambridge academic, and the epitome of *joie de vivre*, because of which she is invited to everything. Willeke is also a Dutch *immigrée* and equally full of life. Andrew and his partner, Nick, have a business in town – a bookshop and café – and frequently host events there, often with interesting speakers.

At one o'clock I left the shop and drove the 20 miles to Kings, the scrap merchant in Stranraer. Last year I replaced the old oil boiler with a more environmentally friendly woodchip boiler and, after considerable effort and time, managed to haul the oil boiler into the back of the van, putting my back out as I did so. I drove it to Kings to cash it in for scrap. It took two men to remove it from the van, and I was reasonably optimistic that I'd receive a handsome sum for it. They gave me £4.80, which I very much doubt would have covered the diesel cost of taking it there.

After I'd dropped the boiler off, I drove to a house in Stranraer to look at books. I was met by a woman in her seventies and her friend. I unwittingly stamped mud (from the scrapyard) all over the pristine carpet of the house. The books were upstairs and neatly laid out on a bed. Very good ornithology collection, with plenty of

New Naturalist monographs and obscure books on raptors, which I know will sell quickly online.

When Anna and I stopped in Biggar last Christmas on the way up to visit my sister in Edinburgh, we dropped in at the bookshop there, Atkinson-Pryce Books. While we were browsing, one of the people who work there – a woman called Sue – recognised Anna. They discussed *Three Things You Need to Know about Rockets* (Anna's book) at length. As we were leaving, she asked me if I

had any New Naturalists. At the time I only had a handful, but now that I've acquired this collection I will contact her and let her know.

Offered £375 for about 100 books. The woman called her son to check that he was happy with the price, but he didn't answer his phone, so – left in limbo – I upped the offer to £425, at which she shook my hand and accepted the offer. I wrote the cheque and packed the books into boxes. I only wanted about half of them, but she insisted that I took everything, including about sixty bound volumes of a magazine called *British Birds* which will, like the old oil boiler, end up being recycled.

Till total £20.50
3 customers

WEDNESDAY, 10 FEBRUARY

Online orders: 2
Books found: 2

Beautiful sunny day. Today's orders were both from the poetry section – very unusual to have any orders from the poetry section, let alone two on the same day.

At 9.45 a.m. my neighbour's mother appeared and told me that she's clearing her parents' house in Dumfries and has a lot of books to dispose of. She told me that they're in bundles, tied up with string. It's odd how often books come into the shop contained this way. There are, essentially, four or five ways people bring books to the shop. The most common is in cardboard boxes, and generally this means of conveyance will contain the best books, and in the best condition. Then there is the plastic laundry basket, which usually means that the books are the relics of a dead great-aunt's house, from which the best have been extracted and the laundry basket is the only means of transporting the books. It strikes me that it's the emotional equivalent of getting the great-aunt's coffin to the crematorium in an Uber. After that there is the Tesco bag, which invariably means the books are slasher crime fiction. Then there's the pile of bin liners, usually splitting, and brought in by a farmer, which inevitably contains dozens of copies of *People's Friends, Friendship Books* and poor-quality fiction from between the 1930s and 1950s without dust jackets and – if lucky – with spines hanging on by a thread. Finally, there's the bundled and tied with garden string category. This normally implies uniformity of size, which again, almost inevitably means that they are sets of Arthur Mee's *Children's Encyclopædias* or *Harmsworth's Home Educator*. The kind of thing you never want to see as a bookseller, particularly after the tightly pulled string has damaged the covers.

A woman in a kaftan came in at 11 a.m. and spent an hour telling me about how much she loves books, then left without buying anything.

Spotted a stone bollard with a hat propped on it on the way to the post office with the orders this morning. I can't decide whether it was phallic or tragic.

Telephoned the woman in Maybole whose books I'm looking at tomorrow to check whether she'd be OK with Caroline, the photographer, coming along to take photographs as part of her project. She was quite happy about it.

A customer walked into the kitchen at 1 p.m., while I was making a sandwich, and put the kettle on. He seemed strangely annoyed when I told him that it wasn't part of the shop and asked him to leave.

Drove to Lockerbie to pick up Emanuela (aka Granny, who used to work in the shop). Dropped in on Galloway Lodge jam factory in Gatehouse of Fleet en route to pick up some apple boxes for tomorrow's book deal. Galloway Lodge is owned by my friend Ruaridh, and the recycling bins are usually full of cardboard boxes which perfectly accommodate about twenty books each. Granny was waiting for me at Lockerbie, wearing a trench coat and smoking a cigarette, and looking every inch the film noir femme fatale. She looked at her watch and said, 'Where you been, you fucking bastard?' I was three minutes late.

Home just after the shop closed. Stayed up late chatting to Granny, who revealed that she's going to write a book called *Three Men and a Goat*. She's very fond of Jerome K. Jerome, but rather than three middle-class men gently rowing down the stream, this book is going to be about a homicidal woman who moves to Scotland and works in a second-hand bookshop. I'm not quite sure where the goat comes into it, but I suspect that there might be a sinister whiff of Aleister Crowley about it. At midnight she told me that it was her birthday, so we opened a bottle of champagne.

Till total £71.00
2 customers

THURSDAY, 11 FEBRUARY

Online orders: 2
Books found: 2

Email from Caroline, the photographer, to say that she no longer needs the extra material and won't be coming to Maybole.

Granny (Emanuela) opened the shop at 8.30 a.m. One of the benefits of having an industrious lodger is the luxury of an occasional lie-in. The sun shone for the few hours of daylight we are blessed with at this time of the year after the solstice.

Eliot appeared at 1 p.m. and told me that he was staying overnight, and hadn't had the time to call me to let me know he was coming. Eliot is the artistic director of Wigtown Book Festival. Despite my occasionally mocking words about him, I value his friendship extremely highly.

I left Granny listing the ornithology books from Tuesday's deal and drove to Maybole to look at books belonging to a retired policewoman with a very yappy dachshund. The books were pretty run-of-the-mill, and I gave her £60 for three boxes. The only interesting title was an auction catalogue of Charles Rennie Mackintosh furniture from 1975. Back to the shop at 5.15 in time to pay Janette, who has industriously cleaned the shop for over twenty years, and go to The Open Book with Eliot and Granny for a short talk about Catalan culture by the two sisters who are running the place for a fortnight. We came back afterwards, and I cooked paella (inspired by a Catalan cookbook which the sisters – Merce and Carme – had given me) and we ate my third-rate food and drank wine until 2 a.m.

Till total £43.50
4 customers

FRIDAY, 12 FEBRUARY

Online orders: 1
Books found: 1

Granny opened the shop while I caught up with emails in the office. It's barely worth opening at the moment, but as John – the previous owner – always said, if customers turn up and you're closed, they won't come back.

Eliot appeared at 9.30 a.m. for a cup of tea and a chat. He's up for a festival committee meeting.

Petra's belly-dancing class began at ten o'clock. I managed to convince Granny to join the other four people who turned up for it (a record number). She wasn't too keen, and told me that 'I am a piece of wood'. I assured her that she'd be fine.

Went to the post office to drop off the mail after lunch and spotted a copy of *New Scientist* with a story about mental health that I thought looked interesting. I picked it up and attempted to open it, only to discover that William had sellotaped it shut to prevent anyone from browsing without buying, as it appeared he had done with every magazine on the stand.

There was a letter in today's post addressed to 'The Book-monger, The Bookshop, The Booktown'.

Granny, after Petra's belly-dancing class, told me, 'My body not ready for this kind of exercise. I am young like a chimpanzee, but tired and sitting under the tree.'

Email in this morning, in relation to an inquiry about *British Dogs*:

I really need the book because I am translating Virginia

13

Woolf's *Flush*, who took much of the information about spaniels she uses in that book from this old book about dogs. I always like to check the original references in my translations. However, I am still undecided about buying it, because our money lost much of its value in relation to other currencies in the period of the last year. And there is the cost of sending it, which, I guess, is not little.

Anyway, if I decide to buy it I will do through the Abebooks site in the next few days. If I do not buy it will be just because it will cost me more than the money I will get from my translation of *Flush*.

Nicky has posted a competition on the shop's Facebook page, asking followers to come up with the best adaptation of a book title by changing just one letter.

Nicky here! for the last time (sob) … farewell friends, you've been fun company but it's time to move on to more sparkling things (Frosty Jack IS involved) so let's end with a competition! Hurrah! And with a nod to 'I'm Sorry I Haven't a Clue' change 1 LETTER ONLY on your favourite book title (Emanuela started us off with *Three Men and a Goat* which is close but has changed 3 letters, just as well) most 'likes' wins the last copy of *Tripe Advisor*!

Nicky, to my great sadness, has decided that her time at The Bookshop has come to its natural conclusion. She's found work managing woodland near Glenluce which is more her thing.

Went to the Bladnoch Inn after work with Eliot and Granny, where we met up with Callum, Petra and Merce and Carme – the two Catalan women who are running The Open Book. We all had fish and chips and far too much to drink. Merce accidentally knocked over a pint, and a tiny bit of beer ended up on Eliot's jumper. He made an enormous fuss about it. When it was his round, he just bought a pint for himself and nobody else. Callum and I ended up seriously out of pocket. Steve Dowling, local stove maker, asked me if I could produce a video to promote his new design of stove. I agreed to do it on Tuesday afternoon.

Eliot kicked his shoes off in the kitchen when we got home. I tripped over them just before I went to bed.

Till total £69.50
4 customers

SATURDAY, 13 FEBRUARY

Online orders: 5
Books found: 5

Granny opened the shop at 8.45 on a beautiful sunny day – the low winter sun streams into the south-facing shop at this time of year: a golden, warming light.

Decided to run a short-story competition with a prize of £100 credit in the shop. Announced it on Facebook and by the end of the day had several submissions. Judges are me, Aine McElwee and John Francis Ward. Every entry has to be exactly 500 words long.

Depressed Welsh man who telephones several times a year looking for early theology telephoned, this time looking for books about fishing villages of the Moray Firth.

Eliot left at noon, after an extensive search for his shoes, which he'd kicked off by the fridge last night.

Today's sign:

In the morning three young women each brought a pile of modern paperback fiction to sell. One lot included a copy of Anna's book, *Three Things You Need to Know about Rockets*. I suspect that they'd already read it, and that's why they were in Wigtown.

A tiny woman wearing patchwork trousers brought in ten boxes of books, mostly Victorian children's novels, which look beautiful but for which there appears to be little or no demand. I gave her £80 for a couple of boxes of reasonably interesting titles. She asked if I could take the lot as she's moving into a smaller house and doesn't have enough space. The shop is now bursting with boxes of books that people have dumped here and I don't want. I'll have to head to the recycling plant in Glasgow soon.

Went to the butcher's to pick up some pork to make a Taiwanese recipe that Alicia (who ran The Open Book for a week in January) had left for me. Bumped into a well-known local farmer's wife who has a reputation as a social climber. She was buying offal and looked sheepish (perhaps muttony) when I saw her basket. Returned to find a customer haggling with Granny over the price of a copy of *Galloway Gossip* that was already heavily reduced (£10 when it should have been £30 – he wanted it for £8). She refused to budge. He eventually coughed up the tenner.

Surprisingly busy day for the time of year, possibly due to the weather. Granny and I went for a short walk down to the salt marsh and along the old railway line in the dying light after I'd shut the shop.

Till total £213.47
12 customers

MONDAY, 15 FEBRUARY

Online orders: 3
Books found: 2

Granny opened the shop again on another cold, sunny day.

MY LOVE OF PIGEONS

**By Arnold Tonks,
1st Midland N.F.C. Angouleme 1978**

May I first thank the editor Mr Harbourne for giving me the opportunity to write a few words for the HOMING WORLD STUD BOOK.

I would like to tell you something of my loft and methods. My loft is 25ft long with four compartments. It has louvres and opening windows with wire mesh inside doors. The loft is cleaned out twice daily in the racing season, and once a day in the winter. It is scrubbed out on Saturdays, and is frequently sprayed with Vykil and Duramitex.

Arnold Tonks holding his M.N.F.C. winner

The Homing World STUD BOOK 1979

Found a book on pigeons in a box that I bought from a customer last year.

Two men came in at 9.15 and spent £60 and £30 on erotica and theology, respectively.

Telephone call at ten o'clock from a very well-spoken man. He was interested in a copy of *The Epic of Gilgamesh*, published in 1930, which we have listed online at £50. After much haggling we agreed on a price of £40. He insisted on next-day delivery, which added £27 to the cost (it's a very large book). When I told him this, he asked, 'What are you sending me, an elephant?'

The shop was busy all morning. After lunch a man asked me if I'd consider selling volume VII of a set of the first *Statistical Account of Scotland* (twenty-one volumes in all, published between 1791 and 1799, and compiled by Church of Scotland ministers from various parishes). I told him that there was no way any bookseller would break a mint twenty-one-volume set unless the customer was prepared to pay the full price for the set for a single volume. For some reason customers seem to think that we're happy to break sets to satisfy their demand for a single volume. This is a relatively new phenomenon. When I bought the shop, nobody expected to be able to extract a single volume from a complete set.

Janette came in at three o'clock to say that she couldn't clean the shop today because she has sciatica. I have considerable sympathy with her, having suffered from it myself.

Email from a couple who are running The Open Book to say that they'll be here at 4 p.m. tomorrow. I have no idea why they felt the need to tell me this.

Closed the shop and went into the garden to begin to clear up the debris following the rigours of winter; snowdrops are poking through and even the daffodils are starting to show signs of life.

Till total £412.14
23 customers

TUESDAY, 16 FEBRUARY

Online orders: 3
Books found: 3

Granny opened the shop. Filthy wet and windy day. When I appeared in the shop, she commented, 'What have happened to your hair?' I washed it last night, and admittedly it looked a bit frizzy, but Granny has the capacity to make you feel as though some sort of malign external force has imposed something horrendous upon you, whether it's when you wash your hair or buy a new item of clothing. Both of which, I admit, happen rarely in my life.

Sandy the tattooed pagan and his friend Elizabeth came in with a pile of walking sticks. Sandy has recently decided that he is a celebrity, although in what capacity I have yet to learn. He sits in the chair that faces the door to the shop and greets visitors like a king greeting his courtiers.

Tall Paul, the Cumbrian antique dealer who always buys sets of leather-bound books and demands discounts which border on the criminal, appeared at eleven o'clock and spotted the eight-volume set of Strickland's *Queens of England*. They came from a large house in the Borders from which I bought books last year, and which I had underpriced at £120. I reluctantly let them go for £100.

The Catalan sisters popped in to remind me that their Taste of Catalonia evening is in The Open Book at 5.30 p.m.

Granny served a customer who spent £80 and asked for a bag. She told him that bags cost 5p. He apparently became extremely agitated and said, 'Seriously? I've just spent £80 and you want to charge me for a bag?' When she told him that it was a legal requirement, he replied, 'I know, but you don't have to do it.'

Email from a book dealer called Larry with a request for a book. He requires an invoice and will pay by cheque on receipt. He and I must be among the few remaining people who trade this way.

A young American couple – Jessie and Derek – who wanted to run The Open Book but couldn't book it because it had already been taken for the week they wanted turned up at four o'clock. They'd emailed me and asked if they could work here instead, so I told them that they were welcome to stay and work in the shop. They're staying in one of my spare rooms. They're about to settle down and are taking the opportunity to do what, I suppose, is the equivalent of the Regency Grand Tour, although possibly without the portraits and pillaging of national treasures.

As the days grow slightly longer, the evening flight of the geese is a little later each day. Today, their return to the salt marsh was just as I closed the shop. A huge, honking skein flew over Wigtown as I was locking up.

Granny and I went to The Open Book for a poetry reading at 5.50 with Merce and Carme, then came back here with everyone for supper. I made sushi and Cullen skink.

After everyone had gone, I showed Derek and Jessie to the spare room and told them they could light the fire since it was a cold night. Ten minutes after they went to bed, Derek appeared in the kitchen to tell me that the room was full of smoke. Clearly a crow has built a nest in the chimney. We opened the windows to avoid asphyxiation, which unsurprisingly had the opposite effect of lighting the fire and reduced the temperature in their bedroom by several degrees.

Bed at 2 a.m.

Till total £289.39
17 customers

WEDNESDAY, 17 FEBRUARY

Online orders: 2
Books found: 2

Granny opened the shop. Jessie and Derek appeared at about 10.30, clearly thankful to have survived the night without freezing or suffering from smoke inhalation. They went for coffee at Reading Lasses, the bookshop and café opposite the shop. When they returned, I showed them to the Scottish room, where they tidied the shelves with a level of enthusiasm matched only by my own torpid indifference to the task.

Went to the RSPB office in Wigtown and asked if they wanted the bound copies of *British Birds* that I picked up from the ornithology deal in Stranraer. Paul, the boss, managed to find space for them, so I took four boxes over and left them there, relieved that the books are no longer my problem.

Found a book called *Greek Dances* in a box from the book deal in Maybole.

At about three, before it began to get dark, Granny and I

went for a walk in the Wood of Cree, a short drive away. For a young woman, she was remarkably slow. She complained incessantly about her knees. After yesterday's rain the thundering floods tumbling down the waterfalls of the narrow burn threw up a hazy mist that formed tiny rainbows over the deep pools, lit by the low winter sun, which poked its dying gaze through the leafless trees. We walked up the damp forest path – snowdrops struggling to push their heads through last autumn's fallen leaves around us.

After the shop closed, I went to The Open Book for a Skype meeting with Merce's English class, who – for reasons that still escape me – wanted to speak to me. Merce teaches a class of teenagers in a school near Barcelona. It's hard to imagine a more terrifying audience than a group of Catalan adolescents, but they were kind and interesting, and curious about Scotland and independence.

Granny cooked supper. It was utterly vile. Revolting dry home-made bread with some sort of burned vegetable on it for the first course; even more foul home-made bread with something which I have yet to identify for the second course. Man cannot live on bread alone, particularly if it's baked by Granny.

Till total £289.39
17 customers

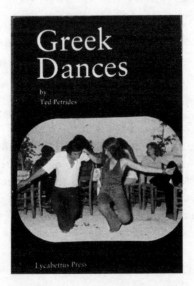

THURSDAY, 18 FEBRUARY

Online orders: 0
Books found: 0

At 9.30 a.m. I went to fill up the log basket from the woodshed and found two customers wandering through the garden. Must set some mantraps for these idiots.

Jessie spent the day sorting through the sci-fi section and putting it in alphabetical order. Derek went through the boxes for recycling to see if there was anything that might be sellable in The Open Book.

Good responses to Nicky's post about changing one letter of a book title to change the meaning.

Jan Archbold: 'A Suitable Bog'
Valentina Mears: 'Hilary Mantel's filthy habits in Bring up
    the Bogies'
Mike Connon: 'Cold Comfort Fart'
Valentina Mears: 'Helen Macdonald's K is for Hawk'
John Francis Ward: 'Finnegan's Cake'
The Bookshop: 'Under Milf Wood'
Jan Archbold: 'Roald Dahl's The Twats'
Aine McElwee: 'The Cunt for Red October'
The Bookshop: 'Watershit Down'
John Francis Ward: 'Charlotte's Wet'
Margi Watters: 'Of Lice and Men'
Adrian Waterworth: 'Or the time that the loo wouldn't
    flush properly – The Curious Incident of the Log in
    the Night-Time.'

After lunch I left Granny in charge and drove to Dumfries to look at a theological library belonging to a retired Church of Scotland minister. This sort of thing I would never have bothered with before, but with Amazon's FBA system it can be quickly scanned and listed (if it has a barcode) then boxed and sent to the Amazon warehouse. Very friendly couple made tea for me. Picked three boxes' worth and gave them £70.

On the way home I stopped at a bungalow in Crocketford

to look at another collection of books. The woman pointed at a pile of boxes and told me that she just wanted £40 for them. They were mainly run-of-the-mill young adult books, but in pristine condition so I agreed on the price and took them away. Home just before closing time.

Till total £84.49
7 customers

FRIDAY, 19 FEBRUARY

Online orders: 2
Books found: 2

Granny opened the shop at 8 a.m.

Two orders for New Naturalist bird books from the ornithology deal, both to the same customer. I emailed Sue from Atkinson-Pryce Books in Biggar, who I know is a collector of New Naturalists, and told her that I had acquired a good collection. She replied immediately with a list of the titles she's after. I told her that I have seven of them and gave her prices.

Harper Lee died today. Blackboard in tribute.

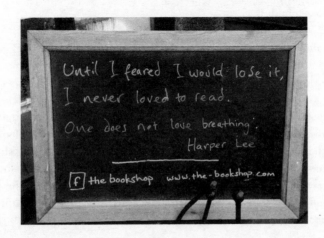

Loaded the van with the books for the recycling plant. Mole-Man was crossing the road towards the shop as I arrived. Mole-Man is one of the shop's few regular customers. He's small, silent and burrows through the shop on his occasional visits.

At 3 p.m. I left Jessie listing the theology books from yesterday on FBA and Derek packing books for the Random Book Club.

The Random Book Club is a subscription service which I set up after the financial crisis of 2008. Members receive a book a month, but have no idea what they will receive.

Meanwhile I drove to Barrhill (20 miles away) to look at a book collection. The woman had called me last week and assured me that the books were all leather-bound. They turned out to be *Reader's Digest* condensed books. I politely declined and drove home. Got back just before closing.

Emailed Aine and John Francis Ward about the short-story competition, and we all agreed on a winner.

Till total £189
8 customers

SATURDAY, 20 FEBRUARY

Online orders: 1
Books found: 1

Granny opened the shop. I wasn't feeling great, so I went back to bed at 9.30. At eleven o'clock Granny knocked on my bedroom door to tell me that Meredith, the student who is going to be here for work experience this summer, was downstairs, so I quickly dressed and came down to meet her and her parents, who had driven her here from Wakefield, in West Yorkshire, to have a look at the place. Meredith emailed me several months ago asking if she could work in the shop to gain experience in the book trade. I'm always happy to help people realise what penury lies before them should they consider a career in the book industry, so I readily agreed to her request.

After Meredith and her parents had left (apparently satisfied that I wasn't running a people-trafficking racket), I was going through a box of books that a customer had dropped in yesterday and found a book called The *Art of Growing Up for Girls Leaving School*. It contains some interesting material.

To give a Good Firm Bustline

Lie face down, with your hands just in front of your shoulders. Take a deep breath, straighten arms, raising your body from the floor, pressing it backwards. Throw your head back, keeping your thighs pressed to the ground.

THE ART OF GROWING UP

Constipation

Change of air can often cause slight constipation, so if you go away for your holidays, don't worry unduly, if all is not as usual. It is quite all right to take a pill on these odd occasions—most people have to. It is only if you have got into such a habit that you find you can never go without a pill, that you will have to take yourself in hand. A few simple bending and stretching exercises such as those given on pages 6 and 7 will help, but really bad chronic constipation calls for a doctor's advice.

Exercise

I have advised you earlier about taking exercise in the fresh air, but even if this is impossible, do take *some* form of exercise. Don't always spend your leisure hours in front of the television or at the cinema. Both viewing and cinema-going are very pleasant and commendable occupations, but, like other good things, should be indulged in with discrimination. Good taste in viewing or cinema-going are dealt with in a later chapter, but I feel I should stress here the point of not over-doing either. To watch till your eyes drop out, or to sit for hours cramped up in a stuffy cinema are not the best way of spending your leisure hours. Do not mistake me, I do not mean that I do not very heartily recommend your watching a good programme, going to see a first-class film, or indeed, curling up with a good book (what could be nicer?) but do not let your leisure hours always be spent in sedentary occupations. Even if the weather is bad for days, there is still table-tennis, dancing and skating to be done indoors.

If you really can't get enough physical exercise to keep you healthy, and if you are on the plump side, there are a few exercises on pages 6 and 7 which will help. They are not very violent and don't look very sensa... I do not do the

25

Derek and Jessie have almost finished tidying the Scottish room. I'm going to have to find something else for them to do. They're so polite and kind that I'm reluctant to ask them to do anything, particularly after I almost asphyxiated them.

While Granny was having lunch and I was covering in the shop, a customer bought two books to the counter: total £9. He gave me £10 and said, 'Keep the £1.' I was so taken aback by this unprecedented generosity that I gave him his £1 change and told him that I wish there were more like him.

Between Granny, Derek, Jessie and me, the house is so full of phones and laptops that there are cables everywhere. Every socket now looks like Medusa's head.

I heard on the news today that Umberto Eco has died. I read *The Name of the Rose* after I'd watched the film, with Sean Connery. According to the brief obituary on the radio this morning, Eco's father was one of thirteen children.

Derek, Granny and Jessie sorted the mail for the Random Book Club, which involved packing about 300 books and labelling them afterwards so that there was no way of knowing who was getting what. I listened in on their conversation as they were packing, and it was clear that neither Jessie nor Derek had a clue what Granny was saying.

In the afternoon I took Derek and Jessie on a tour of the Machars – the peninsula on which Wigtown is perched. We visited the pretty fishing village of the Isle of Whithorn, the ancient castle of Sorbie Tower and the Norman church at Cruggleton before darkness descended.

For the time of year, the shop was remarkably busy again.

Ben and Katie, who run the pub, came round for supper with Callum and a few other friends. Ben managed to offend almost everyone within moments of arriving. I cooked a leg of lamb from the butcher (£26), and Granny made a potato dish which had the texture of sawdust and the flavour of cardboard.

Till total £366.48
28 customers

MONDAY, 22 FEBRUARY

Online orders: 5
Books found: 4

Granny and I opened the shop. Clear, sunny day. Granny decided that she'd organise the poetry section alphabetically. I didn't have the heart to tell her that it is already organised alphabetically.

At 2 p.m. an elderly man brought in a very large box of art books, mainly ex-library. We try to avoid ex-library books, but I gave him £25 for the few that I thought I might have a chance of selling.

Email from Caroline, the photographer, about meeting at the recycling plant in Glasgow. She wants to take some photographs there as part of her degree. I replied, telling her that I intend to go there on Wednesday afternoon and could meet her there.

Jessie and Granny spent much of the day listing books to be sold on FBA.

A man appeared and introduced himself as Adrian, the winner of the shop's short-story competition, so I invited him and his wife,

Glenda, to have a browse and find £100 worth of books. The total came to £114. I waived the £14.

Just before closing the shop I came into the kitchen to find that Jessie and Derek had been shopping for tonight's supper. The Tesco bag on the table had an unfortunate crease.

Postman picked up the six bags for the Random Book Club at closing time, then Derek, Jessie, Granny and I went down to the old railway line for a walk. As we were passing the Martyr's Stake (where two women were drowned for their religious beliefs in 1685), a huge skein of geese flew in from behind us to their night-time sanctuary. Normally they land a good distance from the town and don't come closer until near-darkness, but they landed fairly close to the old railway line. My father is convinced – having witnessed the phenomenon every year for thirty years as a salt marsh farmer – that this is because they instinctively know that the wildfowling season ends on 20 February, so they don't need the protection of darkness, nor do they need to fly far out over the bay to avoid being shot by hidden guns.

Till total £50.50
4 customers

TUESDAY, 23 FEBRUARY

Online orders: 3
Books found: 3

Beautiful sunny day. Ice on the inside of the windows again. Granny opened the shop while I indulged in the luxury of a lie-in and began to read *A Touch of Mistletoe*, by Barbara Comyns, which had been recommended by my friend the journalist Lee Randall. It's published by Virago, a publisher for which I have enormous respect not only as a bookseller (their books fly off the shelves) but also as a reader. They share with few publishers that rarest of things in the publishing world: the capacity to find extraordinarily good writers combined with an appealing aesthetic – their beautiful green bindings with tastefully illustrated covers are a delight. By the second page I was enchanted – the narrator, talking about her grandfather, explains the absence of her grandmother: 'His wife had been mislaid years earlier.'

Joyce, who with her husband, Ian, runs The Old Bank

bookshop in Wigtown, called in at 10.30 to discuss changes to the Spring Festival programme. This is a small festival which the impecunious booksellers of Wigtown arrange around the May bank holiday. With a tiny budget, which is inversely matched by enormous enthusiasm, we manage to pull off something pretty decent every year, although it is a pale shadow of the Wigtown Book Festival in the autumn.

Jessie and Derek left at lunchtime to continue their Grand Tour. I was very sorry to see them go – they were exemplary house guests, and will doubtless charm their way around the rest of Europe.

Derek bought a beautifully bound edition of Byron's works with gilt edges and an unusual engraved pattern to the fore-edge as a wedding present for his friend in Chile. I didn't really want to sell it – it's rare to find such a beautiful book.

Ben and Katie came around looking for an angle grinder, so I took them to the shed, where Ben spotted my bikes and asked if he could buy one of them. I'm quite certain that he would have offered the meanest price that he thought he could get away with, so I said no and told him that I'd look out for one for him.

Drove to Bladnoch after lunch to look at a book collection

that had belonged to a man who was a fanatical cyclist. There were hundreds of books about cycling. His son was dealing with the estate. I recall seeing his father out on one of his many bikes regularly when I cycled the roads of the Machars, even up until last year. He died of a heart attack at the age of seventy-nine. I bought two bikes (one with Ben in mind) and about 200 books. The van is full of boxes and books from previous deals, so I'll empty it and collect the books and bikes tomorrow.

After work I went to The Ploughman to offer Ben the bike I'd bought with him in mind. I told him that he could have it for £100, the price I paid for it. In his typically contrarian manner he told me that he's now decided that he wants a mountain bike rather than a road bike, so I'm stuck with a bike I don't want.

My mother appeared at 4 p.m. with five wheels from the Alvis, a vintage car that my father is rebuilding. I made the mistake of telling my parents that I'm driving up to Glasgow tomorrow and offered to drop the wheels off at the shot-blasting factory in Kilmarnock. My father – since he retired – has occupied much of his time restoring old cars. He rebuilt a 1936 Bentley, and the Alvis he is now working on was built just after the war.

Till total £135.56
3 customers

WEDNESDAY, 24 FEBRUARY

Online orders: 2
Books found: 2

Granny opened the shop on a clear, cold, sunny day.

Set off at 11 a.m. for recycling plant in Glasgow to dump the books that people bring into the shop and which we can't sell, stopping en route at the shot-blasting factory in Kilmarnock (a pretty tricky place to find). Picked up Caroline from Shields Road subway station in Glasgow, conveniently close to the recycling plant. Went to the weighbridge and sat in the van while they weighed us in. Caroline seemed unduly excited when I explained what was going on. She took photographs as I dumped half a ton of books into three huge plastic containers, then weighed out and drove home, the low winter sun shining straight into the cab of the van as we headed south-west. Arrived just in time to find Granny locking up and my mother hovering around the front door of the shop with Sarah, the woman who's running The Open Book this week. She was about to take her to Baldoon Castle, the location of the true story behind *The Bride of Lammermoor* and Donizetti's opera *Lucia di Lammermoor*, a subject about which my mother has written a short book. Said a brief hello, then drove to Airyolland, a farm near to Stranraer, to drop Caroline home.

Back to the shop at about 7 p.m.

Till total £28.50
3 customers

THURSDAY, 25 FEBRUARY

Online orders: 3
Books found: 2

Granny opened the shop and I started sorting through the bicycle books but was interrupted by a couple who came in at 10.30 a.m. and spent an hour raking through the boxes before leaving, muttering, 'There's too much choice.'

Granny and I packed the last of the random books for this month's mail-out, which is now five days overdue.

While Granny was having a lunch break, I sold a book about how to grow marijuana to an elderly local man who once subjected me to a lengthy lecture for drinking a beer with some friends during the ceilidh at the book festival. He had a whiff of contrition about him when he gave me a £5 note. Not sure whether he's eating humble pie or possibly hash brownies.

After lunch I began the process of closing down an FBA shipment and entering the data for delivery. This involves weighing each box and entering the dimensions on the FBA shipment page on Amazon, and printing off labels for the UPS courier. Brought the bathroom scales down. The easiest way to weigh the boxes is to stand on the scales holding a box then deduct my bodyweight, which I notice has stabilised at twelve and a half stone. That's the same weight I was when I left school at the age of eighteen. Just as I'd almost finished doing it, Callum appeared at 5 p.m. and dragged us to the pub for a pint.

Till total £64
5 customers

Online orders: 7
Books found: 7

Granny was already in the shop tidying up the fiction section when I came down to open up at 9 a.m.

Petra appeared for her belly-dancing class at 10 a.m. Only one person turned up – the woman with short pink hair Petra refers to as 'the judge's wife'. I have no idea who she is.

Caroline, the photographer, arrived at 12.30. We spent the day shooting video for her project and editing it on my computer in the snug. Caroline, on hearing her voice on one of the recordings we'd made, commented, 'I sound like I'm from the Machars.' The Machars is the peninsula that Wigtown sits on. The next peninsula to the west, on the far side of Luce Bay – the Rhins – is only a few miles away, yet the two accents (to locals, at least) are noticeably different. I suppose this shouldn't come as a great surprise. Dumfries – in the east of the county – and Carlisle are only 30 miles apart, but the Dumfries accent is clearly Scottish, and Carlisle's is unquestionably English.

In the afternoon an elderly couple brought in three bags of books: Richmal Crompton *Just William*s and a lot of *Highways and Byways*, a well-produced series of local history/topography books from the early twentieth century. Gave them £65.

It's not suggested that he takes up cross-country running, goes on a crash diet, takes the pledge or attends evening classes in yoga.

Are you getting enough?

There are a number of ways of testing how fit you really are. You probably instinctively know already, but try answering these simple q
give you a rough idea of v
need to take more exercis

A man phoned at 10.45 a.m. to 'resign' his membership of the Random Book Club – 'I'm more than happy with the service you provide, but only about one in twelve books is of any interest to me.' Which is ENTIRELY THE POINT.

Granny rescued a book called *Everyday Fitness* from the pile of boxes destined for the recycling plant.

I'd intended to finish off the FBA shipment which Callum had interrupted but I couldn't find the scales to weigh the last few boxes.

Till total £33.50
5 customers

SATURDAY, 27 FEBRUARY

Online orders: 5
Books found: 5

Granny opened the shop on a very cold, clear morning. I lit the wood-burning stove in the shop, although I'm starting to wonder why I bother. Despite a recent surge in footfall, there are normally so few customers at this time of year that it doesn't make financial sense to keep them warm.

At 1.45 an elderly local woman appeared with a bag of books, and after much conspiratorial wobbling of the head and peering over the top of her demi-lunes (which seemed to be her way of suggesting that she knew more about their worth than I did) she asked me to value the contents of the bag, which contained several faded Harry Potters. Some were first editions; all were virtually worthless. When I told her this, she looked incredulous and told me that she'd read in *The Sun* recently that Harry Potter firsts were worth a fortune, and she was expecting at least a four-figure sum. I suggested that she took them to another bookshop for a second opinion.

Searched in vain for the weighing scales. The boxes of FBA books are cluttering up the shop and I need to shift them as soon as possible.

Watched the Scotland–Italy Six Nations rugby with Granny. Scotland won with 36 points to Italy's 20. Granny was furious, particularly after I told her that it was unusual for Italy to even make it onto the scoreboard.

Till total £147.98
12 customers

MONDAY, 29 FEBRUARY

Online orders: 7
Books found: 7

Shortly after I opened the shop, Granny appeared, wearing the white archival gloves she uses when she's tidying the shelves. I told her that she looked like Michael Jackson. She told me to fuck off.

My mother appeared at 10.30 and waffled endlessly about my father's back, which has been a source of considerable pain for decades – and something which he appears to have genetically passed on to me. She's worried that he'll end up in a wheelchair and require a carer. I knew he was suffering, but this is far worse than I had thought.

Still no sign of the weighing scales, so I have ordered another set.

After a dry but grey morning the rain came on at about lunchtime.

This week's volunteer for The Open Book was supposed to be a woman from California called Bess. She made it across America, and the Atlantic, but in Dublin a customs official asked her the purpose of her visit. She made the mistake of telling him that she was going to be 'working in a bookshop'. She didn't have a work permit. He sent her on the first flight back to America.

I imagine that same custom official is at home now, combing his moustache and telling his only friend, Adolf (his cat), all about it before he sits down to a supper of stale cornflakes and spite.

A young woman spent an hour in the garden room and bought

seven fairly expensive books from the ornithology collection I'd picked up from a house in Stranraer a couple of weeks ago. The stereotype of bearded men with binoculars being birdwatchers has largely proved to be true in my experience, although she has exploded the myth. She told me that she works for the RSPB at the Mull of Galloway visitor centre.

Granny and I spent the afternoon organising the sport section to accommodate the cycling books. While we were shelving the books we talked about cycling, and Granny told me, 'I can't cycle a stupid fucking bicycle, my eyesight is too shit and I too uncoordinated.'

Till total £95.49
6 customers

MARCH

The worthy man who taught me how to buy and sell books is now away from his old bookshop, and his stock has been scattered by the auctioneer's hammer. He was very frugal, and indeed miserly. He amassed a small fortune, but lost it by publishing a newspaper, and the worry of it killed him.

R. M. Williamson, *Bits from an Old Bookshop*

There seems to be a literary tradition that booksellers are portrayed in fiction as being frugal: John Baxter in *The Intimate Thoughts of John Baxter, Bookseller*, to name but one. I like to think that it's a question of circumstance rather than choice – not many of us make a sufficiently decent living to amass even 'a small fortune' and by necessity are obliged to live fairly parsimonious lives which define us as poor, rather than miserly. I can't think of any booksellers I've encountered who are anything less than generous with what little they have. The character of Henry Earlforward in Arnold Bennett's splendid *Riceyman Steps* (published in 1923), though, is the perfect example of a miserly bookseller. Not content with selling his wife's expensive wedding ring from her first marriage and buying a cheap one for his betrothal to her, he fell into a panic about her request to visit Madame Tussaud's as a treat on their wedding day because of the ticket price:

> Withal, as he extracted a pound note from his case, he suffered agony – and she was watching him with her bright eyes. It was a new pound note. The paper was white and substantial; not a crease on it. The dim watermarks whispered genuineness. The green and brown of the design were more beautiful than any picture. The majestic representation of the Houses of Parliament on the back gave assurance that the solidity of the whole realm was behind that note. The thing was as lovely and touching as a young virgin daughter. Could he abandon it for ever to the cold, harsh world?

Bennett describes Earlforward's reluctance to spend money as a psychological 'monster' which retreats when Violet, his bride, pays the additional fee to visit the Chamber of Horrors, although notably the 'Relics of Napoleon did not interest them'. Perhaps if Maggs had sold the emperor's penis to the museum rather than to an American book dealer, they might have had a very different day.

I have no idea why it seems normal for people to imagine that second-hand booksellers are sitting on untold piles of wealth. I have friends who mistakenly believe that I am, and certainly customers who – when asked to pay £6 for a hardback that was £18 when new two years ago – are often vocal in their resentment. As always, Dylan Moran's character Bernard Black, in *Black Books*, strikes the perfect note when a customer offers to pay £2 for a book that Bernard has priced at £3: 'Because £3 is just naked profiteering for a book a mere 912 pages long. What will I do with that extra £1? Add an acre to the grounds? Chuck some more Koi carp in my piano-shaped pond? I know: I'll build a wing on the National Gallery with my name on it.'

Even Williamson, most generous of spirit and purse, noted that

> In works of fiction, the second-hand bookseller is a curious compound of imagination and reality. He is invariably an old man of a morose, unsociable temperament. He is of a sceptical disposition; last century he quoted from Voltaire, Hume, and Tom Paine, and nowadays he studies the higher critics. He is miserly, greedy, shabby, and utterly callous as to the world's opinions. He is usually a widower; his charmingly lovely daughter and a black cat are the companions of his solitude.

Later on he comments that

> I was at one time employed by a second-hand dealer in books who was the most miserly, miserable and suspicious man I ever came into close contact with. He dined every day in the back shop on rice and milk; one New Year's morning he presented me with an orange, which was the only gift I ever received from him.

I truly hope that this myth has now been exploded – I doubt that the second-hand book trade is made up of a greater number of misers than any other business, but perhaps because very few of us make more than a subsistence living from it, and because most of us are the sole employee, we are quite visible to our customers in our morose, unsociable shabbiness.

TUESDAY, I MARCH

Online orders: 5
Books found: 2

My mother appeared at 11 to take Granny out for coffee. Once my mother had left the room, Granny said, 'Ha ha, fucking bastard, now you have to do some work,' as she held the shop door open and let the cold wind in to add to my discomfort in her absence.

A woman in her late sixties, with black curly hair peppered with grey, and a faintly American accent, came in after they'd left with a man who I assume is her husband. He is probably around eighty. They visit two or three times a year and pile up books on the table by the fire, then sit in the leather armchairs in front of it and read for the entire day. They are both sweet, and kind, and if it's a cold day like today I always light the fire so that they're warm and comfortable. I don't know their names, or where they're from, but they clearly make a pilgrimage to Wigtown, always spend at least £50 and are incredibly polite about how much they enjoy coming here.

A couple from Girvan brought six boxes of pretty average books down at noon, a mix of fiction and non-fiction. Gave them £25 for a small pile.

The new weighing scales arrived, so I started to weigh the boxes for FBA shipment. When I lifted up the first box to weigh it, I found the missing scales underneath it.

Association of Wigtown Booksellers (AWB) meeting at 5.30 in Curly Tale Books, the shop next door, which specialises in children's books. The discussion revolved – as it always does at this time of year – around the programme for our Spring Festival. It would be far more interesting if there were arguments, banging of fists on tables and slamming of doors, but we all tend to agree and accommodate one another's requirements.

Closing the back door of the shop this evening, I noticed that the pond is full of mating frogs once again. The sound of them when the back door is opened is almost deafening.

Sue from Atkinson-Pryce Books in Biggar called to order two more of the New Naturalists from the deal in Stranraer.

Till total £156.50
4 customers

WEDNESDAY, 2 MARCH

Online orders: 3
Books found: 3

Cold and sunny when I opened the shop. The first job of the day was to call UPS and arrange the uplift of the sixteen boxes to go to the Amazon fulfilment centre in Dunfermline.

My father arrived at 11.30, at the same time as Isabel (to do the accounts) and a woman who had called earlier with books to sell. She was particularly obnoxious and questioned my judgement when I rejected some of her books.

Bought books from a man who came in with two boxes. More *Just William*s and a lot of Mark Twain.

Granny and I spent the afternoon pricing up books and listing some of them online, and putting the rest on the shelves.

After the shop closed, I sat in the snug and read *A Touch of Mistletoe* for a few hours. It's a truly brilliant book, and I can't believe I hadn't come across it before. I've reached the part where we discover that Blanche's husband, Captain Cressy, turns out to be more interested in men than women. Vicky, the narrator, had a premonition that things wouldn't work out before they even married, explaining, 'I knew she would never be happy with Captain Cressy. He was impressive at first sight, but he had a skin like cold-boiled bacon.'

Till total £74
4 customers

THURSDAY, 3 MARCH

Online orders: 3
Books found: 3

Sunny day. Granny indulged in her favourite pastime: she went to the doctor at 9 a.m. She adores going to the doctor because he has no choice but to listen to her numerous complaints, whereas I tend to leave the room when she gets started on her ailments.

Today was World Book Day. I marked the occasion by smashing up a Kindle and nailing it to the front door of the shop with a note saying, 'It's World Book Day. Destroy your Kindle.'

At 9.30 the rep from Nicholson Maps appeared, looking unusually smart. He's been coming to the shop every few months for fifteen years with his van full of OS maps to top up my stock, and I still don't know his name. He's in his fifties and has no facial hair of any sort: eyebrows, beard or hair. Once, when I was climbing with Callum in Glencoe, I bumped into him outside a shop in Ballachulish. He didn't look the least bit surprised. His news today was that Nicholson Maps is bankrupt and the stock has been bought by Birlinn, a Scottish publisher. He has been retained by them but has no idea how much longer he'll have a job.

UPS courier arrived at 11 a.m. to uplift the sixteen boxes to go to FBA.

At ten o'clock the telephone rang. It was a woman from Kirk-cudbright (about 30 miles away). She had some craft books to sell. She appeared at 1.10 with ten bags of books. The books were all in pristine condition. Gave her £100 for them. I spent Granny's lunch break listing them online. Later, an old man came in with a carload of books for sale, all rubbish.

Till total £72.50
8 customers

FRIDAY, 4 MARCH

Online orders: 6
Books found: 6

Granny opened the shop. Petra appeared at 9.45. Nobody turned up for her belly-dancing class but she hung around and had a cup of tea, and chatted to Granny.

Tom showed up at 10.30 to ask if we're going to the pub tonight. I told him that we probably would.

At 11.45 the lorry turned up with a pallet of pellets for the boiler. Unloaded them with the driver.

Delivery of new books from Booksource, our supplier of the handful of new books we stock in the shop. Putting them on the shelf, I spotted a book in the local section that I hadn't seen before: it's called *Big Lang Danner*, by a man called Willie Drennan. Flicking through it, I spotted a mention of my shop:

> In this bookshop they had several beautiful locally crafted sticks made out of blackthorn, hazel and ash. I went for the blackthorn stick as it seemed to be the best fit for me. I asked the young Englishman behind the counter if he would consider accepting my stick as a trade-in. He said no and didn't seem all that amused either.

It wasn't all that amusing, and I'm not English, I'm Scottish.

Janette was in to clean the shop this afternoon. As we were leaving the shop (she to go home, me to take Granny on a trip), an icy blast of wind from the north hit us and she commented, 'She's cold tonight.' I'm not sure that anywhere else I've lived has ascribed a gender to the weather, but it's perfectly normal in Wigtown, and the weather is always female.

After we closed the shop, I took Granny to the cemetery at St Medans, now that it is getting light enough to do things after 5 p.m. Granny has an obsession with graveyards, and the one at St Medans must be one of the most beautiful in Scotland. The crumbling old church is surrounded by broadleaf woodland, and the stones are old and weathered. It was the chapel for the Maxwell family, who lived – and continue to live – in Monreith House, a huge stately home built in 1791. I doubt if there are more than thirty headstones and plots in the tiny burial area, but it is right next to the beach, and has a stunning view across Luce Bay to the South Rhins – the most westerly part of Galloway, and the most southerly tip of Scotland.

I'm taking Granny to Edinburgh airport tomorrow because she has to return to Genoa. She doesn't want to leave. I've asked my friend Mary if she can cover for her in the shop.

Till total £60.49
4 customers

SATURDAY, 5 MARCH

Online orders: 3
Books found: 3

It was a cold, sunny day, so I lit the fire in the shop, showed Mary how the till and card machine work, then at 9.30 drove to Edinburgh airport with Granny. Tearful farewell. Granny has done much for the shop, become a good friend and a part of the fabric of Wigtown. Mary is a voiceover artist who moved to Wigtown several years ago. She's wonderfully entertaining and – unlike everyone else who works in the shop – appears to enjoy chatting to customers. Best of all, though, is the moment they've left the shop: she can mimic them perfectly, particularly – for some reason – Brummie accents.

Home at 3.30. I spent part of the remainder of the afternoon pulling out the rosemary plants which were in the big pots at the front of the shop. After two years they finally succumbed to the unrelenting assault of urine from the poodle that my neighbours own. It pisses on them three times a day when it is being taken for its walk. I replaced them with evergreen azaleas. Let's see how they fare against the bloody poodle. I should probably have put a plant with vicious thorns there instead of the azaleas.

Till total £138.10
12 customers

MONDAY, 7 MARCH

Online orders: 9
Books found: 9

Opened the shop shortly after nine o'clock as I couldn't find the key. It was in the van. It's strange and rather sad not to hear the clacking of Granny's boots on the wooden floors any more. The sun was shining, as it occasionally does at this time of year.

One of today's orders was to Daunt Books in London. I'm sure he's a very nice man, but I don't much care for James Daunt, although I've never met him. He is partly responsible for the homogeneity of the high street and the disappearance of independent bookshops from the landscape.

Most of the orders this morning were for New Naturalists and other books from the ornithology collection from Stranraer that I listed recently.

Realised that I haven't bothered to change the time on the clock in the shop since the clocks changed in autumn. That would explain the look of panic on customers' faces when they spot it.

Left Mary in charge of the shop at eleven o'clock and drove to Lockerbie to catch the 1.15 train to London to look at a library belonging to a retired archaeologist. Took the Tube to Waterloo, then walked to Westminster Bridge, where my friend Elaine met me and drove me to her house, where she had kindly prepared a bed in her spare room. It was wonderful to catch up with her – I hadn't seen her since we went for supper in Edinburgh a couple of years ago.

Till total £46.99
3 customers

TUESDAY, 8 MARCH

Online orders: 6
Books found: 5

Elaine drove me to the archaeologist's house in Notting Hill. The books were gorgeous – a fine collection of rare and antiquarian books, including several copies of Camden's *Britannia*. It was way out of my league financially, and I wondered why he had asked me to come and view it when there are several London dealers with considerably deeper pockets than mine who would have been a far better choice. He explained that his father had lived in Wigtown for several years, and that he always felt a connection with the place, and thought that he'd give me first refusal. I thanked him and explained that I couldn't possibly give him even a fraction of what the books were worth, and advised him to either put them into a specialist auction or contact one of the London dealers – Maggs or Harrington. He generously offered to pay my train fare, but I declined, telling him that it had been worth the cost of the tickets just to see his library.

Finished *A Touch of Mistletoe*. Travel by train affords one the luxury of uninterrupted reading. I must thank Lee for giving me her old copy of the book.

Made it home shortly before 8.30 p.m.

Till total £124
8 customers

WEDNESDAY, 9 MARCH

Online orders: 2
Books found: 2

Spotted the Wigtown Buddhist ambling along at 1 p.m. in nothing but his orange robe and sandals, despite the freezing weather and cold north wind. I think he has something to do with Samye Ling, the Tibetan Buddhist monastery in the wild hills of Eskdalemuir, in the east of the region.

Isabel came in to do the accounts. She brought six boxes of books from her recently deceased uncle's estate.

Following the incident with the short, squat dog a few weeks ago, Captain appears to have revised his strategy regarding the shop's canine visitors. Rather than taunting them, he's taken a decidedly more aggressive position, and now approaches them, hissing, hackles up. To my surprise, and probably his too, most of the dogs back off, whimpering. The fearfulness of the reaction appears to be in inverse proportion to the size of the dog. A woman came in with a chihuahua today, which must have been about half the size of the cat. Captain squared up to the tiny creature and it went berserk, yapping furiously and straining at the leash with all of its feeble might. Captain stood his ground, and eventually the woman scooped the ferocious dog up and left the shop.

One of my few regular customers is a Cockney man who has moved to the area. A few months ago he came in, distraught that he'd finished every Patrick O'Brian novel, and didn't know what to read next. I suggested Alexander Kent and Bernard Cornwell. Today he came in and bought six Alexander Kent novels and two Cornwells and said, 'You've got me addicted.' I gave him a decent discount, largely because he has never asked for one.

Email from a dealer in America to whom we had sent a book:

> As a bookseller of forty years, please advise on why
> your store billed the condition of this book as 'Like new.'
> The book is in only good condition, heavily foxed, which
> makes one wonder if yellowing pages constitute 'Like
> New' in your vocabulary. To add comic insult, the book
> was tossed into a mailing envelope without packaging
> (bubble wrap, newspaper) so the corners were damaged
> on its transatlantic journey. I'm assuming that you are not
> professional booksellers?
> Please advise before I take this up with ABE.

I intensely dislike this kind of adversarial approach to resolving problems, particularly when it's littered with insults, so I asked him to return the book for a full refund.

Till total £120.99
11 customers

THURSDAY, 10 MARCH

Online orders: 4
Books found: 4

There was a scattering of feathers under the kitchen table this morning. This is where Captain prefers to bring his prey to finish it off. Like most cat owners, the one thing I dislike the most is that the creature picks off garden birds – completely unnecessary when he always has food in his bowl, but clearly an instinct that he can't suppress. At least he has the decency to eat them.

One of today's orders was from the ornithology collection; the other was from the craft lot that came in last week – a book about beads, which sold for £30.

Two young American men were waiting outside when I opened the shop at 8.50 this morning. They scooted around for about ten minutes, then one of them came to the counter with two books and a map and asked where the 'washroom' was. As he was paying, I noticed that he had very dirty hands. He clearly saw that I'd noticed, and explained that he'd been metal-detecting in the grounds of a castle after dark last night. I'm not sure whether he had permission, or what he had expected to find.

At about lunchtime, an elderly man came in asking for John Galt and S. R. Crockett titles, so I showed him to the Scottish room. As he was leaving, we had a chat about literature and art – he mentioned F. C. B. Cadell's famous painting *The Orange Blind*. I told him that my sister Lulu lives in the house where *The Orange Blind* was painted, Cadell's old house. Twenty minutes later we were still talking. He was interested in the origins of place-names, as am I, and asked me what the etymology of Wigtown is, so I told him that, as best I knew, it was from the Norse words meaning 'town on the bay'. His wife, it turns out, is a native Gaelic-speaker. They live in the Isle of Lewis and he only travels by bus. He'd been helicoptered from Lewis to Inverness with a suspected heart attack, and once he'd been discharged thought that he might as well make the most of being on the mainland and visit Wigtown. I couldn't help seeing an elderly vision of myself reflected in him.

A middle-aged customer on crutches wandered around reading all the signs out loud while her mother gazed for a while at the shot Kindle before asking me, 'Why did you shoot a calculator?'

Telephone call at 5 p.m. from a man called Homer whose son has set up an auction house in Dumfries. He has forty boxes of books unsold from the last sale. He's bringing them over tomorrow. To say that my expectations are low is an understatement.

Till total £151.48
7 customers

FRIDAY, 11 MARCH

Online orders: 1
Books found: 0

Petra's belly-dancing class. The pink-haired judge's wife was the only client.

At 10 a.m. the old man from yesterday reappeared, looking again for John Galt, Stevenson, Crockett. He bought several of each. I gave him a decent discount partly because he was a very amenable man and partly because neither Galt nor Crockett is a good seller these days. In their lifetimes they were best-sellers, but today they are almost impossible to shift.

Homer appeared with forty boxes of books. We unloaded them, then he left. I suspect that the contents of the boxes are of so little interest and value that he escaped before I could go through them and make him take them away.

Kenny Bell, one of the shop's Facebook followers, turned up. He'd been hillwalking in the area yesterday and had the day off, so he decided to drop in and say hello.

I have a small property on a nearby street which I rebuilt from a ruin about ten years ago. When I say 'I rebuilt', in truth it was a team of Polish builders. It's currently rented out by a tenant – a really lovely man who never complains about anything, but he finally cracked. Every time the wind blows from the west, and it's raining (which is most of the time), the rainwater is driven in under the door, soaking the sitting-room floor. He asked if he could replace the door with something a little less permeable. I readily agreed, and wrote him a cheque for the cost of the replacement door.

At 4.30 three young women came in asking for medical textbooks. I tend not to stock many of these because they become obsolete very quickly, with each new intake at university requiring the very latest editions of everything.

After I closed the shop I went onto Amazon Marketplace to see why we only had one order. It appears that my seller account has been suspended due to too many orders being fulfilled after the twenty-four-hour limit. This is because Granny forgot to click the 'Sent' button on Monsoon after she'd packed and sent the orders out, and it is absolutely my fault for failing to explain the procedure to her. Although all our feedback shows that the books arrived on time, if not earlier than expected, Amazon's algorithm fails to recognise this. I've emailed their appeals system and will hopefully be back online soon.

Till total £82.49
5 customers

SATURDAY, 12 MARCH

Online orders: 0
Books found: 0

No orders today – still suspended from Amazon Marketplace, despite my efforts to get back online again.

Ben appeared at 11 a.m. to invite me to Craft for a sneak preview before they open. It's a little sad that a restaurant opening in town can generate such excitement, but that is part of living in a rural community

Spent the day going through Homer's books. As expected, they were nearly all completely unsellable. Of the forty boxes, I extracted two boxes of sellable books. Called him and offered him £100. Now I am faced with the prospect of the shop being cluttered with boxes of rubbish until I can get to the recycling plant again.

Mother dropped in at 3.45 to say hello. 'I'm in a rush so I can't stay long...' At 4.30 she was still here, then, as she was leaving, she bumped into her friend the local historian Jack Hunter. They chatted in the doorway for a further twenty minutes.

Till total £91
11 customers

Online orders: 2
Books found: 2

Both orders were from ABE. We appear to still be suspended from Amazon Marketplace.

Warm, sunny day. I felt quite invigorated from spending yesterday working in the garden. It finally feels like spring has arrived, although I'm always conscious in March of the saying that it 'comes in like a lion, goes out like a lamb'. It's not unusual to have a heavy snowfall at this time of year. I can remember ski trips to Glenshee in the vomit-inducing school bus. God knows where the school bought that bloody bus from, but it was driven by a Polish refugee who had stayed in Scotland after the war and was known to us as Charlie, although his real name was probably Chwalibog, or something similar.

My friend Cloda called for a chat. After about twenty minutes of telling me about a problem that Leo, her partner, is having with an employee, she casually dropped into the conversation the fact that she's pregnant again. Must write to congratulate her. Cloda and I met about twenty years ago when we both lived in Bristol – she's Irish and runs a pharmacy in Dublin.

A young woman bought several books about knitting. She's staying in one of the cabins on the Carrick shore near Gatehouse. It became fashionable for the great and the good of the area to build small wooden chalets on this pretty bit of the Galloway coastline in the 1920s and to spend the summer there. Some of them survive intact, but have been modernised inside for comfort. Others have been pulled down and replaced by hideous modern structures. Now it looks like a coastal shanty town for wealthy pensioners.

After I'd closed the shop, I drove to the supermarket in Newton Stewart. The Co-op in Wigtown is more than adequate, but sometimes it's worth going 7 miles further afield for a bit of variety. Like fresh fruit and vegetables.

Till total £115
6 customers

TUESDAY, 15 MARCH

Online orders: 1
Books found: 1

I received a telephone call from Amazon shortly after opening the shop, regarding the suspension of my account. I'd sent another message to them using a different email address and they've responded to that, but not to the initial message. I'm not sure which email this call was in response to, but I will have to write an 'Action Plan' to show how I'm going to make sure I'm compliant with their guidelines, which is a euphemistic way of saying 'rules'. They're going to email me with further instructions. It feels like I'm being vetted for a Top Secret job with MI5.

Went to the post office at 10 a.m. to buy some sellotape. I couldn't find my wallet. Finally worked out that I'd left it in the van (unlocked) overnight.

Telephone call from a woman near Edinburgh who has books she wants me to give a probate valuation for. She can only manage Thursday morning, so will probably drive up tomorrow afternoon and stay overnight with my sister Lulu.

I was halfway through my lunch (a Co-op sandwich) in the shop when I coughed and a small piece of chorizo flew through the air and landed on a customer's jacket. Thankfully it was on their back, and near the bottom, so they didn't notice. It was still there when they left an hour later.

During the afternoon I was pricing up books and found a copy of an early title by Richard Holloway. He's a regular speaker at Wigtown Book Festival and now, I hope, a friend. On the back was a photograph of him in much more youthful days, when he still wore a dog collar.

Richard is one of the most cerebral and interesting people I know. He resigned from his position as bishop of Edinburgh (which he'd held since 1986) in 2000. He describes himself as 'after-religionist', which I take to mean agnostic.

Till total £64.55
8 customers

WEDNESDAY, 16 MARCH

Online orders: 2
Books found: 2

Both orders from ABE, still no sign of Amazon letting my inventory back online. Emailed them yet again to ask why I'm still suspended.

Drove to Lockerbie and caught the 4.30 train to Edinburgh for a probate valuation on the contents of a house tomorrow. Mary covered the shop for the afternoon. She spent an hour in the Community Shop (charity shop) this morning and emerged – as always – with a splendid find. She has an uncanny knack of always going to the shop shortly after someone with an interesting collection of rubbish has died and picking off the best of their remains. I don't wish to make her sound like a vulture – she's far from it, she's more of a magpie – but she loves a bargain, particularly if it something that is utterly useless, and even better if it has no identifiable purpose whatsoever. Today she turned up waving a boy's kilt (Hunting Stewart cut from Harris tweed). 'Isn't it fabulous?' Indeed it was, but petite though she is, I suspect it may be too small.

Till total £122.49
6 customers

THURSDAY, 17 MARCH

Online orders: 2
Books found: 1

Arrived at the house at 9 a.m. to evaluate the books for a deceased estate at a very smart house on Regent Terrace. The solicitor met me there. There were approximately 2,000 books, mainly on architecture, including full sets of *Castellated and Domestic Architecture of Scotland* and *Baronial and Ecclesiastical Antiquities of Scotland*, as well as a fine copy of Francis Grose's *The Antiquities of Scotland*, which contains the first ever edition of 'Tam o' Shanter' to appear in a book. I suggested a probate value for the lot of £6,500.

Caught the 12.12 p.m. train back to Lockerbie and drove home. Arrived back at the shop at 2.40. Mary went home, and I worked for the rest of the afternoon. Apparently there has been a recent death in the town, and the Community Shop is expecting to receive the contents of the house. Mary was practically buzzing with excitement.

My friend Tracy arrived at four o'clock and we went for a walk after I'd shut the shop. It was beautifully warm in the evening sunshine of the early spring. Tracy is now working for Majestic Wines in Guildford. She's from Malta, and had a job working for the RSPB in Wigtown for a year. She made a lot of friends when she was here, and comes back whenever she can to catch up with us all. One of her Majestic customers is Mary Quant.

Till total £118.51
9 customers

FRIDAY, 18 MARCH

Online orders: 1
Books found: 1

Still no reply from Amazon to my email about lifting my suspension. I'm starting to enjoy not having to deal with them, and their silence is proving to be more of a relief than a burden.

Petra appeared at 9.50 a.m. for her belly-dancing class. She subjected me to her latest conspiracy theory: she's found some sort of guru, whose every word she takes as gospel. I can't remember his name, but after she showed me his website it was manifestly obvious that he either had serious mental health problems or was a complete charlatan. My money is on the latter. This one was about the vapour trails from aircraft seeding mind-controlling chemicals which fall to earth and keep us under the control of a cartel of some sort.

Nobody turned up for the class, not even the judge's wife, so Tracy volunteered. The now predictably rhythmic thumping lasted its customary hour. There were no customers until after eleven o'clock anyway, so the wailing music and banging noises from upstairs didn't really matter.

After Petra had gone, we had a telephone call from a woman in the nearby village of the Isle of Whithorn, looking for sci-fi titles by David Eddings and Maggie Furey. I found several books by both and called her back. She's going to drop in next week. She sounded extremely excited when I replied to her call.

Callum appeared at noon and rescued me from Tracy, who had remained in the shop after Petra's belly-dancing class and was giving me a lecture on my life and my various failings as a human being.

Finally, a telephone call from Amazon telling me that they would email me with instructions about how to resolve my suspended account. Nothing in the inbox by the end of the day.

At about 3 p.m. an Irish man arrived and bought about forty books on a huge range of subjects, including vivisection and cooking with offal.

Walked to pub in Bladnoch (about a mile away) after I'd closed the shop to have a drink with my friends Tom and Willeke, who kindly gave me a lift home at about eight o'clock.

Till total £150.99
10 customers

SATURDAY, 19 MARCH

Online orders: 0
Books found: 0

Nothing in the inbox from Amazon about my suspended account, so I emailed them again. Every day of suspension is costing me about £40, although it's probably costing Amazon too, as they take about 30 per cent of my online turnover.

At eleven o'clock Steve Wise appeared with his new partner and her children. Steve used to have a bookshop in Wigtown called Creaking Shelves, and ran a taxi as a sideline. He struggled to survive – he arrived just as the financial crisis of 2008 hit, and eventually closed up and moved away.

A young woman and her boyfriend came in just before lunch. She stopped in the front room of the shop, looked around and repeated, 'This is dreamy,' several times. We got chatting about wood-burning stoves after she spotted me putting more logs on. She lives in Dumfries and told me that she really wanted to visit the shop, 'the one everyone always talks about. Everyone says that it looks like there are hardly any books there until you go through into the back and there's thousands.' I was flattered to the point of embarrassment.

After lunch I found a man in the boiler room taking photographs. I asked him what he was doing. It turned out that he's a boiler engineer. We had a surprisingly interesting chat about boilers for about twenty minutes. Considering how frequently the fancy new boiler breaks down, he might be a useful contact.

At 5 p.m., just as I was closing the shop, a woman came in with five bags of books. She'd been in earlier in the week selling cookbooks. Went through the bags and took out about sixty decent contemporary fiction paperbacks. Gave her £30. The Random Book Club shipment is due, and this is perfect stock for it.

Till total £251.95
16 customers

MONDAY, 21 MARCH

Online orders: 0
Books found: 0

Still suspended from Amazon, and no reply to my previous message, so I emailed them again.

Just after I'd opened, a woman wearing a Paddington duffel

coat came in and asked, 'Have you got a mat we can put a jigsaw on?' I suggested that she use a table. She didn't look very pleased. I suppose with a mat you can lift the jigsaw and move it about, but since we don't sell them I couldn't really help. Felt a bit guilty when she stormed out, clearly assuming that I was being facetious, which, in fairness to her, I was.

The book from the angry American dealer arrived back in today's post. It was EXACTLY as we had described it, with no foxing or yellowed pages, or damaged corners. I don't know what he was complaining about – perhaps he'd found a cheaper copy somewhere else. Still, there was no need to suggest that I'm not a proper bookseller.

I spent the morning unloading boxes of books from the van then loading the discarded stock (mainly the rubbish that Homer brought in last week) to take to the recycling plant in Glasgow.

After lunch I drove to Glasgow with Tracy. We dumped the books (which filled four large plastic containers). I left Tracy at Shields Road subway station and said goodbye. She's off back to Guildford on the train. I don't think she likes her new job particularly, although she's clearly good at it, as they've offered to train her up for a managerial position.

Home by 5.10 p.m.

Till total £205.05
8 customers

TUESDAY, 22 MARCH

Online orders: 0
Books found: 0

Still suspended from Amazon, and still nothing by way of help to reverse the suspension.

Phone call from ABE telling me that I've been suspended from their website for posting the offensive email from the American bookseller who complained about the book we sold him. I posted it on Facebook. He wrote to ABE and complained that I'd shared his aggressive email on social media. I've removed the posts about him and emailed ABE to say that I have done so, with a grovellingly insincere apology. I'm starting to seriously dislike almost everything about the internet. I've now been suspended from Amazon, ABE and Facebook, all by algorithms.

Closed the shop early and went for a pint with Callum.

Till total £115.90
17 customers

WEDNESDAY, 23 MARCH

Online orders: 0
Books found: 0

This morning I received an email from ABE saying that they've reinstated my account because I removed the 'confidential' email from the American book dealer, so at least I have one platform for selling books online. I'm increasingly becoming convinced that anonymity is the reason that the internet is so toxic. I very much doubt that the American book dealer would have said any of the things in his email if he'd had to say them to my face. It helps that I'm 6 foot 2 and look as though I've just climbed out of a skip.

The new Open Book people dropped in to say hello and buy a few books.

As I was putting out books in the biography section, I spotted a biography of Mary Quant. I'll post it to Tracy.

Boxes of Spring Festival programmes arrived this afternoon. Now we need to distribute them and hope that we can sell a few tickets.

Till total £77
13 customers

THURSDAY, 24 MARCH

Online orders: 0
Books found: 0

A tall, gloomy-looking customer found a five-volume set of paper-backs about ecclesiastical architecture on the table in the shop. It was unpriced and had been there for a long time, so I told him that he could have them for the heavily discounted price of £20 (original price £55). He replied, 'I'll give you £15.' I reluctantly agreed, just to see the back of the damned things and the back of the customer.

Pretty uneventful day. Spent much of it tidying the shelves and catching up with emails. I think the average age of today's customers was probably between seventy and eighty.

Still nothing more from Amazon about compliance with guidelines.

Till total £199.98
18 customers

FRIDAY, 25 MARCH

Online orders: 1
Books found: 0

Today was Good Friday, and a sunny day with a cloudless blue sky. I'm not in the least bit religious, but holy days are always good for takings in the shop.

No news from Amazon. I think I'm going to cancel my account.

Carol-Ann and Katie (former employees) met up in the shop and went for breakfast at Glaisnock, a guesthouse on the opposite side of the street which has a small café. They brought me back a bacon roll at eleven o'clock. Katie's mother used to have the bookshop which is now The Open Book. She bought it from a man called Ian Langford, who I knew briefly before he moved away from Wigtown. He published natural history books, illustrated by well-known wildlife artists including Keith Brockie and Donald Watson. I always had the impression that he didn't particularly like me. I'm fairly sure that I was right. He also created a tourist business near Newton Stewart whose premise completely bewildered me – a hothouse that contained butterflies and carnivorous plants. Despite our differences, I was sad to read of his death at the age of just sixty-one. His obituary was in *The Guardian*. He did much for Wigtown.

A young woman came in looking for a book called *Clash by Night*, which her father had seen when he was visiting the shop last year. Amazingly, not only was it on the database but it was on the right shelf.

This afternoon my mother dropped off four hanging baskets, which she always plants up for the front of the shop.

Callum and I decided to go to Craft, which was formerly the Wigtown Ploughman, for a pint. Callum and Ben (the chef) haven't really seen eye to eye since the time we were in the pub and Ben criticised Callum for feeding his children chicken that wasn't free-range and organic. Callum – who was at this point a single father – snapped back, 'You fucking well try feeding three teenage boys on a budget of fuck-all.' It came very close to a punch-up. Callum would have won by a considerable margin, although I wouldn't have put it past Ben to play dirty.

Till total £136
13 customers

SATURDAY, 26 MARCH

Online orders: 1
Books found: 0

Easter weekend, and a miserable wet day. The wind was howling from the south, so the windows were leaking from the moment I opened the shop.

I came downstairs after making a cup of tea to find a woman

standing in front of the shot Kindle. She seemed a bit dazed, and repeated, 'I love that,' half a dozen times.

The shop was busy all morning. At eleven o'clock a man in a well-cut tweed suit came in with a box of books. I had high hopes. Given his accent, Range Rover and general demeanour, he clearly intended to pass himself off as mildly aristocratic, but the books were only good for the recycling plant; the few in reasonable condition were *Reader's Digest*s, and the rest – even if they hadn't been damaged by being stored in a loft for years – were of no value. He didn't seem to mind when I told him. In fact, he seemed quite cheery about it and said that he always enjoyed a trip to the local dump.

Alan, a neighbour of my parents, dropped in to say hello. He works (as far as I can tell) in finance and has a small cottage about half a mile from my parents' house. He's an extremely amusing man, and has the most eccentric garden I have ever seen. The cottage is on the Moss of Cree, an ancient raised bog which has been heavily planted with Sitka spruce by the Forestry Commission. Alan's garden creeps into this wet, woody landscape and, besides the well-maintained lawn, has concrete hands poking through the soil, speed limit signs in the middle of bits of woodland, statues of naked women, and baubles hanging from trees, among an abundance of other strange things. At some point it will become a major tourist attraction.

Till total £613.96
58 customers

MONDAY, 28 MARCH

Online orders: 0
Books found: 0

Still suspended from Amazon. Emailed them again.

As I was walking past the poetry section with a pile of books to put in the Scottish room, I overheard three young women discussing their favourite drag queen. I posted the conversation on Facebook. Someone suggested a game where followers suggest drag queen names with literary influences. Best so far from Lindsey 'Dragula' and Lauren 'Tequila Mockingbird' and 'Blanche Dubious'.

Ordered a pallet of pellets for the boiler. I'm starting to wish I'd never bought the damned thing; it is nothing but hard work.

Till total £136
13 customers

TUESDAY, 29 MARCH

Online orders: 0
Books found: 0

The sun was shining when I opened the shop this morning. Checked emails. No great surprise to discover that my account is still suspended from Amazon.

A large customer waddled through the shop like Gogol's 'stately goose', Sobakevich's wife, telling her husband to hurry up, and piling books into his arms as she went.

The same customer later tuttingly accused me of 'hiding' because I wasn't at the counter when she came to pay for her books. I know that working in a shop requires a degree of customer service, but I dislike it when there's an expectation of some sort of servility. It's not how I treat people in shops. I had been upstairs, making a cup of tea, but it has given me an idea – I might start hiding behind shelves and leaping out to startle customers.

Till total £580.38
49 customers

Online orders: 0
Books found: 0

In despair, I finally called Amazon in an effort to have the suspension lifted. A very polite woman told me that different departments within Amazon are not allowed to talk to one another, and that there is no telephone number for the seller performance department, the people who are dealing with my suspension.

Telephone call from a woman in Doune, near Stirling, who wants to sell her late husband's collection of books on microscopes. I have arranged to drive there next Tuesday afternoon to look at them. Doune Castle is, I think, one of the settings for the television drama series *Outlander*.

The shop was busy all day, but at its busiest the delivery of pellets arrived, so I wheelbarrowed them back to the pellet store and occasionally managed to dart into the shop and serve customers.

Particularly offensive post on Facebook from an elderly American man who told me that my page makes me look like 'an arrogant ass'. China Rose and Aine McElwee – two friends on social media and in real life – went to town on him, but not in their usual savage way. They intelligently engaged with him and reduced him to looking like a fool. Perhaps I am an 'arrogant ass'. I like to think that I'm not, though, and I would prefer not to have a stranger's opinion on the question posted on my business page.

My mother and Anna visited and had a cup of tea in the afternoon. I've been summoned to Sunday lunch with my parents this weekend. Anna is back in Wigtown for a few weeks. Although she's moved to Edinburgh, she is still involved with the festival, and makes regular visits for meetings.

My lifelong friend Colin and his daughter Lara came over for supper. They stayed for the night. I have two friends who I've known since before I have any memories – Colin is one of them. He's a giant of a man – 6 foot 5 – and is as loyal a friend as anyone could hope for. He works in Kuwait, and on his rare visits back to Scotland he always finds the time to come over and catch up. Bought a leg of lamb from the butcher, and undercooked it. I think that the only reason Lara comes over is to see Captain, the cat, who she's known since he was a kitten. When she was a child and came to visit with Colin, Captain would always sleep in her bed.

Till total £246.98
19 customers

THURSDAY, 31 MARCH

Online orders: 0
Books found: 0

Still suspended from Amazon and no orders from ABE for days, so I emailed them to ask what's going on.

Colin and Lara left at 10.45, just as the engineer arrived to check a problem with the new boiler, and the people from Samye Ling dropped off five boxes of books. I have an arrangement with the librarian at Samye Ling whereby any donations to their library which she thinks don't fit their ideology are boxed and dropped off at the shop. I sort through them and take what I want, then send them a cheque. There's rarely anything of much value, but I keep doing it because one day something interesting will come my way. Fortunately, yesterday I cleared the books off the table in the front of the shop where I sort through fresh stock, so I have some space to process them.

At lunchtime a huge, burly man came to the counter with an enormous pile of books. He looked like the sort that would rip your head off if you so much as smiled at him, so it came as a bit of a surprise to find that he was buying Spinoza, among other things. It turned out that he has a bookshop in Belgrade, as well as a publishing imprint, both called Magellan. We chatted about the woeful state of both bookselling and publishing, then, to my amazement, he told me that his favourite book was *The Bankrupt Bookseller*. He's the only person I know who has ever even heard of it, let alone read it. He's doing a motorbike tour of the UK with his son, who is studying at Edinburgh University.

I processed the Samye Ling books that arrived yesterday; not a lot of great interest, but there was one called *What a Drag*, which seemed very timely in light of the Facebook activity around drag queens a few days ago.

As I was processing the books on the table in the shop, a customer picked one up and bought it. This is far from unusual: unpriced fresh stock is the easiest thing to sell, although most of the time customers expect to decide the price, rather than ask what I'm prepared to take for the book.

At 4.30 I was subjected to a lengthy telephone call from a man in Holywood, Northern Ireland, who had read about Wigtown in *The Oldie* magazine and was interested in establishing his town as a book town. He spent about twenty minutes asking me questions, apparently unconcerned about whether or not I might be busy with other things. He told me that he'd tried to contact Eliot but had not received anything by way of reply. This is the third time I've heard that complaint this week from as many people. Eliot's a busy man, so I understand why he can't reply to everyone, but it's slightly irritating that I have to take the blame for this.

Closed the shop and went for supper at Craft with Liam and Rosie, who are in The Open Book this week. They're both enthusiastic Escape Room gamers. I'm tempted to put a bolt on the door of The Open Book when they're in there tomorrow and see how they fare.

Till total £250.13
13 customers

APRIL

The pleasure to be derived from poking about an old book shop is like drinking from a well whose waters are ever bubbling forth pure and cool. Every time one visits the place there is some fresh volume added, some new treasure to be examined, some interesting theme to talk about with the bookseller. Even if there be no new books, are not the old ones like dear friends ever waiting to be looked at? There is a delight in just being in the presence of old books; one feels at home in the best society; the smell of the old leather binding is good, the homely honest letterpress is better, but the carrying away in one's pocket the volume as one's very own is best of all.

R. M. Williamson, *Bits from an Old Bookshop*

There is no question that we have – well over one hundred years later – customers who share Williamson's opinion. Some people come to the shop with no intention of buying anything. For them the mere fact that they are surrounded by old books provides some kind of sensory gratification, and possibly a form of therapy. Jen Campbell noted in *The Bookshop Book* that there is a chemical reason that old books have a particular smell, and more recently – in an article in *The Guardian* – Claire Armistead discussed a paper published by researchers at UCL in which 'Cecilia Bembibre and Matija Strlič describe how they analysed samples from an old book, picked up in a second-hand shop, and developed an "historic book odour wheel", which connects identifiable chemicals with people's reactions to them'. In recent years two neologisms have appeared to describe the smell of old books: Oliver Tearle came up with 'bibliosmia' in 2014, combining the Greek words for 'book' and 'smell', and a year earlier John Koenig, in his *Dictionary of Obscure Sorrows*, invented 'vellichor: the strange wistfulness of used book stores', which, rather than connoting the smell itself, is the emotion that the smell invokes. The example he gives is: 'There's a bookshop on the corner and just walking past fills me with a sense of vellichor.'

Williamson's other observation about 'some fresh volume' is something that, in the case of my shop, is a real phenomenon which I could never have anticipated. It's extraordinary, but among the

100,000 titles we have on the shelves, customers – even those who have never set foot in the shop – seem to be drawn to the books we have put out most recently.

After twenty years in the trade, I still feel my pulse quickening on the rare occasions in which I visit another second-hand bookshop. It's not quite the same as a house clearance or sorting through a private library, but there's something about bookshops that fires the imagination. Sandy the tattooed pagan, one of my few regular customers, always has a look on his face when he visits the shop that is almost reminiscent of a child in a sweet shop; he knows that I never stop buying books to refresh my stock, and consequently he is possessed of a thinly veiled excitement whenever he comes here, and rarely leaves empty-handed.

FRIDAY, I APRIL

Online orders: 1
Books found: 1

It was raining when I opened the shop, and it poured incessantly until lunchtime.

ABE order for a copy of *Galloway, A Land Apart*, by Andrew McCulloch, from a customer in Canada. Most of our orders from Canadian customers are about Scottish history, largely – I suspect – because of the Nova Scotia connection and the emigration of so many Scots after the clearances.

A man with a Middle Eastern accent bought several paperbacks and left, only to reappear a moment later asking if he could use the bathroom. It was clearly a matter of some urgency, so I showed him to the loo (normally not for customers). Shortly afterwards he came to the counter and thanked me, saying, 'My prostate's not what it used to be.'

At one o'clock Gerard Brookes and Peter Dance appeared. Gerard is a book dealer who specialises in natural history, and Peter is a collector of fine, rare books. He always brings a torch which he shines on every book in the antiquarian section because the lighting there is pretty limited. They descend on the rare books like locusts, and paw and molest their way through the stock. Occasionally one of them will buy something, but I suspect today they were out on a bit of a jolly; neither bought anything.

When I was closing the shop I noticed that the boiler screen had a warning that the pressure in the system was too low. I checked the new meter and noticed it was leaking, so I emailed the people from whom I bought it and told them. Until it is fixed we will have no hot water or central heating.

Nicky and Anna came round after I'd shut the shop. We watched Nicky's favourite film, *A Knight's Tale*. I don't think I've ever seen such a dreadful film.

Till total £380.50
30 customers

SATURDAY, 2 APRIL

Online orders: 1
Books found: 1

Today's solitary order was from ABE, another Scottish book (T. C. Smout's *A History of the Scottish People*), to go to a customer in New Zealand. The Scottish diaspora appears to have settled in Canada in the northern hemisphere and New Zealand in the southern. No doubt the climates are similar.

I use the term loosely, but my 'friend' Ruaridh turned up at 11 a.m. with a box of biscuits from Chile which Christian had brought over. Ruaridh has a business making jam, marmalade and chutney in Gatehouse, about 20 miles away. His father set it up, and Christian (his half-brother) is one of my oldest friends. Christian married a Chilean woman about ten years ago, and has lived in Santiago since then. I made a pot of tea and we ate the biscuits.

Meredith, who has made a singularly ill-judged decision to become a bookseller and an even worse choice to seek my counsel on the subject by way of work experience, arrived at 3.30 p.m. I showed her to the spare bedroom and helped her with her bags.

The shop was busy all day, mainly young families, which can only mean that the schools are on holiday.

A young woman brought in a bag of books. She wants to move to California, and her daughter is keen to move to Sweden. I gave her £20 for the handful of titles that I wanted. As I was going through them it became obvious that many of them had been bought from this shop, which means I probably paid £1 for each one several years ago then sold them for £4, and now the cycle repeats itself, but this time the values have gone down in the intervening period rather than up.

Till total £423.33
28 customers

MONDAY, 4 APRIL

Online orders: 1
Books found: 1

Dreadful wet morning. Meredith was already up and about and had made herself breakfast by the time I opened the shop.

Customer: 'Is there any order to the books in this shop?'

Yes: every single shelf has a label.

Amazon has reinstated our FBA stock, and today there were several orders, but the shop's stock (Amazon Marketplace) is still suspended so I emailed them again.

Radio 3 has Vaughan Williams as Composer of the Week. *Fantasia on a Theme by Thomas Tallis* came on during Meredith's lunch break, with predictable consequences: it never fails to reduce me to tears.

Meredith seems like a very nice young woman, although she clearly hasn't grown out of the phase of life during which any sort of authority figure is ripe for mockery. I'm about as far from an authority figure as it's possible to be, but I sense that I'm in the firing line anyway.

Till total £887.45
38 customers

TUESDAY, 5 APRIL

Online orders: 0
Books found: 0

For the time of year it was surprisingly warm and sunny. Opened the shop and checked the emails, then Amazon. We're still suspended, so I asked Meredith if she could try to work out how to have our account reinstated.

Anna and I drove to Dumfries for the fortnightly general auction, at which I bought two boxes of books. After I'd paid for the books, we drove on to Doune to look at the scientific instrument collection. The house was in a neat, modern estate of expensive-looking bungalows. I rang the bell (which had sophisticated security intercom with a video camera). After a few minutes a woman's voice answered and I explained who I was. She buzzed me in and I could immediately see why it had taken her so long to answer the buzzer. She was a frail, elderly woman pushing a trolley on which she clearly relied for her mobility. She showed me to the bookcase while she and Anna chatted. Inside, the house was exactly what you would expect from a house whose exterior was immaculate and tidy – everything in its place and rigidly organised. The books were in her late husband's office: a roomful of old microscopes in beautiful wooden boxes, and other antique optical equipment.

Everything was in pristine condition, including the books, which were of such specific and niche subjects that I was fairly confident that the print runs would have been small and consequently likely to command a reasonably decent price online. I gave her £350 for five boxes, which was clearly considerably more than she had been expecting. She and Anna chatted away, but I could tell that she wasn't as relaxed and friendly as Anna. I eavesdropped as they discussed her late husband, who had been an engineer. They had lived in Paisley for most of their lives and moved to the pretty town of Doune in retirement, where, not long afterwards, he discovered that he had terminal lung cancer from working with asbestos for much of his career. He was clearly an intensely private person as he didn't tell any of their friends, nor did they know about his obsession with microscopes. From the photographs he looked like a kind man, moon-faced and bearded. Before we left, she showed us an astrolabe which he had built from scratch. We visited Doune Castle on the way home. It was still light when we got home at seven o'clock. This time of year, with the lengthening days, is unquestionably my favourite.

I made toad-in-the-hole for supper and shouted up to Meredith (who scuttles off up to her room as soon as the shop closes and stays there until the morning) to see whether she'd like to join us. She declined.

Till total £218.44
18 customers

WEDNESDAY, 6 APRIL

Online orders: 0
Books found: 0

Opened the shop and asked Meredith what our Amazon Marketplace status is. We're still suspended.

The blossom on the fruit trees is starting to open, and the flowers on the magnolia have almost opened up.

Meredith started listing the microscope books. Some are online at fairly high prices, but unless we can get back on Amazon Marketplace they are never going to sell. They definitely won't sell in the shop.

My friend the antique dealer Mary P dropped in a box of books. Very nice series by Blackie from the early twentieth century, illustrated travel guides in decorative bindings. Among them was a copy of *First Impressions of Florence*, by Selina Cole. It contained a letter from Cole to her cousin, whose father had illustrated the book. Sadly there's nothing of great value in the box.

Till total £532.98
34 customers

THURSDAY, 7 APRIL

Online orders: 0
Books found: 0

We're still suspended from Amazon Marketplace. It has definitely had an impact on our turnover, but oddly – because Amazon is so greedy – not a huge dent in our profit, and it has certainly had an impact on my state of mind. Following the initial panic, and frantic efforts to reinstate our account, I've become rather Zen about the whole situation, and not having to deal with the mean-spirited customers who use Amazon has proved to be quite refreshing. I'm contemplating making the situation permanent.

Meredith worked in the shop all day, so I took the morning off and drove to Galloway House Gardens to pick wild garlic. On the way home I went to Sainsbury's and picked up olive oil, walnuts and Parmesan and made wild garlic pesto in the afternoon.

We've run out of the canvas bags with The Bookshop branding on them, so I've ordered more. The first lot, which I ordered a couple of years ago, were flimsy and cheap, so this time I've decided to spend a bit more and get some of a considerably higher quality.

Till total £305.25
29 customers

FRIDAY, 8 APRIL

Online orders: 1
Books found: 1

I opened the shop just before 9 a.m. – it was one of those sunny spring days which almost wipe out the memory of the dank misery of winter and fill you with optimism. The daffodils around the bowling green are starting to open. Meredith appeared just after I'd opened and shot me a surly scowl when I wished her good morning.

As I was sorting through a box of books, I came across one called *Manners for Men*, published by James Bowden in London in 1897. It was impossible to resist flicking through it. The author was Charlotte Eliza Humphry, or 'Madge of Truth', as she called herself. Here are her observations on how to behave on the street:

> I once saw a Lord Mayor of London enter his carriage before his wife, who scrambled in after him as though well accustomed to do so. One does not expect the refinement of good manners from civic dignitaries, as a rule, but this little action told the spectators more about the man than they would ever have found out in the newspapers. They at once perceived that he was unversed in the ways of good society.

At least she was spared the sight of our current Prime Minister when he was Mayor of London during the 2012 Olympics dangling – waving plastic flags – 'like a damp towel slung over a washing line on a soggy day', as a passer-by, Rebecca Denton, told the *Guardian*.

Now that the weather is a little warmer, I've decided that from now on – unless we encounter a blast of particularly cold weather – I won't light the fire again until winter.

Despite my offer to cook for her every night, Meredith consistently refuses. I hear her get up regularly at about midnight and go to the kitchen and microwave something – I have no idea what.

Till total £208
14 customers

SATURDAY, 9 APRIL

Online orders: 2
Books found: 2

According to Meredith we're still suspended from Amazon, but at least we had two ABE orders today, totalling £75. I've pretty much given up on Amazon; every message I send about reinstating the account receives a reply clearly created by an algorithm, and it is impossible to speak to a human being in their Marketplace department. They don't have a telephone number, and all communication is by email. Although Amazon bought ABE in 2008, ABE still retains some of the integrity and loyalty to booksellers that Amazon completely lacks. I still dislike selling through the site, though, because Bezos owns it.

It was another sunny spring day, and the first Wigtown market of the year. The market consists of a dozen or so tented stalls in the middle of the square. I had hoped, when the idea of a Wigtown market was first suggested, that it would be a blend of a farmers' market and possibly some local crafts. Instead it is mainly people selling Country and Western CDs, and synthetic cushions, but at least it is there, and who knows what it might evolve into.

Chitra Ramaswamy called in to say hello. She's been to the festival and chaired events a few times, and her excellent book *Expecting: The Inner Life of Pregnancy* has just come out. We had a cup of tea and a catch-up.

While I was having my lunch, a man came to the counter and insisted that I come down from the office, so Meredith came upstairs and asked me if I'd be prepared to meet him. He spent twenty minutes trying to convince me to stock his self-published children's book about a livery of talking trains. When I pointed out that the Revd W. Awdry did that in1946 with *Thomas the Tank Engine*, he looked blankly at me and asked what I was talking about.

At 3 p.m. a woman brought in 200 railway books which had belonged to her late husband. No *Thomas the Tank Engines* in this collection – mainly books about the LMS. I gave her £175 for them. Just after she'd left, a man came in with 300 military history books, all in Tesco bags. This is normally a good subject, but the shelves are full at the moment, and a lot of his books were missing dust jackets and not in particularly good condition. I selected about thirty of them and gave him £50. He insisted on leaving the whole lot, and told me that they had belonged to his brother, who had served in the Gordon Highlanders. He was clearing his brother's house, as he'd been moved into a care home.

Till total £263.60
11 customers

MONDAY, 11 APRIL

Online orders: 0
Books found: 0

Before I opened the shop, I boxed up the bags of military history books that were dumped on us on Saturday and tidied the place up. Meredith checked the online value of the books I wanted to keep and priced them up. There were far fewer customers today, now that the schools have gone back after the Easter break.

Meredith found quite a few reasonably valuable books from the railway collection, but without Amazon Marketplace (still suspended) it's going to be hard to sell them well. I'll put them in the shop at significantly lower than the Amazon prices.

Two customers asked what 'Home Front Novels' are. This is one of Nicky's many legacies: she was prone to creating categories where none needed to be created, and – on finding a few books of romantic fiction set during the First and Second World Wars – decided, unilaterally, to create a genre of 'Home Front Novels'. Even though she no longer works in the shop, I haven't managed to reorganise things so that customers aren't baffled by her system of categorisation.

Callum brought ten sacks of logs. This is his latest business venture. He once confided in me that the moment he realises that he is good at something, he instantly becomes bored with it and decides to switch to a career about which he knows literally nothing. Since leaving university he has been a geologist, a financial adviser, a builder and now has ventured into solid fuel.

Locked up at 5 and went for a walk down to the salt marsh. Meredith went to her room and didn't appear again. She seems to like the solitude of her space. Either that or she just doesn't like me. On brief reflection, I suspect it's the latter.

Till total £132
11 customers

TUESDAY, 12 APRIL

Online orders: 0
Books found: 0

Meredith appeared at 9.30. Anna and Nicky came in at ten o'clock and told me that they were going to visit the Gem Rock Museum in Creetown, one of the area's most (surprisingly) popular tourist attractions. The last time I was there was about thirty years ago, and it was like walking into someone's grandmother's sitting room, but with a few not very precious stones on a table, and a papier mâché volcano mounted on a bit of plywood. Admittedly, if you pushed a button a bit of smoke came out of the volcano, but as the region's most popular tourist attraction, it was a bit underwhelming. Nicky told me that she and Anna are planning to found the Wigtown Gold Mining Company, and are going to the Gem Rock Museum for inspiration.

After lunch I left Meredith in charge and drove to Dumfries to look at a collection of books left to a widow by her husband. He had worked for the NHS and had been in charge of dentistry for the region. Often in these situations – particularly when someone has been recently bereaved – there is an emotional barrier; they don't want to acknowledge that they are disposing of a loved one's life's collection, but on this occasion she could not have been kinder, and we chatted at length about her husband, and about her own life.

On the journey home I notice that the fields, which have been greening up for the past few weeks, have assumed a sort of pinstripe. When farmers apply fertiliser to boost the spring growth, they normally roll the fields with huge rollers drawn behind tractors afterwards to push the fertiliser granules into the soil, and the result is a rather aesthetically pleasing pattern, the sort you might expect on the lawn of a formal garden, but on a much larger scale.

Home at 6 p.m.

Till total £335.50
28 customers

WEDNESDAY, 13 APRIL

Online orders: 0
Books found: 0

Sandy the tattooed pagan dropped in with some walking sticks at 10.45. Meredith spent the morning treating the leather bindings in the antiquarian section. They're prone to drying out and cracking if they're not kept in a suitable environment. This normally happens when books have been kept in a house that is too warm and too dry. Neither of these conditions applies to the shop, but I like to make sure that they're given regular maintenance. We use leather food – saddle soap or other things that moisturise the bindings and provide nutrients which keep the leather looking bright and fresh.

Sandy has been busy with his metal-detector, but has found little of interest recently, although in the past few years he's unearthed belt buckles, bullet cases and a variety of relics from the Viking era to today. Coke cans are regular finds. He takes a remarkably ethical approach to his hobby and always asks permission from farmers to trawl their fields, and tells them if and when he's found anything of interest.

Isabel came in to catch up with the accounts. She and George, her husband, have decided to start breeding Belted Galloways, cattle native to this region, which are famously good-natured and delicious.

Till total £102.45
12 customers

THURSDAY, 14 APRIL

Online orders: 0
Books found: 0

On the doorstep this morning was a large bag which had the words 'Unlucky Dip, £1 per go' written on it. The bag was filled with shredded newspaper. It was clearly a present from Graeme and Sarah at Craigard Gallery, just a few doors down from the shop. I spent a good two minutes ferreting about in there before realising there was nothing in it.

Meredith opened the shop, and I headed off towards Glenluce first thing to look at the book collection of the late Lord Devaird. He and his wife lived in a beautiful farmhouse on the coast near Auchenmalg, about half an hour from Wigtown. He was a regular customer and a very pleasant – if slightly distant – man who died in December last year. He'd been a QC, a judge and a law lecturer, whose career had been blighted by a scandal. I liked him a great deal; he was always kind and interested in what was going on in the shop. The books were in a shed, and were mostly paperback crime novels. There were about 3,000 of them. I sorted through and picked out enough to fill the van and came home. Jane, his widow, was good enough to offer me a cup of tea – a courtesy that is surprisingly rare when you're in someone's house, but one which I always offer to anyone who visits the shop in a professional capacity.

Eliot arrived at 4 p.m. We spent the evening discussing the next book festival. I felt, as always, that my brain had been mined. Managed to avoid tripping over his shoes, which he'd kicked off just outside the downstairs loo.

Till total £244.50
15 customers

FRIDAY, 15 APRIL

Online orders: 0
Books found: 0

Petra arrived at 9.50 a.m. for her belly-dancing class. Today there were no takers, so she spent an hour in the shop chatting to Meredith and me about her latest conspiracy theories; I think this one involved aliens, but in truth I can't remember.

An old man arrived with two boxes of books at 11 a.m. and left them for us to check. I sorted through them and Meredith checked them online. He returned after half an hour. I offered him £20 for them. He replied, '£20! You're joking?' If I had been joking, it would have been on the side of generosity. He took them away and told us that he was going to a 'more reputable establishment'.

An hour after he'd left another elderly man with a car full of books arrived. They were all paperbacks in poor condition, with a few old book club hardbacks. After delving through them, I discovered three local history books, none of any significant value. I offered him £15 for them. He told me that he'd never been so insulted and that he was going to donate them to the Old Bank bookshop. It's remarkable that a man who was clearly in his eighties had 'never been so insulted'. I'd been on the receiving end of considerably worse insults by the time I was five years old.

After Meredith's lunch break, I went to The Glaisnock, a B&B on the other side of the square with a restaurant, for lunch with Anna, then drove her to Lockerbie to catch a flight from Glasgow to Boston to visit her parents.

Home at 6 p.m. Meredith was in her room watching a horror film on her laptop. Either that or she was torturing the cat, to judge from the sounds.

Till total £139.40
10 customers

SATURDAY, 16 APRIL

Online orders: 0
Books found: 0

Opened the shop at 9 a.m. Meredith appeared shortly afterwards and took over with her customary scowl. My old housemate Martin is visiting Callum for the weekend. They turned up at eleven o'clock and we went upstairs for a cup of tea. Martin and I left Bristol at the same time, in 2001. He was looking for somewhere to live, so I suggested that he could move in and stay in one of the spare rooms – it gave me a small income in rent. He told me that he'd be here for a few months and moved out seven years later.

A Spanish couple came to the shop and told me that they'd both read Anna's book, and were curious to see the sights of the area, so I left Meredith in charge and drove them around the peninsula. We visited the stone circle, the Isle of Whithorn, Cruggleton Church and Sorbie Tower, and the stunning graveyard at Monreith.

Thankfully, the weather was kind to us. Returned to the shop as Meredith was hovering with the key in her hand, about to lock us out. I invited them to stay for supper, and cooked Cullen skink. They ended up spending the night in the spare room.

Late night, bed at about 2 a.m.

Till total £258.06
18 customers

MONDAY, 18 APRIL

Online orders: 3
Books found: 3

The Spanish couple left on the 11.15 a.m. bus from Newton Stewart to Dumfries. It's a pretty tortuous journey, stopping (understandably) at every possible town and village on the way.

Went to the post office when the shop was empty at one o'clock and exchanged five £20 notes for 100 £1 coins. William was having his afternoon nap.

Found another interesting note in Madge of Truth's guide to *Manners for Men*. Apparently, after leading the 'senior of the party' to a carriage with his right arm, a gentleman conveys instructions to the coachman, and if invited in to accompany the ladies, 'he always takes the back seat – that is, with his back to the horses'.

Spotted Bum-Bag Dave shuffling onto the bus to Newton Stewart as I was closing up. He hasn't set foot in the shop for quite a while. I think I may have offended him. I certainly hope so.

Till total £310
12 customers

TUESDAY, 19 APRIL

Online orders: 2
Books found: 2

Meredith opened the shop on a fairly quiet day. She went to Reading Lasses for lunch, during which I covered in the shop and dipped further into Madge of Truth's *Manners for Men*. She has much to say about hairstyles.

> 'Who is that long-haired fellow?' is the question invariably asked about any man whose visits to the barber are infrequent. 'Must be an artist or a music man' is the frequent commentary. Sometimes he is merely careless of conventionalities, and by being so proves that he is rather out of it where good society is concerned. The rule appears to be that directly a man finds that he has any hair worth brushing, he must immediately go and have it cut.

Lord knows what she'd make of my unruly mop.

When she got back from lunch, I had the following conversation with Meredith:

> Me: 'Meredith, would you mind putting the books on the
> table out on the shelves?'
> Meredith (reluctantly): 'OK.'

An hour later and there was still no sign of activity. She has the makings of a fine bookseller.

The spring seems to have brought sunshine with it this year – another beautiful day. It's been warm enough to heat up the ground sufficiently for me to have to cut the grass for the first time this year after I closed the shop. I think we're at the 'out like a lamb' end of the spring aphorism.

The number of geese flighting to the salt marsh seems to be lower than they were a month ago – some of them must have started their journey north for the summer.

Till total £149
12 customers

Online orders: o
Books found: o

Meredith left to go home to Wakefield for a break this morning. She picked a nice day to leave: the sun was shining and it was warm. I wished her a safe journey. She looked back at me as she left the shop and said, 'Yeah.'

A young American woman came to the counter with our entire stock of the Folio Society's works of Shakespeare which I bought from a house in Fife two years ago. It was complete, but I've sold odd volumes since I bought it, but she clearly decided that she was going to scoop up what remained of it. Normally people who are travelling pick up the odd paperback, but rarely anything large or heavy because of baggage restrictions. The Folio Society published Shakespeare's works individually, in slip cases between 1950 and 1976. They're all different colours, and are known as 'The Rainbow Shakespeare'.

A customer wearing a yellow duffel coat was loitering by the antiquarian section and asked, 'Are we allowed to touch?'

As long as you don't touch me, yes.

A group of four people (clearly very wealthy) came in at 3 p.m. looking for books about the Somme. They're heading there in late May for a battlefield tour. I wonder if it is run by my friend Rob Twigger's friend Mike. He set up a business a few years ago taking people on tours of battlefields and other sites of wartime importance, all accompanied by academics who give lectures on the locations.

Till total £193.49
13 customers

THURSDAY, 21 APRIL

Online orders: 0
Books found: 0

Norrie came in to cover the shop today, although the cost of his wages was significantly more than the day's takings. He worked in the shop for several years shortly after I'd bought the business. He was a godsend – incredibly capable, he fixed everything that needed to be repaired, and between us we completely re-shelved the shop.

I left the shop at 9 a.m. and drove to Glasgow with my father. A couple of years ago he came up with an idea to monitor the numbers of migratory fish returning to Scottish rivers. I pitched it to Strathclyde University, and their engineering department made a prototype. Today the students who had produced it were demonstrating how it works, and invited us up to see it in action. I decided to take the narrow road over the Galloway Hills, much to my father's concern. The blind corners and occasional forestry lorries, heavily loaded with recently felled trees, seemed to make him anxious, although he visibly swelled with pride when we arrived at the demonstration and he was treated like a visiting dignitary by the students.

We left Glasgow at three o'clock and were home by six, in the last of the lingering daylight.

Till total £26
4 customers

FRIDAY, 22 APRIL

Online orders: 1
Books found: 1

Petra appeared shortly before 10 a.m. for her belly-dancing class. She's absorbed considerably more conspiracy theories since last week, and is not afraid to share them. I think today's may have been about moon landings, but to be honest I stopped listening pretty quickly. They are so profoundly improbable that I'm astonished that such an intelligent woman would even entertain them. Nobody turned up for her class, possibly because the lizards have discovered that she knows too much and have reprogrammed humanity to steer clear of her.

Today we had an order for *The Trafalgar Companion*. Meredith had listed it at £50. Thanks to online price-matching software it sold today for £10. It's a very heavy book, and is shipping to the USA, so we will make a net loss on it.

A young hipster couple dropped off a box of books then left. I don't think they want any money for them. Mostly decent paperback fiction which will sell quickly in the shop or can go into the Random Book Club. One of the joys of living in Wigtown is that it is a place almost oblivious to the fickle whims of trends and fashions. While areas of Glasgow and London are being colonised by bearded, sleeve-tattooed quinoa ambassadors, Wigtown remains much the same as it has always been.

Till total £186.50
10 customers

SATURDAY, 23 APRIL

Online orders: 2
Books found: 2

Opened the shop half an hour late because I couldn't find the key. It had fallen into the waste paper basket when I totalled up the till last night – the force of the opening till had pushed it from the counter and into the bin. There was a fairly irritated man waiting by the door when I unlocked it. He'd been there since 9 a.m. and had brought forty boxes of books, which he hastily unloaded from his rusty van and drove off. We didn't have time to discuss whether he was donating them or was expecting to be paid before he left.

A retired Church of Scotland minister dropped off twelve plastic crates of theology books in the afternoon. Theology is a dog when it comes to sales in the shop, and I generally avoid buying any books on the subject, but he was leaving his manse and clearly wanted to dispose of them, so I agreed to take them but refused to pay for them.

There's clearly an election coming up; Aileen McLeod from the SNP called in with some leaflets, shortly followed by Alex Fergusson from the Scottish Conservative Party. I make a point of keeping politics and business apart, so all the propaganda ended up in the pile of paper which I use to light the fire.

At 3.30 a woman from Ayrshire telephoned about disposing of her parents' book collections. I've arranged to drive north to see her on Wednesday.

Till total £204.89
18 customers

MONDAY, 25 APRIL

Online orders: 1
Books found: 0

At 9 a.m. a woman telephoned to ask if she could come around with theology books to sell. I really don't need any more, after the twelve plastic crates that came in on Saturday, but I told her that I'd be happy to look at them if she was prepared to take them home with her if they were unsuitable for the shop. There's always a chance with theology that there might be something very old and potentially valuable, but it is so rare that it's easier just to say no when people call wanting to sell religious books.

At 9.10 a.m. the woman from Ayrshire who called last week telephoned to make sure that I'm still coming to see her on Wednesday. I told her that I'd be there by noon.

I was tidying the children's section at 11 a.m. when I noticed an appalling smell – it was the woman who had phoned earlier about the theology books. There was very little of interest, but I fished out a few about the pope being the Antichrist, which I was certain would appeal to some of my more bigoted Northern Irish customers, and gave her £20 for them.

My parents turned up with my father's cousin and his wife for lunch. I had completely forgotten about their visit, and all I could offer them was toasted stale bread (which I hastily scraped the mould from when they were admiring the cornicing in the drawing room) and some duck and orange pâté which I retrieved from the back of the fridge. My father's cousin used to work for Rolls-Royce, and I'm sure that they were expecting oysters and champagne. No such luck. The best that they can realistically expect from their culinary experience above The Bookshop is that they've dodged a case of listeria.

Till total £242.47
19 customers

TUESDAY, 26 APRIL

Online orders: 0
Books found: 0

Today's first customer appeared at 11.55 a.m. and complained that he was unable to buy caviar from the Co-op. The second customer came to the counter with a copy of *Biggles Delivers the Goods* for his grandson. He took an unreasonable amount of time to locate his wallet, and a further two minutes to find the £6.50 to pay for it.

The woman whose books I was supposed to look at in Ayrshire tomorrow called to say that she has a virus and has to postpone. I had arranged to look at another collection in Dumfriesshire tomorrow and had hoped to combine the two, but that no longer looks like an option.

I went through the forty boxes of books that came in on Saturday. Almost all were unsellable. More than half of them were in German and in terrible condition, so I telephoned the man with the van up to let him know. He sounded very disappointed that I'd only managed to find three boxes of material that I could sell from his collection. I offered him £50 for them. He said he'd come down to collect the rest; I told him that I can save him a trip and drop them off next time I'm passing Biggar, where he lives.

Till total £174.98
4 customers

WEDNESDAY, 27 APRIL

Online orders: 0
Books found: 0

Mary covered the shop this morning so that I could go to a house near Thornhill (an hour away) to look at a library. It belonged to a middle-aged couple downsizing from a very big house, and contained some good antiquarian Scottish material. I offered them £2,000; they told me that they are going to think about it and get back to me. Got home at about lunchtime, just in time for Mary to visit the Community Shop. She came back and proudly showed me a chopping board shaped like a fish, with a metal head (£4). I told her that my mother had given it to me for Christmas three years ago, and that – never having used it – I'd dropped it off at the charity shop a month ago.

A woman whose house I had visited to buy books from five years ago brought in two boxes of Terry Pratchett paperbacks. Within ten minutes of her leaving, a customer (black jeans, white trainers) had bought three of them.

After work I drove to Prestwick airport to pick up Granny. She's decided to move to Scotland permanently. As we were going through the Galloway Hills at 9 p.m., two Mountain Rescue Land Rovers raced past us in the opposite direction with blue lights flashing. No doubt some hillwalkers had lost their way. There's still snow on the summits. Granny's staying in the spare room until she can find a place of her own, and although she's incredibly hard-working and very entertaining company, I've decided not to let her work in the shop – she needs to find her own way in the world.

Meredith appeared at 6 p.m. after her weekend away. Which started nearly ten days ago.

Till total £228.98
17 customers

THURSDAY, 28 APRIL

Online orders: 1
Books found: 1

I spent the morning listing books on the computer in the shop, which meant that I had my back to customers. An elderly York-shireman came in, spotted me and said, 'I'm looking for the railway books, love.' Must cut my hair – my toes are curled so tight after the experience that I don't think that I'll ever walk again, and I'll be shuddering for at least a month.

Mary came in at lunchtime and took over so that I could look at a book collection in Minnigaff, near Newton Stewart. It belonged to a woman who used to go to the auction in Dumfries, and who I know only from that. The books were all about art, and in very good condition. I gave her £200 for them. My back is not in great shape, and since art books tend to weigh quite a lot (photographic paper is heavier than ordinary paper), I was almost bent double by the time I'd filled the van.

Mary told me that she'd bought a vegetable spiraliser (only used once) and 'a large chrome collar' (I didn't ask) from the Community Shop yesterday, before she left to walk her dogs on the beach at four o'clock.

Till total £40.49
4 customers

FRIDAY, 29 APRIL

Online orders: 0
Books found: 0

Petra turned up for her belly-dancing class at 10 a.m. Nobody turned up, not even the pink-haired judge's wife, who – for reasons which remain unknown to me, and which I could scarcely care less about – never talks to me on the rare occasions when she deigns to grace the premises.

Picked up *Manners for Men* again and discovered Madge of Truth's advice on riding costumes for the park: 'Only quite old-fashioned people ride in black coats, the usual gear consisting of knickerbocker suits with Norfolk, or other country jacket, brown tops and bowler hats.' I may adopt this style for mountain-biking. Madge continues: 'Many an old statesman is still to be seen in the park riding in frock-coat and tall hat, just as John Leech depicted the men of his day.' Leech (who died in 1864) was possibly Punch's most famous illustrator. He also produced work for some of Dickens's novels, notably *A Christmas Carol*. Large-format volumes of his illustrations used to sell well in the shop, as did those of his contemporary George Cruikshank, but they are both out of fashion these days, possibly because they produced work depicting highly prejudiced racial stereotypes, primarily anti-Semitic, and painting Irish rebels as barely more than monkeys and Chinese characters as barbarians. Cruikshank in the context of today's mores is particularly unacceptable for his anti-abolitionist political stance on slavery, and the illustrations he produced to support his position.

Four retired customers from Yorkshire who holiday up here several times a year appeared at 11 a.m. One of them has a house near Gatehouse, and they are regular visitors. I'm unfairly dismissive of them, but they're kind and loyal customers. Today they spotted me tidying up the Scottish room and one of them commented, 'Oh good; he's here.' If I'd had anywhere to run to, I'd have legged it, but I didn't, and I live in a state of permanent irritation that I haven't set up a speed dial to the shop telephone from my mobile so that I can run to the counter, answer it and invent an urgent emergency that requires me to desert my post.

Tomorrow is the start of our Spring Festival.

Till total £97.40
12 customers

SATURDAY, 30 APRIL

Online orders: 2
Books found: 2

Meredith opened the shop. I spent the morning preparing the drawing room for events for our Spring Book Festival. Moved the table and chairs around for events which will be unlikely to sell more than three tickets.

After lunch, I took Granny to the tiny town of Sorbie (about 5 miles away), whose population can't be more than 200 souls, most of whom aren't many years from the grave. We went to meet Morag and Andrea (Italian), the owners of a fabulous restaurant, to see whether they were prepared to offer her work. To my astonishment, they were.

Raced back to the shop to host Sandy the tattooed pagan's poetry event at 3 p.m. We sold twelve tickets, and – surprisingly – twelve people turned up. I thought that at least one of them would have died during the period between when tickets became available and the event itself.

Till total £398.70
41 customers

MAY

When we ventured within the precincts of the establishment a young man appeared from some back region to attend to our modest wants, but our ideal bookseller never rose from his chair or deigned to look our way. When we boys planned our future vocations in life, we one and all decided to be booksellers. We did not mean to be young men selling halfpenny-worths of slate pencils, or penny bottles of ink to little boys, but we meant to be fully-fledged booksellers right off. How jolly it would be to sit in a chair doing nothing all day, or no master's tawse to fear; to have an unlimited supply of stories to read, a young man to do all the work, and the privilege of talking to and smiling at a real nobleman's daughter!

R. M. Williamson, *Bits from an Old Bookshop*

I don't think I had a single schoolfriend who had it in mind that being a bookseller was their vocation in life. It was only when – aged thirty – I told my friends in Bristol that I was moving back to Scotland to run a bookshop that all of their inner booksellers came to the surface and they told me that running a bookshop had always been a dream.

Shortly after I moved back and took over the shop, an American photographer who was writing a feature for *Condé Nast Traveller* magazine asked me if I'd agree to doing a piece with some photos for the magazine. Hungry for any publicity for the shop, I agreed. It's almost unimaginable to think that only twenty years ago he shot the photos on a 35 mm film SLR, and sent me copies of them a month later by post on slides. During the shoot he told me that I was very young for a bookseller. The thought that it was a job predominantly occupied by those more advanced in years had never even occurred to me, but as other booksellers came to pillage my stock over that first year, it became increasingly obvious that for many of them – though by no means all – it was almost a retirement hobby. At one point Williamson mentions that

the bookseller who owned the shop was an old gentleman of mild aspect, whose dress, manners, and tone of voice were in our eyes the perfection of respectability. We thought him a far greater and wealthier man than the minister, and the doctor was nobody compared to him. He seemed to spend his time writing, reading, and meditating. We never saw him cleaning the windows, sweeping the floor, or dusting the shop.

If only this were true. For something perceived as genteel, book-selling is back-breaking work, and the constant driving long distances, and lugging of heavy boxes of books from the houses of the dead down flights of stairs and into the van takes its toll. Even the elderly Mr Pumpherston in *The Intimate Thoughts of John Baxter, Bookseller* is fairly industrious, and Arnold Bennett's Henry Earlforward in *Riceyman Steps* seems rarely to be caught sitting idly in his chair by his miser's fire, reading.

SUNDAY, I MAY

Online orders: 1
Books found: 1

Opened the shop at 9 a.m. and lit the stove, as well as the fire in the big room above the shop, in preparation for Andy Nicholson's event at noon. Andy is the county archaeologist and an accom-plished public speaker. He came to talk about the Galloway Hoard, a huge collection of treasure unearthed by a metal-detectorist in 2014 and swiftly removed to the National Museum of Scotland.

A customer came to the counter with six books and asked for a trade discount. First time in ages that I've had a trade sale, apart from a couple of regulars.

An elderly couple came to the counter with a copy of Thomas Garnett's *Observations on a Tour Through the Highlands*, from 1811, priced at £450, which we listed online years ago. I suspected that it was overpriced, so I checked comparable copies and let them have it for £200.

Nicky arrived about half an hour before Andy's talk about the Galloway Hoard expecting to be able to attend, even though she didn't have a ticket. About ten other people did the same thing, despite the event selling out days ago. I asked her if she could introduce Andy and take tickets at the door.

After Andy's hugely popular and fascinating talk, Sara Maitland – author of the superb *A Book of Silence* – came to the shop and spoke to another packed room (people turn up at the last minute during our Spring Festival). Sara lives in the wilderness of the hills behind nearby Glenluce, and has become a friend over the years. She and Bill Clinton were friends when he was a Rhodes Scholar at Oxford and she was reading English there.

Till total £122.65
10 customers

MONDAY, 2 MAY

Online orders: 1
Books found: 1

Before I opened the shop this morning I moved the furniture back in the big room to the more domestic arrangement we had before the talks here yesterday afternoon.

Telephone call this morning from a woman in London whose Portuguese home I cleared in 2014. She is looking for a large, illustrated book on the history of art for her grandchildren. She and her husband had worked overseas for most of their working lives, and were both keen readers. They'd amassed a considerable library when the time came for retirement, and they bought a bungalow in Amarante, a beautiful town in northern Portugal. Sadly, shortly after they'd moved, he died and she moved back to London to be closer to friends and family, leaving the house full of their possessions. She telephoned me in 2013 and told me that I could have the books for nothing provided I could clear them, so I called my friend Rob Twigger and asked if he'd be up for an adventure. I drove the van down from Scotland and met him in Portsmouth on a wet and windy January day, and we boarded the ferry and set off.

If there's one piece of advice that I ought to have listened to, it is that of my friend Angus, a retired submariner, who told me: 'Never cross the Bay of Biscay in January.' It was an incredibly rough crossing, and while we were waiting for the wind to drop enough for us to be able to enter the harbour, we were tossed about so much that the dog pound flooded, drowning the dogs. We eventually made port, and set off for Amarante – 500 miles away – in the driving rain and found a hotel. The following day we drove to the house and were let in by a young French woman who told us that every heroin addict in the area had broken in and stolen everything apart from the books, which, ironically, were probably the most valuable things in the place.

The journey home was eventful. The Biscay ferry was cancelled, so we had to drive to Caen, which involved a rather unpleasant encounter with a customs officer at the Spanish–French border and a further 500 miles of driving. The books probably just about covered the cost of the trip, but it was worth it, for no other reason than to have an adventure with Rob.

The woman who was disposing of the books had been good to me, so I told her to leave the quest for the book about the history of art with me, and promised to see what I could find. She was delightful, and repeated, 'I knew I could rely on you,' several times. When I asked for her address, she told me that she's in a BUPA nursing home – 'dreadful people'. I don't know whether she was referring to the staff or the other inmates.

Till total £216.99
18 customers

TUESDAY, 3 MAY

Online orders: 2
Books found: 2

Mary came in to cover the shop today. Yesterday she bought a gavel and two pottery bongos in the Community Shop. I'm not sure whether she has a change of career in mind, but if she does, it involves either becoming the Speaker of the House of Commons or joining a calypso band.

Book deal in Ayrshire in the afternoon: a woman whose house reeked of damp dogs, and was full of budgie cages. She was about my age and we quickly discovered that we have several mutual friends, although I wouldn't say that she was particularly friendly. In fact, I'd probably go further and say that she was a little hostile. Perhaps Our Mutual Friends weren't that mutual after all.

She was disposing of her parents' books. Her father had been the factor of a large estate in Perthshire and they had retired to a flat in Ayr to be close to her and her family. There were some reasonable books, but by far the most outstanding item was a limited edition of *The Wind in the Willows*, signed by E. H. Shepard. I took Meredith with me so she could see another side of the bookselling business and asked her what she thought the collection (minus the Shepard) was worth. In my head I had come up with a figure of £150, which was exactly the figure she arrived at. There were quite a few Folio Society titles in slip cases, and we have gaps on the shelves of the Folio section at the moment, so I grabbed them, and a decent collection of Arthur Ransomes in reasonable condition.

Made it back home at 6 p.m. Meredith went straight to her bedroom. When I passed her door, I could hear the sound of chainsaws and screaming coming from her laptop.

Till total £263
18 customers

WEDNESDAY, 4 MAY

Online orders: 1
Books found: 1

Opened the shop at 9.05 a.m. Meredith appeared shortly afterwards, and we unloaded the books from Ayr from the van.

Isabel came in today to undertake the unenviable task of balancing the shop's books. Financial books.

While I was covering Meredith's lunch break, a customer came to the counter to pay for three Malcolm Saville paperbacks, and sneezed in my face so closely that I had to clean my glasses after she'd left.

Cooked carbonara for supper and shouted up to Meredith, who had, as usual, retreated to her room the moment the shop shut. I was met with the customary, 'No, thanks.'

Till total £168.94
19 customers

THURSDAY, 5 MAY

Online orders: 2
Books found: 2

Meredith and I were sorting through the books we'd bought in Ayrshire on Tuesday when she picked up a 1929 edition of Oliver Goldsmith's *The Vicar of Wakefield*, hugely popular with the Victorians, illustrated by Arthur Rackham. Her face lit up when she saw the title, and – with as much excitement as she's capable of mustering (which isn't a great deal) – she said, 'Oooh, look, a book about Wakefield!' Despite being from Wakefield, in west Yorkshire, astonishingly, Meredith hadn't heard of this famous book. I fear for her future in the book trade.

We only sold two books today – a copy of Gavin Maxwell's *Ring of Bright Water* and a copy of *West over the Waves*, a book that is begging to be made into a film, written by Jayne who has the shop next door. It is a biography of the impetuous Scottish aristocrat Elsie Mackay, who defied the conventions of the 1920s and attempted to defy the laws of physics by flying across the Atlantic only a few years after the Wright brothers had managed the first powered flight.

Till total £12.99
2 customers

Online orders: 0
Books found: 0

Warm day, with a smell of damp spring growth in the air. Opened the shop and left the door open for the first time this year.

The local Bernard Cornwell collector was in this morning. He bought six non-fiction books on maritime history. I think his exposure to the fictional worlds of Patrick O'Brian and Alexander Kent has given him a thirst for more knowledge.

In the afternoon, after several hours, I managed to work out how to do live chat with Amazon, and their rep, Ramil, has assured me that the seller performance team will be in touch within twenty-four hours.

No sign of Meredith all day. Even her noisy laptop seems to have become silent.

Went to the pub with Callum after work for a quick pint.

When I got home, I noticed that the setting sun had lit the few clouds in the sky a glorious pink, so I decided to take a photograph of it by standing on the balcony wall, which afforded me a little extra height and a much better view. While I was (admittedly a little unsteadily) attempting to manoeuvre myself into the best position to take an Instagrammable photograph, I stumbled on a plant pot (dill) and fell over. I landed on the bothy roof with a heavy fall. Suspect I may have broken at least one rib.

Till total £244.49
16 customers

SATURDAY, 7 MAY

Online orders: 1
Books found: 1

Opened the shop at nine o'clock as usual. Expected to see Meredith by ten, but she still appears to be in hibernation. I'm pretty sure that she's still alive because I heard the ping of the microwave at midnight.

I've definitely broken a rib. I barely slept last night because of the pain.

Overheard two customers, a man and a woman, chatting by the history section:

'I want something to read, but I don't want to pay for it, if you know what I mean.'

So, you're either going to a library or you're about to steal a book.

Picked and packed the remaining random books and took the bags over to Wilma in the post office. She told me that there's a rumour that William is selling the business, but she told me not to get too excited. Similar rumours have been circulating for years and are – mostly – a case of wishful thinking.

Till total £297.88
26 customers

MONDAY, 9 MAY

Online orders: 2
Books found: 1

Meredith reappeared at 11 a.m. after her leave of absence. She'd been ill for a couple of days but was feeling better this morning, so I left her in charge of the shop and went into the garden to cut the grass and do some weeding. When I was covering her lunch break, Bum-Bag Dave appeared and asked me what time the bus to Newton Stewart leaves. We had our usual argument about whether or not I'm providing a public service, and precisely what duties he – as a long-term unemployed man – felt I ought to be performing.

Till total £25
3 customers

TUESDAY, 10 MAY

Online orders: 3
Books found: 1

A customer wearing a thick tweed skirt was waiting outside the shop when I opened at 9 a.m. She pointed theatrically at her watch and said, 'What time do you call this?' I pointed at the clock tower on the county buildings and said, 'Nine o'clock,' at which she produced an even more theatrical sigh and pushed past me into the shop. After about an hour she came to the counter and said, 'I see you don't have any books about cooking with roadkill.' I replied that I was unaware that such a book even existed, to which she responded, 'Ahh, that's where you're wrong. There is an excellent one, and I know that because I wrote it. I really think that you ought to stock it.' As politely as I was capable of in the face of her exceptional rudeness, I told her that we only really stock new books about local history. She repeated the dramatic sigh from our earlier conversation and left in a tweedy flout.

Meredith spent the day reorganising the crime section. Customers tend to have a slightly cavalier disregard for putting books back in alphabetical order.

Till total £259.45
18 customers

WEDNESDAY, 11 MAY

Online orders: 1
Books found: 1

Meredith was having breakfast when I came down to the kitchen to make a cup of tea before opening the shop. She's perfectly friendly when she's not in her room, where it appears she spends much of her time watching horror films and chatting to her friends on Skype.

Caravan season is upon us again. When I opened the shop, there was an enormous motorhome parked in front of the shop. I wandered across the street to see quite how massive it was. Even from the bus stop – about 50 metres away – I couldn't see any of the ground floor of the building. I'm starting to wonder if I'm on some sort of Pokemon-type list where members of the Caravan Club gain points for taking a photo of their hideous vehicles in front of the shop.

Mole-Man came in after lunch and silently burrowed his way through the shop, picking up his usual assortment of books on completely unconnected titles: today's haul included crochet, poetry, two books about Scottish railways and a Jean Plaidy historical fiction novel from her Plantagenet Saga.

The motorhome was still there when I locked up.

Till total £134.80
13 customers

THURSDAY, 12 MAY

Online orders: 2
Books found: 2

Woken by Captain at 7 a.m. He jumped onto my bed, then walked over me and sat on my chest. This usually means that he's run out of food, so I got up and fed him, then went back to bed.

Opened the shop with Meredith at 9 a.m. The giant motorhome is still there in front of the shop, taunting me. Kate the postie arrived at ten o'clock with the usual assortment of bills, but among them was a small parcel from one of my old Bristol friends. It contained a copy of a novella by E. M. Forster called *The Machine Stops*, and a note telling me that I would almost certainly like it. I'd never heard of it. I will read it when I have time.

At eleven o'clock a family (parents, three children) came in after a walk on the salt marsh. It was obvious that that was where they'd been because the heavy clay mud is quite distinctive (it dries a light grey colour) and they'd clearly made absolutely no effort to wash their boots before descending on the shop and trailing mud through every room. One of the children – a small boy – bought a copy of Enid Blyton's *The Caravan Family*. I wonder if they're the owners of the accursed vehicle that is still parked in front of the shop.

Till total £37
6 customers

FRIDAY, 13 MAY

Online orders: 1
Books found: 0

I opened the shop, and Meredith appeared shortly afterwards and complained about the motorhome. She's clearly recovered from her illness. At eleven o'clock a young woman brought in three boxes of books, mainly modern paperback fiction and quite decent material: Toni Morrison, Kurt Vonnegut, Kazuo Ishiguro, Haruki Murakami, Iris Murdoch, Evelyn Waugh and many others whose works are loosely described as literary fiction, all in excellent condition. I gave her £75 for them. They're all authors who I like to have in stock, but once the gaps on the shelves are filled, the remainder can go to the Random Book Club customers.

Nipped out after lunch for a haircut at the hairdresser's (three doors down). Richard, the large man who used to cut hair, has given up and it has been taken over by a young woman called Naomi. Thankfully she's almost as fast as Richard and has stuck to his low prices. For me, it costs about £5, which I have calculated translates to about 50p per minute. She asked me how I wanted her to cut my hair. I hadn't really thought about it, so I shrugged and said that I'd leave it up to her to decide. I left her salon after ten minutes looking like a ginger pineapple.

Returned to the shop and sorted through the books which came in this morning. Meredith priced them up and put them out.

Till total £239.48
23 customers

SATURDAY, 14 MAY

Online orders: 1
Books found: 1

I suspect that Meredith is planning to leave soon; she has become increasingly rude to me over the period of her time here – not offensive, but definitely lacking in even the slightest measure of respect. I think I may have successfully put her off a career in bookselling.

When Meredith was having her lunch break, a man dressed entirely in black with long white hair and a white beard came in with a small bag of books to sell. He looked like a budget Billy Connolly. The books were largely modern hardback fiction and not terribly interesting, but he has more, so I arranged to visit him next Thursday to look at them.

This afternoon I discovered the full horror of Meredith's 'system' for putting books on shelves according to their subject: a copy of *Swallows and Amazons* in the ornithology section.

Elderly couple came in at lunchtime and, as they were passing, the husband spotted a copy of a first edition of H. G. Wells's *The First Men in the Moon*, in a blue cloth gilt-decorated binding, published by Newnes in 1901. A discussion followed between them, during which they reminisced about having seen the film, and they both decided that they'd like to read the book. I was sorting through a box of books at the time. The husband walked over with the copy of the book and asked, 'How much is that?' I think he was expecting that it would be £2 or £3: he looked quite shocked when I told him that it was £400, and told me that it was 'a little more than I expected'. At least he had the decency to put it like that, rather than the usual, 'Bloody hell, it was tuppence when it came out.'

Till total £90.49
13 customers

MONDAY, 16 MAY

Online orders: 4
Books found: 2

Meredith and I spent about two hours trying to locate the missing orders: a book called *The Behavioural Effects of Canine Castration: An Owner's Guide* and another whose title is *The Heyday of the Welsh Narrow Gauge*. We emailed to apologise and issued refunds. Thankfully we're still suspended from Amazon, and the orders were on ABE, which doesn't offer a customer feedback facility, one of the most abused and unfair features of Bezos's website. Meredith was fairly critical of my 'system' for finding online orders. We're only managing to fulfil about 50 per cent of them. The only way to get close to 100 per cent is to have a warehouse to which the public has no access – having online stock in the shop is always going to cause problems. For a small business, it's a difficult problem to solve; we would require another property, and a dedicated member of staff whose job was to deal with listing and dealing with orders. When we tried this before, it barely broke even financially, and caused me considerable administrative headaches, so I wound it up and sold the stock to another dealer, who ended up having exactly the same problems and winding up his online business.

We gave up our search for the books about castration and Welsh railways at lunchtime. Meredith went to Reading Lasses for her lunch break and I covered in the shop. She has now broken the record for the shop's longest lunch break: she came back at 2.30, two hours after she'd left.

At about 12.45 an elderly couple came in. The woman was obviously partially sighted and accompanied by a guide dog – a friendly-looking golden Labrador. Captain, who had been sitting on the counter for most of the morning, took one look at the dog and leapt, snarling and hackles up, towards the creature, which – clearly trained to deal with aggressive cats – sat down silently and stared at him. I grabbed the hissing feline by the scruff of the neck and managed to escape with just a few bites and scratches before I locked him in the kitchen. I apologised profusely to the customers, who were remarkably sanguine about it and were generous enough to say that Captain was just defending his territory.

Till total £130.50
10 customers

TUESDAY, 17 MAY

Online orders: 2
Books found: 2

Granny, who has been sleeping in the spare room for months now, has found work in The Pheasant, a restaurant about 5 miles away, in the tiny village of Sorbie. It is run by a local woman called Morag and her Italian husband, Andrea. They've done a fantastic job of turning what was, when I was young, a run-down pub into a stylish restaurant with excellent food. When my parents moved to Scotland before I was born, the pub was called The Fair Seat but known to locals as 'The Sair Feet' because it's a fairly long walk from everywhere.

Today was Granny's first day, and she left on the bus at 9 a.m. She was standing at the bus stop (opposite the shop) smoking a cigarette when I opened the shop, and as soon as she saw me she raised her middle finger at me and mouthed, 'Fuck off, you shitty fucking bastard.'

Meredith asked if she could take today and tomorrow off to go to Coventry to see her former flatmates (musicians) perform in their finals. I say 'asked', but she presented it to me as a fait accompli, and jumped into her car and left shortly after I opened the shop and before I'd had a chance to agree.

My sister and her children called into the shop at 11 a.m. They're down visiting my parents for a couple of nights.

As I was sorting through boxes of books, I found a sick note for someone called Holly Jarvis, from Fettes College, dated 1986, in a six-volume set of Boswell's *Life of Johnson*.

The new batch of bookshop bags arrived. They're a significant improvement on the last lot. They cost £3.50 each, so I'll sell them in the shop for £5.

At lunchtime I sold eight Arthur Ransome titles from the Ayr deal a week or two ago to a middle-aged couple who, at the counter, told me that 'You can do better than this. I mean £8.50 each is a bit steep.' It really isn't, not for Arthur Ransome first editions in dust jackets, so I offered to give them a £1 discount. He replied, 'That's more like it, so £7.50 each then.' I had – as he inferred – intended to give them £1 off per volume, but his sense of smugness that he could dictate the terms of the contract irked me, so I told him that the discount was on the total, not per volume. I could see his brow furrowing in silent fury, but he clearly wanted the books, and knew that he was already on the receiving end of a bargain before he began his negotiation. He put the books on the counter, visibly seething, and wandered off to browse more. His wife found six green Penguin Simenons (Georges Simenon wrote the Maigret novels), and this time didn't ask for a discount.

Till total £304.47
25 customers

WEDNESDAY, 18 MAY

Online orders: 2
Books found: 2

Granny was in her trench coat smoking a cigarette at the bus stop when I opened the shop. We went through what I suspect will become a daily ritual of whoever spots the other first raising their middle finger and cursing the other.

Customer brought in a paperback copy of *Spring Fever*, by P. G. Wodehouse, which he'd bought last week for £2.50. 'I've read this one now, can I swap it for another £2.50 book?'

Drove to Galloway House Gardens for a walk after I'd closed the shop. The sweet smell of freshly cut grass filled the air almost all the way from the shop to Garlieston. It's the first cut of silage for most farmers, and the deep green fields are now a light yellow, with rows of dark green, awaiting the arrival of the forage harvester tomorrow or the following day.

Till total £304.47
25 customers

THURSDAY, 19 MAY

Online orders: 2
Books found: 2

Two old women arrived with three boxes of books to sell. They came to the counter (I was reading *Manners for Men*) and accused me of being asleep, presumably because I didn't leap to attention when they appeared. The books were fairly average, mostly paperback fiction from the 1950s. Gave them £20.

Young couple bought a copy of Stevenson's *Virginibus Puerisque*. It was from the Tusitala edition. She was American, he was Scottish and they were here with his parents. They discussed the relative merits of Kindle v. books. He has a Kindle; she refuses to touch it and only reads books.

Tusitala is a Samoan word which translates roughly as 'teller of tales', and is how the Samoans referred to Stevenson when he spent time recuperating there. He suffered from breathing problems for most of his life, and his doctor suggested that he move to the South Pacific for the benefit of his health. Heinemann published his complete works in a blue cloth binding in the 1920s. When I bought the shop, the Tusitala set would regularly sell for about £80. Now nobody seems to want it. I can't remember when I last sold a set.

Drove to Glenluce after lunch to look at books. Granny had a day off from The Pheasant and covered for me in the shop. The books were in a former council house on the side of a windswept hill. The building appeared to have been converted from a house into a series of single-room bedsits, apparently designed by someone who was more accustomed to building prison cells than homes. Paul, the man with the black clothes and white hair who was in the shop earlier this week, was selling his books because he is moving to California. He showed me to his room, which can't have been more than 6ft by 6ft and was completely dark with a mezzanine bed under which it was too low to stand. Most of the books were modern fiction, and aside from a television and a laptop, the tiny space seemed mainly full of junk: ornaments, broken guitars, photographs and ashtrays. He clearly spends most of his life here smoking and listening to classical music. Debussy and a fog of smoke filled the acrid air when I arrived. There was nothing of great interest – a few signed copies of books by people I'd never heard of and some barely sellable shop stock. I gave him £70 for two boxes, and was very happy to emerge into the light and the fresh air, and pick my way through the pile of rusting children's bicycles and broken washing machines that littered the garden. It ranks fairly highly in the top ten most depressing places from which I've ever bought books.

Back in the shop about twenty minutes later, where a woman bought *The World's Greatest Golf Courses* for her ninety-nine-year-old father. It's a book that accompanies a TV series which her father likes to watch, and she thinks he'll enjoy it more if he can look at the aerial photos of the courses while he's watching the series.

Meredith was supposed to be back yesterday, but still no sign of her.

Till total £227.49
22 customers

FRIDAY, 20 MAY

Online orders: 3
Books found: 3

Petra's belly-dancing class at 10 a.m. Nobody turned up, but she decided to sit in the drawing room above the shop for an hour, 'Just in case.'

Customer bought a copy of the superbly titled *Donald McLeod's Gloomy Memories*. I'm sure I've sold a copy of it before. Must read it.

It was Tuesday morning when Meredith asked, 'Is it OK if I take today and tomorrow off?'

Me: 'Yes, of course.'

It's now Friday and there's still no sign of her, nor any word from her. I salute her cavalier approach to the world of employment.

Spent the evening reading E. M. Forster's *The Machine Stops*. It's a fantastic novella, published in 1909 and remarkably prescient in its dystopian vision of a future in which humanity has become entirely disconnected from itself. Everyone lives in their own underground cell, and is entirely dependent on the Machine. Human contact is through devices that look strikingly like the internet, and physical contact has become so alien that when Vashti – one of the two characters – has to travel by airship, and is about to fall over, she exclaims, 'How dare you! You forget yourself!' when a stewardess on the airship attempts to catch her. Forster explains that the stewardess 'was confused, and apologised for not having let her fall. People never touched one another. The custom had become obsolete, owing to the Machine.'

Till total £77
6 customers

Online orders: 0
Books found: 0

Granny and I had our customary exchange across the street when I opened the shop. Today she held her cigarette between gritted teeth and raised the middle finger of both hands in hostile salute.

At 10.30 a.m. a customer asked where the hardback fiction section was – he was looking for books by H. Rider Haggard. Five minutes later, while he was leaning against a stepladder, he asked, 'Is there something I can stand on to get to a higher shelf?'

We had no internet until noon. I suspect that there was an engineer tinkering with the exchange.

At two o'clock a customer asked for a copy of *Paradise Lost*. Showed him a two-volume set from 1824 in a slightly tatty calf binding which had come in a week ago from a customer who was clearing his late father's house in Kirkinner (4 miles away).

> Customer: 'How much?'
> Me: 'It's £17.' (Thinking to myself, 'Bloody hell, that's cheap'.)
> Customer: 'Oh no. There's no way I'm paying that much for an old book.'

Still no sign of Meredith when I shut the shop.

When Granny got home from The Pheasant, she commented that we seem to have lost some cutlery and crockery. I hadn't really noticed, but as soon as she mentioned it I could see that the drawers and cupboards were significantly depleted. I expect my mother may have borrowed it for a lunch party.

Till total £187.50
19 customers

Online orders: 3
Books found: 3

Granny had already headed off to work when I opened the shop
this morning. She told me last night that she's now made friends
with the bus driver, who has taken to lecturing her about smoking.
When she gets on the bus in the morning she's smoking, and when
she's waiting at the bus stop in Sorbie to come home at the end of
the day, she has a cigarette on the go.

A customer spent an hour wandering around the shop,
whistling tunelessly. I was reaching for the customer-beating stick
when he came to the counter with £120 worth of books, at which
point my scowl swiftly became a friendly smile.

Spent the afternoon flicking through *The Machine Stops* again.
When the Machine begins to break down, and Vashti's equivalent
of Spotify stops working properly, she complains to the Machine.
It rapidly becomes evident that both the Committee of Mending
Apparatus and the Central Committee are the 1909 equivalent of
an Amazon algorithm:

> 'If you don't mend it at once, I shall complain to the Central
> Committee.'
> 'No personal complaints are received by the Central
> Committee,' the Committee of the Mending Apparatus
> replied.
> 'Through whom am I to make my complaint, then?'
> 'Through us.'
> 'I complain then.'
> 'Your complaint shall be forwarded in its turn.'
> 'Have others complained?'
> This question was unmechanical and the Committee of the
> Mending Apparatus refused to answer it.

When I first read this, I was compelled to re-read my correspondence with Amazon when I was first suspended, and my efforts to
have my account reactivated:

Me: Please could someone contact me regarding this case. I have been suspended since last year and although I have submitted an action plan which addressed the problem several times, I have not been able to reinstate my account. The damage this has done to my business is extremely serious and I would appreciate any help getting my account reinstated. I have been selling successfully on Amazon for several years.

Amazon Seller Support: Hello Shaun, this is [...] the Seller Support that you have chatted earlier. I understand that you would like to reinstate your account that has been suspended. As we've discussed, I highly suggest you to send an email directly to our Performance team for you to reinstate your suspended account.

Amazon Seller Performance Team: Hello Shaun, This is an automated response to confirm that we have received your email. Please do not respond to this auto-generated email. Your email will be reviewed by the Amazon.co.uk Seller Performance Team...

There is no telephone number for the Seller Performance Team. Even other departments within Amazon are unable to speak with them directly.

Meredith returned at 4 p.m., almost a week after she left for 'two days off'. Impressively, she offered no explanation for her absence.

Till total £40.50
16 customers

TUESDAY, 24 MAY

Online orders: 2
Books found: 2

Sunny spring day. I opened the shop, then Meredith took over at 9.30 with a scowl that could have melted granite. She still hasn't told me about her mini-break. I've grown rather fond of her absolute disregard for my authority.

Spent most of the day in the van driving to Glasgow with a load of dead stock for recycling. As usual, weighed in, unloaded and weighed out again. I expect I'll receive my cheque for around £40 for roughly 2,000 books which will be put on the conveyor belt, shredded, baled and sent to China. I usually have a chat with the young woman who works there; she spends her holidays in a caravan site not too far from Wigtown, but she wasn't there today.

I stopped near Kilmarnock to look at a collection of Burns books that belonged to a one-legged Church of Scotland minister. It was a fairly decent lot, so I offered him £600 for it. He laughed and told me that he'd been offered that for just one of the 100 or so titles in the collection. If he has, then someone is about to make a very costly mistake: the most valuable of the books in his library was worth £50 at the very most. I left empty-handed, but with £600 still in my pocket. This is far from unusual with collections on a single theme. People who collect on the same subject often know far more about it than I do, but with Burns there's a basic rule of thumb: anything published before he died (1796) tends to be of value, but very little published after that is worth much, unless it's in a fine binding. He will perish with his collection of Burns.

Home at 2 p.m. I gave Meredith a break. A customer asked for the wifi password. I couldn't be bothered to go upstairs and get the card, so I told him that we're not connected to the internet. Shortly afterwards I spotted him taking photographs of books then putting them back on the shelf. At least he won't be using my wifi when he orders them online.

Till total £137.97
17 customers

WEDNESDAY, 25 MAY

Online orders: 4
Books found: 3

Shortly after I opened the shop there was a telephone call from a customer with a strong Irish accent who asked, 'Hello. I'm looking for a book written about himself by the black fella who lived on Robben Island. Do you have a copy?'

Can it possibly get worse?

Meredith appeared at ten o'clock, yawned, stretched and told me that she's decided that I have no further wisdom to impart to her regarding the world of bookselling, so she's going home on Saturday.

Two elderly women came into the shop after lunch. One of them spotted Captain, who had just come in from the rain and was damp and smelly; cue several double entendres involving the word 'pussy', which – childish though I am – are not worthy of repetition.

Found another superb passage from *Manners for Men*. This time Madge is advising the young gentleman wishing to make his mark on 'society' on the correct way to behave 'In or on an Omnibus':

> In a carriage one is seldom crowded up to the degree that often occurs in the plebeian 'bus'. In fact, there are far more opportunities for the display of good manners in the latter than the former. Many of them are of a negative character. True courtesy, for instance, will prevent a man from infringing the rights of his neighbours on either side by occupying more than his own allotted space. Very stout men are obliged to do so, but at least they need not spread out their knees in a way that is calculated to aggravate the evil.

And so, in 1897, Madge may well have been the first person in the world to highlight the offence of 'manspreading' on public transport.

Till total £382.30
25 customers

THURSDAY, 26 MAY

Online orders: 2
Books found: 2

Opened the shop with Meredith at 9 a.m. She seems remarkably cheery to be leaving.

Isabel came in at 2 p.m. to do the accounts. I always try to hide when I see her car approaching because she spends the day asking me questions about the business accounts that I really ought to be able to answer but rarely can. I probably shouldn't be running a business. Annoyingly, today she spotted me and collared me.

My friend the artist Davy Brown arrived at the same time as Isabel. I've offered to let him use the drawing room as a gallery for Spring Fling, so he spent the afternoon setting up, lugging large display boards and paintings from his car up the stairs to the room. Spring Fling is an event in which artists open up their studios to visitors. It has been going on for about twenty years, and brings a remarkable number of visitors to the area, some just curious to see how artists work, and others – perhaps more astute – to buy work directly from artists without having to pay the gallery commission, which is now almost 50 per cent. For a couple of years I've rented the space that used to be the warehouse for our online stock to a young artist called Emily Nash. Her mother works for the Wigtown Book Festival Company. Emily is a charming young woman, but terribly shy. She's managed to secure a place in this year's Spring Fling programme and is exhibiting her work in the old warehouse in the back garden of the shop. This means that between Davy and Emily the shop should be busy this weekend.

Meredith disappeared up to her room when I shut the shop, not to be seen again – as always – until tomorrow morning. The microwave will ping at midnight, like an irritating Big Ben.

Till total £113.03
20 customers

Online orders: 0
Books found: 0

Meredith was late up, and so managed to avoid the first customer
of the day who asked, 'Have you got a section on Spain, other than
in the travel section?'

Me: 'No.'

Customer continued to stare at me, grinning, for a further
thirty seconds, as though I might change my mind.

Gerard, one of the few book dealers who still visits and occasionally buys books, turned up with his friend Peter. They often
appear together, as Gerard visits him on his way north to trawl
the bookshops of Scotland for buried treasure, and brings him to
Wigtown from Carlisle, as Peter no longer drives. Gerard bought
the eleven-volume *English Botany* set dated 1832 from Lord
Devaird's collection for £250; Peter bought a folio limited edition
of Poe's *The Bells* illustrated by Dulac in a Yapp binding. A Yapp
binding is a limp bound book. Usually the soft card boards are
covered in a sort of suede which extends over all of the edges. It
was introduced to the world of binding by British binder William
Yapp in the nineteenth century and was predominantly used for
Bibles, although over the years I've found numerous small, pocket-
sized volumes of poetry in Yapp bindings too. I can't say that I'm
particularly fond of it: it has an unfinished look, and the books
don't sit neatly on the shelves because they lack a straight bottom
edge. *The Bells* is the first Folio Society title I've seen bound in a
Yapp binding.

After I closed the shop, I tidied up the garden for Spring
Fling opening night. Visitors will be able to access Davy's show
through the shop, then wander through the garden to Emily's
show in Lochancroft, the building where I used to have my online
stock.

Davy and Emily had a private viewing of their shows, so we
kept the shop open until 9 p.m. so that visitors could come and
view and – hopefully – buy some paintings. Davy's work used to be
fairly abstract, but he's turned to landscapes in the past few years;

he paints very much in the style of the Glasgow School, and his work is bright and colourful. When I closed, I went upstairs for a chat with him. I think he expected to sell more than he did, but there were a few red stickers dotted around the place to denote sales. However, as he pointed out, they were mainly on lower-value prints, rather than the higher-value originals. The high till total for today is explained by the fact that some of Davy's art sales went through the card machine and consequently through the till. The actual figure for book sales is closer to £140.

Till total £734.99
13 customers

SATURDAY, 28 MAY

Online orders: o
Books found: o

Today was Meredith's final day in the shop. We opened up together. Once the shop was open I went to make us both a cup of tea. While I was waiting for it to brew, she shouted up from downstairs:

'Shaun! There's some old woman here who wants to sell you books.'

Her training is complete.

Today was the official opening of Spring Fling, and Davy appeared at 10 a.m. to be on duty, charming visitors and hopefully selling some of his work to them. I needed to be around in the morning to help in the event of there being some sort of crisis. As it happens, Davy has done this several times now and is well prepared, but Meredith was kind enough to postpone her departure until the afternoon to cover the shop for the morning. She left at 2.30, and while I will be sad not to have her help in the shop, there were no tears and hugs, or promises of returning. She's a curious young woman, perfectly polite and friendly, but it was almost as though she created her own island while she was here – not even eating with Granny and me, never coming to the pub and keeping herself to herself. It was, though, extremely helpful having her here.

Till total £187.50
19 customers

SUNDAY, 29 MAY

Online orders: 1
Books found: 1

Second day of Spring Fling, so I had to open the shop at nine o'clock, but now without the help of Meredith. Managed to find today's order, which was for another book from the Stranraer ornithology collection. It's always rewarding when you spend a lot on a decent library and can recover most of it fairly quickly but books from it continue to sell over a longer period. Often with book deals the best material sells very quickly, and what's left eventually ends up in the recycling after three years of gathering dust on the shelves.

Granny kindly brought me a piece of cake from Reading Lasses, and while I was eating it at lunchtime, a customer appeared and asked if we had any books on American Civil War quilting. To my astonishment, we had two. I've bought some large Civil War collections over the past couple of years – it's a good subject for the shop and always sells well, as do books on quilting. Combining the two is a winning formula.

At two o'clock a man wearing a straw fedora brought in two boxes of books, mostly Penguin drama. Drama is possibly the worst-selling subject in my shop, so I picked out a few and rejected the rest. He looked a bit annoyed. He had clearly spent several years putting the collection together and was expecting rich rewards.

A customer bought the Morden map of Scotland. It had been hanging – in a black and gold Hogarth frame – on the wall of the first landing on the stairs for a couple of years. Robert Morden was a cartographer who was commissioned to produce county maps for Camden's *Britannia*, a huge work which broke the UK (or England and Wales, to be more accurate) into chapters by county, each accompanied by a Morden map. His map of Scotland was produced in 1695. Over the years I've had three seventeenth-century copies of Camden's *Britannia*, all of which have had the maps removed.

Granny has shown remarkable compassion today: not only did she bring me some cake but she offered to cover the shop for the afternoon. I suspect she may be coming down with a fever.

Till total £1,778.98*
28 customers

MONDAY, 30 MAY

Online orders: 1
Books found: 1

Sunny day, and warm. The garden is exploding with colour and scent: the fruit trees and the *Viburnum Burkwoodii* with its glorious aroma, and the clematis *Montana Wilsonii*, with its chocolate fragrance, make walking through the space feel like being in a sweet shop.

At eleven o'clock I went to the cellar to find a light bulb to replace one that had died on the chandelier. I was startled to discover a small boy hiding there. I shouted something blasphemous and stepped backwards, at which point he put his finger to his lips to shush me, and whispered that he and his sister were playing hide and seek. To be fair to him, there is nothing to indicate that the cellar is private, but the door handle is notoriously unreliable, and if I hadn't been down there in search of a new light bulb, it's quite possible that he might have been stuck there for several months. At least there's a fairly decent supply of wine.

The RBC books which Meredith and I had packed were sitting

---

* Again, today's total includes sales put through for Davy's paintings. The shop total was £449.78.

in piles on the table in the shop, so I started to bag them up before taking them over to the post office. A customer watched me for a few minutes before asking, 'Are you doing a mailout?'

After I closed the shop I drove to Glenwhan Gardens, a stunning hillside garden created by friends of my parents. It's about a half-hour drive from Wigtown. Tessa, who owns it, had asked me if I could make a promotional video for them, so I filmed for an hour in the golden sunlight of the evening.

Till total £126.39
14 customers

TUESDAY, 31 MAY

Online orders: o
Books found: o

At 10 a.m. a woman brought in two bags of books, almost all unsellable – *CAMRA Good Pub guide 1987*, Reader's Digest Condensed Books, Jeffrey Archer. When I told her that I didn't want them, she didn't seem in the least bit surprised. They'd belonged to her late husband, who, she told me – with undisguised delight – had appalling taste in literature.

Davy spent the day removing his paintings and display stands from the drawing room. I don't think he was particularly pleased with sales over the weekend.

I was rummaging around behind the counter in an unsuccessful search for a pencil sharpener at 11 a.m. when I heard someone say, 'I collect old Ordnance Survey maps.' Even with my head stuck between two shelves behind the counter, I could pretty much have guaranteed that when I reluctantly turned to face the customer, he would be in his sixties and have a beard and a cardigan.

I had some jobs to do in the garden – painting fences, weeding etc. – so I enlisted the help of Willie, a very decent if largely unreliable local man a few years older than I am, to give me a hand while Granny covered in the shop. I'm trying to tidy the garden up, and have ordered 50 metres of concrete path edging. Willie is going to dig a trench and set the path border in it.

I spent the evening putting the furniture and paintings back in the drawing room, and making it look more like my home than an art gallery.

Till total £176.80
17 customers

JUNE

Few books have given so much pleasure and gone through so many editions as The Compleat Angler, by Izaak Walton. The first edition, 12mo, 1653, published at 1s 6d, sold in 1896 for £414.

The gentle art of book hunting is an art well worth learning. Some say that the pleasure enjoyed by the angler is not so much the joy of catching fish, as the delight of wandering amidst lovely scenery, and breathing the fresh ozone of the country. Is it not equally true that the book hunter finds his sweetest happiness while looking for the books he desires, even though he never finds them?

Half the pleasure would be gone from the art of book hunting if one had nothing to do but simply order one's agent to procure the special books and editions one required.

R. M. Williamson, *Bits from an Old Bookshop*

Walton's *The Compleat Angler* is widely regarded as one of the finest books ever written about fishing: it contains numerous engravings of fish, as well as two pages of music for 'The Angler's Song', by Henry Lawes, with one page printed upside down (as intended) to enable two singers to face one another while singing together. It is highly sought after, and at the time of writing the cheapest copy I could find online was offered by a New York dealer at a price of £47,221.25. I'm sure he would have been prepared to drop the 25p for the right customer. Walton's work is often incorrectly credited as being the first book in the English language about fishing. That honour belongs to *Boke of Seynt Albans*, by Juliana Berners, about whom very little is known. It's a work that covers hawking, hunting, field sports and – in the 1496 edition – a chapter titled 'Treatyse of fysshynge wyth an Angle'. Berners is believed to have been a nobleman's daughter who became the prioress of Sopwell Nunnery, and a woman well versed in the world of hunting, fishing and horse riding.

Williamson's observation that it is from the chase rather than the kill that both fishermen and book hunters derive the greatest pleasure is undoubtedly true in all but the most bloodthirsty. This is ground over which I've been before, but it is worth further scrutiny. There is a rather unpalatable gender stereotype that men go fishing to escape from their wives. Apart from the fact that it is patently not true (at least in my experience), it singularly fails to explain the abundance of fisherwomen. I think, with both fishing and book hunting, there is something far more primal at work: the hunter-gatherer instinct which, according to recent archaeological evidence and anthropological theory, was never an exclusively male preserve. It is odd, then, that in the twenty or so years in which I've been in the book trade, the overwhelming majority of what Williamson refers to as 'book hunters' have been male. I suspect that men are more drawn to utterly pointless pursuits (like stamp collecting) than women are. I have no idea why, but as far as collecting things goes, I would agree with Williamson that

> Those who make a hobby of collecting and preserving anything that is curious and interesting are worthy of praise. The desire to collect begins when, as children, we hoard buttons, beads, or marbles and as children of a larger growth we collect picture postcards or postage stamps. We have collectors of book plates, china, quaint furniture, church tokens, engravings, antiquities, pictures, clocks, guns, swords, antique silver, old keys, miniature portraits, violins, and curios of every kind. The collector of books is, we think, the prince of all collectors. His work is a work which never can be completed, his collection can never be perfected: and the delights of collecting books can be indulged in by almost anyone.

Williamson's further observation that the pleasure of book hunting would disappear if one simply had to procure the services of an agent to track down the desired volume is precisely the joy that the internet has sucked from the world. The thrill of the hunt is gone; no adversity needs to be faced, no mountains of books must be climbed, no travel to exotic locations like Inverness and Hull, nor conversations with interesting people are required in the quest for one's personal literary Shangri-La. Instead, instant gratification can be achieved by the soulless click of a button. Where's the fun in that?

Online orders: 0
Books found: 0

Opened the shop at 9 a.m. Granny was working at The Pheasant today. She was enjoying her post-breakfast cigarette at the bus stop when I opened the door. As usual, she mouthed something offensive at me and raised the middle finger of her right hand. She's normally very well dressed, but today – in her trench coat and beret – she bore a remarkable resemblance to a twenty-seven-year-old female Inspector Clouseau.

I spent much of the morning dragging the mail sacks of random books across the road to the post office. Thankfully William was having his mid-morning nap and I managed to sneak them into the back room with the complicit assistance of Wilma.

After lunch a teenage girl bought a book about Josef Fritzl. She asked if she could have a bag to conceal it because it was a gift for her father.

A very tall young man with long ponytail and trilby bought several books about bee-keeping.

Decided to tidy up Meredith's room in the event that we have any visitors in the next few weeks. Granny – back from The Pheasant after lunch – kindly offered to help. I swept and hoovered while she stripped the bed. It's a box bed which I built several years ago, and has a piece of fabric which overhangs the space between the mattress and the floor. While I was hoovering, I heard Granny shout, 'Fucking hell, look at this!' The mystery of the missing cutlery and crockery was solved in that moment. Under the bed were around twenty plates, knives, forks and empty tin pie trays. Meredith had clearly been having midnight feasts and hadn't bothered to wash up after herself.

Today was a beautiful day, and the evening was warm and sunny. It was the Annual General Meeting of the Association of Wigtown Booksellers. Laura kindly agreed to host it in her shop, Byre Books. When I arrived, she had put chairs out in her garden, so we sat out in the evening sun and she produced a bottle of wine. It was the best AWB meeting we've ever had, by a long chalk.

After a couple of glasses of wine, we all agreed that the office bearers should continue in office, particularly since none of them was there.

Till total £291
27 customers

THURSDAY, 2 JUNE

Online orders: 3
Books found: 2

Opened the shop at 9 a.m. Since Meredith has left and Granny is working at The Pheasant, I need some help in the shop, so I asked my friend Stuart (who organises a music event called The Dark Outside) if his daughter Lucy might want to work here for the summer. She's studying music in Perth and has the summer free, and readily agreed. Like her father, she's very quiet and – I hope neither of them will object to this description – unusual. I sometimes wonder if their minds exist in a parallel universe while their bodies are trapped in ours.

Shortly after I'd shown Lucy how to work the primitive cash-collecting devices in the shop, a swarm of pensioners arrived at 9.30. Lucy kept her cool, in spite of the tsunami of grey hair, grey clothes and grey slip-ons washing through the shop. In the end, only one of them bought a book, and it took him six minutes to locate his wallet, by which time the rest of the pestilent mob had moved on to suck the life from pastures new.

At 12.30 I told Lucy that she was welcome to a lunch break, so she walked the short distance home, had something to eat and was back by 1 p.m. – a refreshingly brief absence from the shop after Meredith's lengthy lunches.

The shop was busy all afternoon, but the undoubted highlight was a middle-aged woman who wandered around the shop saying, 'Look, Rufus, cookery books. And over here, military.' This went on through every section of the shop. Rufus was her dog: a bemused

West Highland terrier whose literary curiosity I suspect extends no further than chewing her copy of the *Daily Mail*.

Till total £256.99
27 customers

Online orders: 2
Books found: 2

Both orders were for fishing books. Lucy managed to find them remarkably quickly. She lacks the jaded eye of experience.

At ten o'clock I drove down to Penkiln sawmill, about a mile away, to pick up some timber to make a new shelf. As I was reversing to leave, I managed to hit a pile of concrete blocks and smash one of my brake lights. Jerry, who works there, delights in the misfortunes of others, and I don't think I've seen such a satisfied grin on his face since I overloaded the van with timber and it all fell out on the road just outside the sawmill several years ago.

Willie was in the garden again. The path edging arrived this morning; we hauled it into the garden with wheelbarrows.

At four o'clock a customer brought in four boxes of books to sell – 'This one has gardening books in it, and that one is full of craft books, that one has art books, and this one contains history books. They're all in fairly good condition.' I sometimes wonder if people like this – and I know they're trying to be helpful – wander around the supermarket pointing at various fruit and vegetables and telling other customers, 'This bit has got bananas in it, those red things are tomatoes, and the round orange things are oranges.'

Ben and Beth, the Bookshop Band, arrived for a visit. Put them in the spare room. Had a lovely evening catching up and ploughing through a few bottles of red wine.

Till total £192.91
21 customers

SATURDAY, 4 JUNE

Online orders: 0
Books found: 0

Lucy was waiting outside at nine o'clock. I may have to give her a key so that my occasional breaches of punctuality when it comes to opening time don't mean that she's stuck outside like an advertisement for my indolence.

At eleven o'clock we had four customers in the shop, one of whom decided to have a look at the bottom shelf of the military history section, which is right in front of the counter. His shorts were halfway down his backside, exposing so much flesh and hair that *Das Rheingold* has started playing in my head.

Left Lucy in charge (with a key) and drove to Edinburgh to celebrate the thirtieth birthday of former employee and good friend Carol-Ann.

Till total £294.97
35 customers

MONDAY, 6 JUNE

Online orders: 4
Books found: 2

Returned from Edinburgh last night. At the age of forty-five I am no longer suited to partying with thirty-year-olds. I couldn't hear anything, didn't want to dance and was ready for bed by eleven.

My friends Cloda and Leo came over from Ireland with their daughter, Elsa, for a few days. They arrived at 11 a.m. It was a warm, sunny day, so after lunch Ben and Beth, Cloda and Leo and I went to the beach for a picnic and a swim.

Till total £361.35
26 customers

TUESDAY, 7 JUNE

Online orders: 3
Books found: 3

Lucy in. Asked her if she had any interesting news. She shrugged her shoulders and turned to the computer to see if we had any orders, then set about looking for them. She's uncanny in her ability to find orders which – most likely out of idleness – I could never find.

There must have been a radio adaptation or something, but *Paradise Lost* – a poem which I've only been asked for a handful of times over the past twenty years – appears to have gathered considerable popularity if the number of times I'm asked for a copy is anything to go by. We have a beautiful calf-bound four-volume set of Milton's works, dated 1824 and published by Parker and Whittaker, which is priced at £200, morocco-bound with the most stunning gilt tooling and dentelles. It has been on the shelves for at least a decade. The customer took one look at it and said, 'Tell you what, I'll give you £40 for it', as though he was doing me a favour. There are few things that I dislike more than customers telling me what they'll pay for my stock, particularly when it is framed in such a way as to suggest that I have no choice because they're 'telling me what'. There's only one thing that could have made that 'offer' worse, and that would have been if he'd added 'mate' to the end of the sentence. The insincerity of the word 'mate' is nails on a blackboard to me, unless it is being used by David Attenborough to describe some sort of preying mantis sex ritual. The moment a complete (or relative) stranger uses it, I am suspicious. If it is intended to have a disarming amicability, it has precisely the opposite effect.

Found a book called *Nil Desperandum, a Dictionary of Latin Tags and Phrases* while I was tidying up the Classics section. Favourite so far is *Timeo hominem unius libri*, which translates as 'I fear the man of one book'. I might have this carved on my headstone, which will – five minutes later – have been graffitied over with the words 'pretentious tosser'.

Ben and Beth left for Bath. I think they might be planning to move to Wigtown. Rent is certainly considerably cheaper.

Lucy and I worked in the shop, tidying up in the morning, then I drove to Newton Stewart for a meeting with the bank manager in the afternoon. She's remarkably decent and clearly understands the perils of cash flow when it comes to the survival of small businesses.

Till total £303.99
21 customers

WEDNESDAY, 8 JUNE

Online orders: 1
Books found: 1

Today's order was for a book called *The Art of John Berkley*. Sold on ABE for £50 to an American customer. Lucy found it within seconds. She still hasn't said more than a couple of sentences since she started working in the shop. I'm torn between admiration for her coolness and curiosity about her interests and personality.

A woman who'd spent a while in the fiction section staring up at one of the higher shelves came to the counter and – instead of asking for help – simply said, 'You'll have to get that book for me.' It was a signed first of Martin Amis's *London Fields*. She pawed through it, then put it on the counter and told me that '£50 is far too much for that.'

As if that wasn't enough, as we were about to close, an old woman came to the counter (the shop was busy, as an event we had on upstairs about the history of farming in the Machars had just ended). She thrust a copy of Nigel Tranter's *Spanish Galleon* in my face and said, 'This says it's £15. It can't be. The price is wrong; it's just an old book. I'll give you £5 for it.'

The moment the door swung shut behind her, I increased the price to £25.

Till total £117.49
9 customers

Online orders: 1
Books found: 0

Lucy was waiting outside as usual when I opened the shop, and Granny was in position at the bus stop, a cloud of smoke engulfing her head, but she could still see me well enough to raise her middle finger at me and mouth some obscenity.

After lunch a customer brought in a box of music journals called *Clavichord International*. I offered him £40 for them and said, 'Baroque and Roll.' He looked blankly back at me, took the £40 and left without a word. As is often the case, I felt like a fool.

Lucy sold a set of *The Statistical Account of Scotland* (1799) to a delighted elderly man for £400. Apparently he'd been looking for it for years. We have four sets of them. This set was calf-bound, but had clearly been above the fireplace in a country house library for years, and the leather had dried out and cracked, and many of the boards were loose.

Granny came back from work early – it was a nice day so I told Lucy she could go home early if she wanted to. Granny offered to cover for the afternoon.

Willie came in again and finished setting the path edging. It looks considerably better than the rotting timber which had served the purpose before, and at least I won't have to replace it. I suspect that over the past few weeks I've spent more time making cups of tea for Willie than he has working.

I edited the Glenwhan Gardens video from closing the shop until ten o'clock. The drone footage looks stunning.

Till total £657
24 customers

FRIDAY, 10 JUNE

Online orders: 0
Books found: 0

The sun was shining again when I opened the shop. It has been a glorious spring, with barely a drop of rain. The fields, normally cut for silage at this time of year, are turning yellow with drought.

Telephone call from a man in North Ayrshire who has books to sell. Have agreed to visit him next week.

Here I've had to delete a diary entry about a friend because he requested that I take any reference to him out. I only mentioned him briefly, and in the most affectionate of terms, but for some reason he has insisted that I make no reference to him. I'm convinced that there's some correlation between the inflated egos of the people who insist on this and the unutterable dullness of their lives.

Till total £219.98
15 customers

SATURDAY, 11 JUNE

Online orders: 0
Books found: 0

The person who requested that I remove him from the book dropped in for a cup of tea. Granny covered the shop while we chatted about the house that he's not building, and the time we didn't climb Mont Blanc and the fishing trip we aren't planning.

A customer smelling heavily of talcum powder spent a couple of hours in the shop but bought nothing. The moment he left I attempted to trace his footsteps by following a trail of white powder, but sadly couldn't find any.

Till total £420
34 customers

MONDAY, 13 JUNE

Online orders: 1
Books found: 1

Granny opened the shop and I cut the grass in the garden in the morning. Granny has been co-opted into babysitting duties at The Pheasant. Andrea and Morag have a small child, a boy called Duncan. She told me today that, 'He run to give me a hug, then I discover that he just wanted to clean his nose on my shorts.'

Lucy appeared at nine o'clock. She and Granny spent an hour looking for today's solitary ABE order: a book about painting pottery for children. It rained for the first time in a month, just after I'd finished cutting the grass. I really ought to chase up Amazon about reinstating my seller account, but the feeling of freedom I've experienced since they suspended it has been more liberating than I could have possibly imagined, and I no longer think that the stress of dealing with the Bezos machine is worthwhile.

Two days ago I started reading *We*, by Yevgeny Zamyatin, first published in English in 1924. I'm sure Zamyatin must have read Forster's *The Machine Stops*: so many similar themes run through both novels. *We* deals with – among other things – the question of whether it is better to be 'free' and outside the city walls or 'happy' within the rules set by 'The Table' inside the city walls. Huxley's *Brave New World* (1932) and Orwell's *Nineteen Eighty-Four* (1949) also address similar themes: whether a reasonably comfortable life within a totalitarian regime is worth settling for when freedom outside it is burdened with uncertainty.

I am in absolutely no doubt now. I've had enough of the Machine that is Amazon and I'm dropping out of it.

Till total £287
15 customers

Online orders: 2
Books found: 2

Sunny day. Left Lucy in charge of the shop at 9 a.m. and drove to
Beith in North Ayrshire (almost as far as Glasgow). North Ayrshire
is a strange place for someone from Galloway. It has a certain
beauty, but it is pockmarked by open-cast mines and the remains of
factories. The communities that once depended on them have been
devastated by the decline of heavy industry. All through the county
there is enormous wealth perched above abject poverty. Perhaps
the best example of this is Dumfries House, a beautiful Palladian
country house, stuffed with the finest Chippendale furniture, that
sits above the town of Cumnock. In 2004 Cumnock was declared
top of the UK poverty league, with 20 per cent of households in the
town surviving on under £5,000 a year. The town was once home
to Keir Hardie, the first leader of the Labour Party, who worked
on the *Cumnock News* at the end of the nineteenth century. At one
time it was clearly a prosperous place. I know what it is like to live
in a town that has fallen on hard times, and I know Cumnock –
like Wigtown – has enough people with drive and ambition to pull
it out of the slough of despond.

    Arrived at the house shortly after eleven o'clock. It was a fine,
single-storey Georgian building surrounded by several acres of
pasture, so my expectations may have been unreasonably high.
They were. Inside, the place was utterly revolting: the carpets
were sticky, there was dog hair everywhere and it was clearly a
decade (at least) since anyone had made the slightest attempt to
clean anything. All of the beautiful period detail had been ripped
out: the fine Georgian wallpaper had been scribbled over by the
parents and the six children who tore about the place while I was
there. Thankfully the library had been spared the horrors of the
artistic endeavours of the family, and I rapidly extracted as much
antiquarian material as I could. The books had belonged to the
previous owner. He'd been a fanatical collector of books on Scottish
history, and while there was plenty of material that took up vast
amounts of space and is almost impossible to sell (*Register of the*

Great Seal of Scotland, *Scots Law Times Reports*, etc.) there was much of both value and interest: eighteenth-century county histories with maps and copperplate illustrations, regimental histories, statistical accounts and almost everything in decent calf bindings. I made Matthew, the owner and the son of the previous owner, an offer of £2,500. He told me that he'd 'think about it'.

Made it home just before closing time to find Lucy locking up. I said hello. She said goodbye and walked off.

Till total £274.19
18 customers

WEDNESDAY, 15 JUNE

Online orders: 1
Books found: 1

Lucy in on a morning on which black clouds hung ominously overhead. Decided that it was about time to do another blackboard. Came up with this:

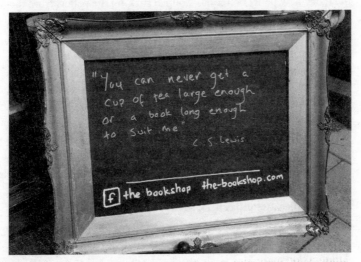

The two women who are running The Open Book called in to say hello just after we'd opened. They were charming, Alice and Lucy. They've been pen pals for years, and have become good friends. Almost without exception, the people who come to run The Open Book have an almost infectious enthusiasm that even the most battle-weary bookseller can't suppress. Believe me, I've tried.

After they'd gone, I started to sand down the edge of the front door; in damp weather the wood swells up and it's impossible to open the door. As I was removing the handle there was a rumble of thunder and it began to rain torrentially. My toolbox has suffered from lending things to neighbours and friends; I couldn't find the correct size screwdriver to unscrew the brass fitting of the handle, so I drove to Home Hardware in Newton Stewart and bought one.

When Meredith arrived all those months ago, I set up a direct debit to give her a living allowance. Today I realised that I was still paying it, so I dropped into the bank (conveniently opposite Home Hardware) and cancelled it.

Today was a day of technological disasters; I somehow managed to trip the fuse for the whole building while I was changing a light bulb. Normally it just trips the lighting ring, but for some reason everything went down. When I reset it, the modem refused to connect to the internet, so Lucy spent the day trying to fix that, and the fancy new pellet boiler has stopped sucking the pellets from the hopper again, so we have no hot water. I did manage to remove the front door handle, though, and finished sanding the edge.

After work, the AWB had a meeting at Beltie Books & Café about *Eggheads*, a television quiz show that we have been asked to supply a team of booksellers for. Afterwards I met up with Granny and The Open Book residents, Alice and Lucy, for a drink in The Ploughman.

After this morning's thundery start, the day turned out to be sunny with occasional spells of torrential rain, after six dry, sunny weeks. The farmers will be delighted; the grass will shoot away now with the rain. They've been having to buy in feed for cattle and sheep because it has been so dry, and at the time of year when normally there's an abundance of grass.

Till total £117.40
15 customers

THURSDAY, 16 JUNE

Online orders: 1
Books found: 1

Lucy in. More broken weather, but at least it was warm. We managed to get back online after half an hour of tinkering and switching things on and off.

Charming email from an online customer: 'I want a refund for book monkey planet.' It's almost as though he'd used a random word generator to write the message. I don't recall the book, but I replied and asked him to return it if he wants a refund.

The women in The Open Book are keen to explore the area by bike, so I drove to Garlieston to borrow a couple from my friends Finn and Ella, as my bikes are the wrong size. Finn and Ella have four children, which means that they have almost every size of bicycle.

Now that I've successfully (I hope) sanded the shop door to a size where it won't jam in the damp weather, I decided to give it a lick of paint. Possibly not the best idea to do it on a busy day when there's a steady stream of customers passing through.

Till total £299.07
24 customers

FRIDAY, 17 JUNE

Online orders: 1
Books found: 1

Lucy was off today. I think she has a college thing in Perth.

Petra appeared at ten o'clock for her dance class. Nobody came. It's starting to feel a bit like Eleanor Rigby's funeral.

Today's order was for a book called *The Treasure of Auchinleck*. After a twenty-minute search I eventually spotted it about four shelves away from where it ought to have been. It sold for £35 on ABE but was on sale for £6 in the shop. Lucy would have found it in seconds.

A customer came to the counter with a pile of books just before lunchtime and asked:

'Will you accept a swap?'
Me (hesitantly): 'What have you got?'
Customer: 'An antique fire extinguisher.'

Deal. The barter economy is alive and well.

Till total £159.50
14 customers

SATURDAY, 18 JUNE

Online orders: 2
Books found: 1

Matthew from Beith called to say that his family is happy with my offer for the books. I've arranged to go and collect them next week.

Fairly busy day in the shop; managed to catch up with emails.

Found a book called *The Traveller in France, Useful Phrases and Words in French*, compiled by J. Chevalier. This is page 82:

I want some tobacco
I want some light shag
We have English, American and French cigarettes
I want pipe tobacco
I want a packet of English cigarettes
I want a box of matches
Have you any good cigars?
I want some petrol for my lighter
Some flints, please
I want some cigarette paper
I always smoke cork-tipped cigarettes

I want light tobacco
Dark tobacco
I want some good snuff
Ash-tray

Till total £224.41
12 customers

MONDAY, 20 JUNE

Online orders: 1
Books found: 1

Lucy was waiting patiently by the front door when I opened at
9.05. There was a trail of dog shit outside, clearly the produce of
a very small dog, and most likely the poodle that lives about three
doors down the street. When Nicky worked in the shop, that little
dog was her nemesis. She blamed it for killing the potted azalea
outside the front door of the shop, and for numerous other petty
crimes.

After lunch I picked up Alice and Lucy from The Open Book
in the van, after I'd removed the empty crisp packets and empty
Coke bottles in an unconvincing attempt to make it look less like
a mobile dustbin. I'd offered to take them on a Machars tour. This
includes the Torhouse Stone Circle, the Old Place of Mochrum (an
ancient castle), Mochrum Loch, then along a winding road through
fields of Belted Galloway cattle and down to the sea, looking across
Luce Bay to the Mull of Galloway, Scotland's most southerly point,
then on through Port William, past Barsalloch hill fort, down to
the Isle of Whithorn and back to Garlieston via Cruggleton Church
– a Norman ruin that was established by Fergus of Galloway
and rebuilt by the third marquess of Bute in 1890 – then on to
Galloway House Gardens and finally Sorbie Tower, an impressive
sixteenth-century castle built by the Clan Hannay. The whole trip
takes about two hours, and not only is it an insider's guide to the
peninsula for visitors who would probably not have discovered a

single one of the locations, but it also serves as a reminder to me of what we have on our doorstep.

Till total £182.48
18 customers

TUESDAY, 21 JUNE

Online orders: o
Books found: o

Granny wasn't working at The Pheasant today, so she kindly opened the shop so that I could sleep in for a while. She and Lucy spent the day sorting through the hardback fiction section, which never stays organised for very long before customers helpfully rearrange it.

A young couple who have decided to open a second-hand bookshop in Surrey came in to buy stock. I took them upstairs for a cup of tea and a chat. While it would have been tempting to try to sell them a load of my dead stock, I remember how kind and decent people in the trade were to me when I started, so I explained how I run my business – not that it is necessarily a model to be followed – and suggested other (less expensive) means by which they might acquire stock. I truly hope that they succeed.

After they'd gone, I drove to Dumfries to buy a new laptop for Isabel. She's coming in to do the accounts tomorrow and has been complaining that the old one has pretty much ground to a halt. Went to Currys and found something that ought to do the trick. It would probably have been simpler to buy something on Amazon, but I've found the way they dealt with my suspension so objectionable, and recent reports about the way they treat their staff even more so, that even if it means considerable inconvenience to me, I won't buy anything from them again unless I'm faced with no alternative.

Till total £222.30
22 customers

WEDNESDAY, 22 JUNE

Online orders: 0
Books found: 0

Granny was working at The Pheasant today. Duncan threw sticks and insisted that she fetch them for him.

Telephone call at 10 from a woman on Mull who has books to dispose of urgently, so I booked a place on the ferry from Oban to Craignure tomorrow morning, and asked Mary to cover the shop.

A customer came to the counter at eleven o'clock with a massive handwritten list of books he claims to have found on our 'online shop'. He asked me to find them for him while he went for a cup of tea. Apart from the fact that we don't have an online shop, the books were all priced at between a penny and 25p, so for roughly forty books the total was £6.59. Even my business acumen isn't quite that diabolical. When he returned from his cup of tea, I explained to him that he must have confused my business with another online shop, and that we've been suspended from Amazon Marketplace for months. Initially he seemed disappointed but swiftly switched gears and became irascible, telling me that he'd travelled from Carlisle to hunt down these books. When I asked him if he'd telephoned to check that we were the right shop before he set off, he shook his head and left.

Till total £257.48
21 customers

THURSDAY, 23 JUNE

Online orders: 0
Books found: 0

Up at 7 a.m. to vote, drove to Kirkinner to register Callum's proxy vote in the Brexit referendum. He's in Spain at the moment. Headed north to catch the 12.30. CalMac ferry from Oban to

Craignure. Left Lucy in charge of the shop.

I almost missed the ferry because of the hundreds of motorhomes pottering along up the side of Loch Lomond at 30 m.p.h., but made it to Oban with minutes to spare.

Drove through Mull to Tobermory, where I eventually found the ancient farmhouse and an almost equally ancient woman with a stick who walked incredibly slowly and stank of urine. Tethered to a post at the front door was a yapping Yorkshire terrier, and as soon as I entered the kitchen, a sleek Irish setter jumped up excitedly and almost knocked me over.

The house, the elderly woman proudly told me, had been visited by Boswell and Johnson on their tour of the Western Isles. Neither had liked it particularly, and I suspect that it probably hadn't been cleaned since their visit in 1773. A thick layer of dust and grime covered almost every surface, particularly the books, which were housed in a large room at the gable end furthest from the front door. The house had been modernised unsympathetically and very cheaply. The elderly woman was a widow whose husband had died a few years ago. They were farmers, specialising in Shetland ponies and Galloway cattle. The place was chaotic, with piles of paperwork on the floor and broken tools and sacks of animal feed in every room. The books were mediocre, but I managed to salvage six boxes of reasonable material from the place. Every time I picked up anything that I thought might have any value, the widow waved her stick at me and snatched it from my hand, snapping, 'I'm keeping that one.' I gave her £200 and managed to navigate my way carefully past the tethered dog as I loaded the van. Every time I passed the cursed creature, it seemed determined to ensnare my legs in its leash.

Once I'd loaded the van and said goodbye to the elderly widow I headed for The Mishnish, where I intended to have a shower to wash off the grime of the farmhouse. En route I managed to brush against an oncoming BT Openreach van on one of the winding streets of Tobermory and successfully removed its wing mirror. The driver appeared to be convinced that it was my fault, and for a short while I thought that there might be a fight, which I would certainly have lost, but after exchanging insurance details he calmed down and we parted company.

Settled down in The Mishnish with a pint and began to read *By Grand Central Station I Sat Down and Wept* by Elizabeth Smart. It was one of the few books from the hovel that I'd always intended to read, in part because the title is so intriguing. I can't imagine that anyone could fail to want to know more. I admit that I found it a little hard to begin with. I suspect that I'm not equipped with the intellectual stamina to deal with it. It is beautifully written, though. When she's describing the wife of her lover, who – I think – has lost a baby (although I'm not sure because the book is written entirely from the perspective of the mind of the author and makes very few references to what is actually happening; rather, she explains her emotional reactions to events), she writes of her: 'Her shoulders have always the attitude of grieving, and her thin breasts are pitiful like Virgin Shrines that have been robbed.'

Went to bed at 10.30. In the background I had the television on with the referendum results and analysis. When Northumberland – the first constituency to return a vote, and predicted to be a Remain county – gave a strong majority to leave the EU, I switched off the television, fairly sure that things would not go the way I had hoped.

Till total £135.50
19 customers

FRIDAY, 24 JUNE

Online orders: 0
Books found: 0

Up at 9 a.m. to the news that the UK has voted to leave the EU. The only comfort to be drawn from this is that not a single constituency in Scotland voted to leave. Overall, 62 per cent of voters in Scotland voted to remain.

Over breakfast I received a call from Lucy, who had managed to switch the computer off and was wondering how to get Monsoon (our online database) to open. This requires a convoluted series of tricks which I explained to her until it was working. Still no orders. I'm worried that I may have been suspended by ABE again as well as Amazon. If this is the case, then I have no online presence at all, but I'm still paying monthly fees to Amazon, ABE and Monsoon.

Drove to Craignure after breakfast. Managed to book a space on the noon ferry crossing, so I made it to Oban at 12.40. Carried on reading *By Grand Central Station* on the boat. It's an unusual book, and by halfway through I gave up on looking for any sort of sense of what was going on by hoping for descriptions of events. Rather, the clues are there in her abstract explanations of what is going on in her mind. Again, about her lover's wife: 'I have broken her heart like a robin's egg. Its wreck reaches her finite horizon.'

Now that I've almost got to grips with her style, I can begin to appreciate what an extraordinary writer she was. Her descriptions of love and loss are profoundly moving. I am considerably out of my depth, though. I'm a simple creature and need to be whacked on the head with narrative signposts.

Docked at Oban, then drove to Lockerbie, left the van in the car park and caught the train to Waverley for Finn's fiftieth birthday party in Howie's. Finn isn't afraid to push the boat out when it comes to parties, and this was a mightily impressive affair. There must have been 150 people there. Bumped into Dylan Moran at the bar and briefly chatted with him. As usual, I was like a schoolboy talking to the headmaster.

Back to Lulu and Scott's at 1 a.m. for a few whiskies then bed.

Till total £166.50
16 customers

SATURDAY, 25 JUNE

Online orders: 0
Books found: 0

Left my sister's flat at 10 a.m., then caught the Lockerbie train and made it home by 3 p.m. Granny covered the shop. As soon as I made it back, she looked me up and down with a disparaging expression and said, 'Enjoy your 'oliday, fucking bastard?'

Telephone call in the afternoon from a man in the Borders who is moving house and wants to dispose of his library. I visited him before a year or two ago to have a look at the collection. I've agreed to go over next week and take what I can. If I remember, it was a large country house, and he and I got on very well.

Finished *By Grand Central Station*. I don't think that I've ever read anything like it. By the kitchen table I sat down and wept at the final sentence: 'My dear, my darling, do you hear me where you sleep?'

Till total £269.13
23 customers

MONDAY, 27 JUNE

Online orders: 0
Books found: 0

Opened the shop for the first time since Wednesday. Granny

worked for the morning while I unloaded the van and began sorting through the sticky, dusty books from the Tobermory farmhouse.

After lunch I left Lucy in charge of the shop while I took Granny to the Jobcentre in Stranraer to organise a National Insurance number for her. I left her arguing with a middle-aged man about it and went the supermarket, where I bumped into Sandy the tattooed pagan. I was at the fish counter trying to work out what to have for supper when I heard the familiar cry of 'Seamus! How are you, son?' We had a brief chat during which he asked about 'Florentina' (he never remembers Emanuela's name) and we discussed walking sticks – we're running low, as we always do at this time of year, so he's going to drop some more off soon. Bought some smoked haddock.

Afterwards, on my way to pick Granny up, Kirsty, my former tenant on Lochancroft Lane, ran out in front of the van – I hit the brakes and narrowly avoided running her over, then instantly regretted it.

Home at four o'clock. The shop was quiet all day. Made Cullen skink for supper, one of Granny's favourites.

Till total £113
15 customers

TUESDAY, 28 JUNE

Online orders: 0
Books found: 0

Granny was working at The Pheasant this morning, so I left Lucy in charge and drove to Gatehouse to look at some books belonging to family friends. I went to their new house – a modern bungalow – and picked up the daughter, Ruby, who announced, when we arrived at the old house, that she had forgotten the keys, so we drove back to the new house, where I waited in the van for half an hour while she looked for them. Eventually she found them and we drove to the old house where the books were. She failed to give me any directions, even though she was sitting next to me in the van, and we missed every turning and had to go back once again. We drove past the house while she chatted about her new interest in baking, and a mile along a road before we reached a dead end and I asked her where to go, at which point she told me that we needed to turn around and go back.

The books were interesting enough, with many privately bound in half-morocco with beautiful gilt tooling. I gave her a cheque for £100 for a couple of boxes of them. As we were leaving the house I spotted three calf-bound folios – had a look at them and they contained stunning black-and-white original Victorian photographs of expeditions to Egypt that her great grandfather had taken. Sadly, but completely understandably, she was unwilling to part with them.

Home in time for lunch. When Lucy got back from her break, we got to work cleaning up the books from the Tobermory deal with soapy water, rags and leather food.

After supper I started reading *Everything is Illuminated* by Jonathan Safran Foer. I know nothing about it, but it's published by Penguin, which is usually (although not always) a sign of reasonable quality, and I was as intrigued by the title as I had been by *By Grand Central Station I Sat Down and Wept*.

Till total £197.03
12 customers

WEDNESDAY, 29 JUNE

Online orders: 1
Books found: 1

Left Granny in charge of the shop and set off for Jedburgh at 9, arriving at Glenburn Hall at noon. Christopher and his wife, Nonie, were both home, and showed me where the various books were – it rained incessantly while I was there.

I packed the books into boxes and loaded them into the van with the help of Jeff, their gardener. Sadly, most of what they wished to dispose of wasn't much use for the shop or for selling online. I suspect they kept the better material. Still, it was great to have a wander around the beautiful house, and they were engaging company.

Left Glenburn at two o'clock, home just after five to discover that the takings today were very good. This is normally the case when I'm away from the shop.

Till total £459.45
23 customers

THURSDAY, 30 JUNE

Online orders: 0
Books found: 0

Lucy in. She was even more taciturn than usual. Boxes of books are starting to pile up in the shop, so I asked Lucy to price up the books on the table and put them on the shelves while I sorted through the boxes and organised them into books to be sent out in the Random Book Club, books to list online and books to go straight onto the shelves. We made significant progress, particularly now that we're no longer wiping grease and dog hair from the Tobermory books.

Sandy the tattooed pagan arrived while Lucy was having her lunch break. He was wielding a bundle of walking sticks, which he theatrically dropped into the stick stand. He always demands credit in the shop, rather than cash – another example of the barter economy at work. Don't tell the taxman.

Till total £459.45
23 customers

JULY

What are called 'knock-out' sales are sometimes carried out by the trade. The plan is illegal, dishonest, and selfish. The booksellers, previous to the sale, agree among themselves not to outbid each other, but to manage so that no one outside the charmed circle will get a book under its value. After the sale is over the conspirators adjourn to a room in some hotel, and the books are re-sold to the highest bidder in the company, and the profits divided.

Another worthy has an original way of making a bid. He just opens and shuts his mouth by way of assent. Many and varied are the devices resorted to by 'cute dealers to keep their brothers in the trade from thinking they are bidding. A wink of the eye, a facile twitch, a movement of a finger are enough for the auctioneer.

R. M. Williamson, *Bits from an Old Bookshop*

How little has changed since Williamson's days at the book sales. Although I rarely attend specialist book auctions because I don't have much trouble acquiring decent stock either through the shop or the private sale of the libraries of deceased estates, I do go to auctions regularly. When I bought the shop, the accommodation above it – an expansive four-bedroom flat – was completely unfurnished. Unwilling to fill the fine Georgian building with flatpack Scandi-navian furniture, I decided that the best, and cheapest, option was to attend the local saleroom and pick up period pieces of furniture as they appeared, and when I could afford them. It has taken me nearly twenty years, but I suspect that the contents of the house now are not far away from those which would have filled it 200 years ago, although owing to my tight budget, they may have a few more chips and scratches than they might. The 'knock-out' sales still go on, much to the chagrin of the salerooms. On a number of occasions I've heard the auctioneer in our local auction angrily point out that it is illegal when the most shamelessly obvious incidents of this occur. What is frustrating for the saleroom is that while it is clear that a 'ring' is operating, it is almost impossible to prove, which is why – over 100 years after Williamson's condemnation of the practice – it continues. It happens in auctions of all sorts: art, furniture, silver, jewellery and books, and I doubt it will ever cease.

Perhaps the guppy-like dealer who conceals his bids from his fellow booksellers by opening and closing his mouth was one who has chosen not to join the ring, and bids secretly so that his fellows do not suspect him of undermining their code. I've always found that the best way to keep an eye on what's happening in the room is to stand at the back – that way it's easy to spot hands being raised, or heads being nodded between you and the hammer, and to know when it is wise to keep bidding or to bow out. Once, though, this tactic let me down badly; it was a hot day in summer at a fine furniture sale, and I had my eye on a few lots. During a lull between them, I found myself chatting at the back of the room to my friend Robin, a farmer who exports antiques to America. I had my back to the auctioneer, and was deep in discussion with Robin about the potential hammer price of a Georgian chest commode that I was determined to buy. I was fanning myself with the catalogue as we chatted while behind me I heard the price of a chandelier that I had no desire to buy racing rapidly upwards. Eventually Robin stopped our conversation and said, 'You know you're up to £2,200 on that chandelier? I don't think it's worth that.' Thankfully, the auctioneer realised that I hadn't been bidding, politely made me look like an idiot and began the bidding again.

Auctions are not for the faint-hearted, and it's remarkably easy to let the moment run away with you. Williamson describes a sale of theological texts that an inexperienced minister attended:

He seemed amazed when he saw some of his favourite authors being sold at what seemed to him ridiculously low prices. He got quite excited and began to bid. He would not let a bargain pass him, and when, at the close of the sale, he had come to his senses, and stood beside a great pile of books with his account in his hand and an empty purse, he looked very unlike the trim, jolly parson who had entered that room two hours before.

FRIDAY, I JULY

Online orders: 2
Books found: 1

The swallow chicks in the nest in the close between my house and my neighbours have fledged. This is Captain's favourite time of the year, as the poor fledglings often end up on the ground after tumbling from the nest and, not sure quite what to do next, they make easy prey for fat cats.

Lucy was in today. Granny was at The Pheasant.

One of today's emails was in response to a message in which I apologised to a customer because we didn't have the book he was after. I replied to his message which ended with the words, 'Take care.' I had intended to write, 'You too,' in response, but thanks to a slip of the finger ended up writing, 'You tool,' and pressed 'Send' before I noticed.

Till total £305
21 customers

SATURDAY, 2 JULY

Online orders: 1
Books found: 1

Lucy ran the shop today – I sneaked off and went fishing after heavy rain last night. The river was perfect, but despite my best efforts, I caught nothing. A small degree of comfort could be drawn from the fact that the three other people I bumped into on the river had also failed to catch anything.

Got home in time for Lucy to go for lunch, and unloaded the Glenburn books from the van. It feels that we're always fighting a losing battle when it comes to stock coming in, but I think we're finally making a little progress.

My father's cousin Rachel visited. It's always a pleasure to see her. She lives in Shropshire and is friendly with Anna Dreda, whose wonderful bookshop in Much Wenlock sadly closed recently.

Till total £322.47
26 customers

MONDAY, 4 JULY

Online orders: 3
Books found: 3

Lucy had to deal with the first customer of the day today. He came into the shop at 11 a.m.

> Lucy: 'Good morning.'
> Customer: silence.

Ten minutes later he came to the till with four books and put them on the counter, saying nothing. Lucy added them up and told him that the total was £12. No response other than to push his credit card towards Lucy. Lucy processed everything, said thank you and goodbye, only to be met with a stony face and complete silence.

When Lucy was on her lunch break, I received a telephone call from Amazon about reactivating my account – they asked me to send photographs of bank statements and a letter from HMRC. I'm not sure I can be bothered: I've rather enjoyed not having to dance to their digital algorithmic tune.

Till total £294.97
35 customers

TUESDAY, 5 JULY

Online orders: 3
Books found: 3

Opened the shop at 9 a.m. as usual, Granny took over shortly afterwards so that I could drive to Beith to collect the books I'd looked at last week. Spent a couple of hours boxing and loading them into the van. The driveway was so narrow that the van barely fitted down it, and I had to hack my way through a fuchsia to gain access to the side door of the van to load up. I couldn't use the back doors as I'd loaded the back with boxes of books to take to the recycling plant in Glasgow. By the time I'd finished, I was covered in fuchsia flowers and scratches.

Left the house in Beith at 1.30 and drove to the recycling plant in Glasgow to ditch thirty-four boxes of books. Home at 9.30. It was still light when I got back.

Till total £167.49
17 customers

WEDNESDAY, 6 JULY

Online orders: 3
Books found: 2

Lucy in. I managed to open a bit early, so the door was open when she arrived.

I spent the day unloading the boxes of Scottish antiquarian material from the Beith deal, while Lucy cleaned and treated the bindings with leather food.

Two different customers brought in boxes of books, one of which was a collection of cookery books, primarily on dieting. It's curious to note that, for the large part, people who bring in dieting books to sell have clearly failed to stick rigidly to the recipes contained within them. Perhaps they're selling them because they've given up.

The other customer, a man with a springer spaniel, brought in two boxes containing a mixed selection, including quite a few books about gundog training, a subject that sells surprisingly well. I wrote a cheque for £40 for them. As I handed him the cheque, the spaniel squatted down on the floor and urinated. Both she and her owner looked equally embarrassed. So much for books on training dogs. After they'd left, the air thick with apologies, I ran upstairs and grabbed the mop.

Till total £361.35
26 customers

THURSDAY, 7 JULY

Online orders: 3
Books found: 3

Lucy and I spent the day working our way through the Beith books again. They're pretty grotty, but with a bit of effort we've managed to make them look quite presentable.

Customer came to the counter with a rare and quite valuable paperback copy of the 1966 Olympia Press edition of William S. Burroughs's *Junkie*. She made a ten-minute fuss over the £40 price tag, including the usual ritual of pointing at the original price and asking how it was possible that it could have gone up in value.

I explained that the Gutenberg Bible sold for 30 florins when it was first produced in 1455. A copy sold in 1987 for $5.4 million, but she didn't seem particularly interested in my thoughts and kept stabbing her index finger at the book, which she'd laid face-down on the counter, and saying, 'Why? Why? Why?'

After a while she loudly proclaimed to the increasingly curious audience of customers who were pretending to read books but clearly had far more interest in the theatre playing out in front of them, that there was no way she was prepared to pay that much 'for a bloody paperback' then marched defiantly back to the paperback section and made a show of stuffing it unceremoniously back on the shelf. I'd forgotten that I'd read Burroughs when I was a student – it's often unpleasant encounters such as this that remind me of books I've read. *Naked Lunch* and *Junkie* were both fairly hard work, I remember. Perhaps I should read them again, now that I'm infinitely wiser than I was then.

The Olympia Press paperbacks are (usually) a uniform style: green paper covers with black-and-white borders whose only difference is the title of each publication. The press tended towards publishing the salacious, banking on the fact that, being based in liberal Paris, they were less likely to attract litigation than if they'd been in the UK or the USA. Their neat, attractive Traveller's Companion books were all published in English, but only sold in the safe space of Paris (although often smuggled across borders to be sold in underground bookshops by runners); Olympia was the first publisher to go to press with Nabokov's *Lolita*, in 1955. Looking through their list recently, I was surprised to discover that I'd read quite a few books that they were the first to publish, by authors including J. P. Donleavy, Nabokov, Alexander Trocchi, William S. Burroughs, Oscar Wilde, the Marquis de Sade and Lawrence Durrell. Inevitably the press attracted controversy, not least over copyright issues with its authors. It was eventually bought out by Donleavy's wife.

Till total £459.80
28 customers

FRIDAY, 8 JULY

Online orders: 2
Books found: 1

Lucy in.

Just before lunch, a customer brought in a box of cookery books, including a copy of a book called *Good Potato Dishes*, by someone called Ambrose Heath. Flicking through it, I spotted the list of his previous publications:

Good Food	Good Soups
More Good Food	Good Sweets
Good Food on the Aga	The Book of the Onion
Good Savouries	

It's hard not to be impressed with the directness of his titles.

Sandy the tattooed pagan appeared at 2 p.m. with another bundle of sticks: 'Seamus, old son, how the hell are you?' He then asked Lucy to make him a cup of tea. She refused, so I made him one. I found him in the Scottish room singing a traditional Scottish folk song about witches to an alarmed-looking customer.

Till total £261.99
19 customers

SATURDAY, 9 JULY

Online orders: 3
Books found: 3

I found another small dogshit on the doorstep when I opened the shop. I'm pretty sure that Nicky was right that the culprit is that bloody poodle from three doors down the street. I remember when she spotted it pissing on the azalea in the plant pot in front of the shop. We had had a brief discussion about connecting the pot to a high-voltage power supply.

First customer of the day: 'Oh look, here's a book about Descartes' (pronounced it dess carts). 'Aren't they the ones with the high voices in the choir? That should be in the music section, not philosophy.'

I despair.

Till total £547.70
38 customers

MONDAY, 11 JULY

Online orders: 3
Books found: 3

Opened the shop, left Lucy in charge with Granny on hand to help if necessary. Drove to Prestwick airport and caught a flight to Mallorca, where my sister and brother-in-law have rented a house. My other sister and her family are invited too, so it will be the first time we've all been on holiday together since we were children.

Till total £154.77
22 customers

TUESDAY, 12 JULY

Online orders: 3
Books found: 3

Everything was working fine in the shop when I left yesterday afternoon.

Message from Granny this morning: 'We can't get the mouse to work – it's just stopped all of a sudden.'

So, no online orders can be processed, no new stock listed. What further disasters will befall my beloved business before I return?

Till total £144.55
10 customers

MONDAY, 18 JULY

Online orders: 5
Books found: 3

Arrived back in Prestwick at 4 p.m. yesterday, home just after six.

Two of the five orders today were from overseas. We normally see a spike in overseas sales when the pound is weak, making it relatively cheap for customers from abroad to buy from the UK.

Lucy packed and labelled RBC books. Fairly quiet day in the shop.

Found a copy of *Advice to Young Men*, by William Cobbett (author of *Rural Rides*), in a box from the Beith collection:

> The things which you ought to desire in a wife are, 1. Chastity; 2. Sobriety; 3. Industry; 4. Frugality; 5. Cleanliness; 6. Knowledge of domestic affairs; 7. Good temper; 8. Beauty.

Warm evening, so I made burgers and Granny and I had a barbecue, followed by a game of badminton in the garden. Every time I won a point, she spent about thirty seconds cursing me in a colourful blend of Italian and broken English. We played until it was too dark to continue, at about 11 p.m.

Anna and I would occasionally play badminton of an evening. I remember clearly the time she first suggested a game of 'Bad Mitten'. Once I'd stopped laughing, I realised that this was what she thought the game was called. She'd been to a 'progressive' school in Massachusetts, where spelling was given little weight.

160

Beautiful herringbone sunset sky.

Till total £202.50
16 customers

TUESDAY, 19 JULY

Online orders: 1
Books found: 1

Glorious sunny day, so Granny decided to sunbathe all day instead of 'doing the shop'. She refused to admit it when I suggested that it was in revenge for me thrashing her at badminton last night, saying, 'It's your stupid bloody shop, maybe sometimes you fink about doing some work?' before flicking the middle finger at me and walking out to the garden with her towel and her sun lotion.

I was sorting through the shelves to clear dead stock and decided to throw away a tatty Folio Society copy of Philip Francis's edition of *John Evelyn's Diary* (1963). The moment I put it in the box to go to the recycling, an elderly man picked it up and said, 'How extraordinary, I've been looking for that for years', so I sold it to him for £8.50.

Lucy continued to pack up and label the random books.

Nancy, the American woman who is in The Open Book this week, came over to say hello, and asked me if I'd take a look at the satnav in her hire car. For some reason, the rental company had set the language to Japanese. After about half an hour of tinkering we managed to reset it to English.

Till total £219.49
13 customers

WEDNESDAY, 20 JULY

Online orders: 1
Books found: 1

The back door of the shop was wide open this morning when I opened up. It was raining heavily, but thankfully none of the numerous leaks in the roof or chimneys appeared to be causing any problems.

Granny found a book called *The Women's Guide to Self Defence*. She was particularly pleased with this photograph, and assured me that one day she would surprise me – like Cato in *The Pink Panther* – and execute it to perfection.

Customer: 'Do you buy books in?'
Me: 'We do.'
Customer: 'Amazing.'
Me: 'Do you have books to sell?'
Customer: 'No, I don't really read books. I just wondered how it worked.'

The torrential rain stopped at 10 a.m. and the sun came out.

At 5.15 I switched off all the lights and told customers we were closed. One went right back through the shop and turned them all back on. When I told him again that we were closed, he went into the front room and climbed a ladder and started reading a book from the Irish section. He eventually left at 5.30 p.m.

Till total £382.98
43 customers

Online orders: 4
Books found: 4

Telephone call from the friend of a man whose wife died recently. He has 300 of her craft books to sell.

At 11.30 a well-dressed young man who I'd overheard earlier discussing investment banking with one of his companions asked, 'Excuse me, how are these books priced?'

> Me: 'Well, you see the yellow price sticker on the dust jacket with a price on it?'
> Customer: 'Yes.'
> Me: 'That's the price.'
> Customer: 'Really? Well I never. How clever.'

Good lord, I think it might be time to start stuffing the daily takings into a mattress if this is the benchmark for investment bankers.

After lunch I went to the post office with four bags of random books. Wilma was just back from her lunch break, so mercifully I avoided the deliberately drawn-out torture of being served by William. The bloody poodle who defiles my doorstep would manage to process my mail faster than William does, and he makes no disguise of the fact that he is doing it as slowly as possible just to annoy me. The more urgent you appear, the slower he goes.

Went fishing on the Minnoch. Didn't catch anything.

Peggy and Colin were in Wigtown for a holiday. Peggy chairs events during the festival, and Colin does the social media. Went for supper with them at Craft.

Till total £189
27 customers

FRIDAY, 22 JULY

Online orders: 3
Books found: 2

Lucy opened the shop, and sold a book called *Phallic Worship* at 9.15.
It was in a box of books from the Beith deal, and I'd been meaning to
put it aside for Sandy the tattooed pagan, but a sale's a sale.

Postcard in this morning, a picture of Robert Burns with
the score and lyrics to one of his songs beneath it. On the back, a
message in the unmistakable hand of Nicky. She'd made an unconvincing effort to copy Burns's handwriting style, but it clearly came
from her. This was the message:

> Why don't you spend more time painting your nails
> and plucking your pretty little eyebrows instead of
> boring us rigid with postcards. Hmmm?
>
> Rab

A young girl spent ten minutes wandering through the shop
repeating the words 'I'm a robot' in a dull monotone. I'm going to
test Asimov's second law by telling her to shut up.

After lunch I went to the river with my father. He caught two
salmon – I caught nothing. Rained in the evening, so there may be
enough water to go again tomorrow.

Till total £101.98
17 customers

SATURDAY, 23 JULY

Online orders: 0
Books found: 0

Granny opened the shop. I went to the Minnoch after lunch, but
the water from last night hadn't raised the river enough to make it

worth fishing. Granny: 'Oh yes, you go fishing and leave the poor Granny here to do your work, you bastard.'

When I got back to the shop at three o'clock I sorted through some books and found a note which had been used as a bookmark: 'Darling – I've saved it in Word on the desktop. Just touch the ESCAPE button to bring it up.'

Customer picked up a copy of a book called *Jews Without Jehovah* which had been on the table for about a week, unpriced. He asked how much it was – I considered letting him have it for £8, then thought that there seemed to be something unusual about it, whether it was the cover illustration or the title and the date (1934), so went upstairs and checked. Very scarce title, withdrawn because it was semi-autobiographical and some of the characters took legal action against the author. Understandably, the customer declined my price of £400, so I listed it online for £600.

Till total £487.15
30 customers

Online orders: 4
Books found: 2

Opened the emails this morning to find an order for *Jews Without Jehovah* from a customer in America.

When Lucy was having her lunch break, a man wearing a Parka (it was a very warm day) came to the counter and stood there with his mouth open for five minutes. He was holding a four-pack of Co-op loo roll. I suspect that he may have been part of some sort of art project.

It rained again last night, and Granny spent the morning complaining that I've never taken her fishing, so we went to the Minnoch. To my astonishment, she mastered the art of casting remarkably quickly, and I was concerned that she might catch a fish, but mercifully, she didn't.

When we got back to the shop, I was sorting through some books which a customer had dropped off while we were fishing and discovered a black-and-white photograph of a man in naval uniform from the 1950s in a first edition of Graham Greene's *The Quiet American*. These things always throw me – clearly this photograph meant something to someone, whether it was the subject of the photograph or the person who took it, or perhaps it belonged to another family member. To me, though, it is pretty meaningless, other than as the subject of speculation. I tend to leave ephemera in the books in which I find them – perhaps they may find their way home.

Till total £373.48
28 customers

Online orders: 0
Books found: 0

Lucy in. We spent the morning tidying up books. I found a copy of *The Colour of Her Panties*, by Piers Anthony.

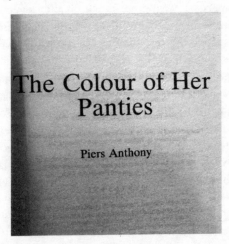

Found a letter in a copy of *Middle East* from the same collection as the photograph of the man in naval uniform, from the wife of Philip Guedalla – a historian and prolific biographer, and the man who came up with the phrase 'History repeats itself. Historians repeat each other.' He died two days after this letter was written by his wife. It was written to Wing Commander Dodds, and it was in a copy of Guedalla's last book – a book about the RAF.

Lucy left at three o'clock, and Granny closed the shop while I went on yet another unsuccessful fishing trip to the river.

Till total £251.19
19 customers

Online orders: 3
Books found: 2

Lucy opened up the shop. I went to the loch at Elrig and caught four small wild brown trout. Came back to find the shop absolutely full of customers.

Email from someone at Expedia who is doing a feature on bookshops and wanted some photos of the shop, so I sent him some of Caroline's, with her permission.

After the shop closed, Granny and I made a video of me walking backwards through the shop throwing books, and singing The Bookshop Band's *In a Shop with Books In*, backwards. Reversed it and put it on Facebook. It's remarkably difficult to learn how to say something as simple as 'In a shop with books in' backwards.

When we'd finished, I cooked the trout I'd caught in the morning. Granny took one look at them and said, 'These are a baby fish. Why you not catch a adult fish?'

Till total £628.50
23 customers

Online orders: 1
Books found: 1

Lucy in. Carried on unpacking the books from the Beith deal. I think we've hit the dustiest and dirtiest box. I'm pretty sure they were on the bookshelves above the fireplace.

Order today was for a book called *The Sparrowhawk*, which came from the Stranraer ornithology collection. Sent to a customer in the Russian Federation.

Lucy overheard a young boy telling his mother, 'There's a badger and a cat in this shop!'

Mother: 'A stuffed badger?'

A family with four over-indulged children came in just before closing. One of them spent ten minutes mauling an 1824 calf-bound edition of *Paradise Lost*, repeating, 'Mummy, look at this book.'

Till total £378.89
40 customers

FRIDAY, 29 JULY

Online orders: 2
Books found: 1

Lucy in. We carried on sorting through the Beith deal. It has taken considerably more time to process than I had anticipated, largely due to the condition. The books in the cases above the fireplace were – as is often the case – both dusty and dry. The leather is invariably cracked and requires treatment to restore it to something resembling a reasonable condition.

The sun shone all day, and in the afternoon, as a few clouds appeared, my father picked me up and we went to Loch Elrig for a couple of hours. We decided to take the boat, which involves driving up to the House of Elrig to pick up the key to the boathouse. The naturalist and writer Gavin Maxwell grew up there, and wrote a book called *The House of Elrig* about his childhood there. It's a beautiful house, in the wild moors of the Machars, and although it looks much older, the stone-built house dates back to 1912. It is surrounded by ancient carved stones, the remains of a medieval chapel, and the foundations of a crannog can be seen in the loch when the water is low. The Austrian artist Oskar Kokoschka spent a summer there with the Korner family after he'd fled Europe during the war. Professor Emil Korner saw the first clouds of the gathering storm over Europe in the 1930s and had the presence of mind to move with his family to Scotland, to the House of Elrig.

We caught six fish, one of which Granny kindly decided was 'a adult fish'.

Till total £167.50
13 customers

SATURDAY, 30 JULY

Online orders: 0
Books found: 0

Opened slightly late as I forgot to charge my phone and it died during the night, so the alarm didn't go off. Mole-Man was waiting outside when I opened the shop in my pyjamas. I let him in and went upstairs to make a cup of tea. He was engrossed in the Classics section when I came downstairs, and clearly didn't hear me approaching. When I said, 'Excuse me', he leapt about a foot in the air and scuttled off.

Shortly before lunchtime, a young man in a pristine white tracksuit appeared at the counter and asked, 'Have you got any books of papers about Wigtown going back to the 1900s?'

After several minutes of conversation, it turned out that 'books of papers' meant 'books'.

Finished *Everything Is Illuminated*. Loved it. Jonathan Safran Foer wrote it when he was a student. The dialogue between Jonathan and his Ukrainian translator/chauffeur Alex is exquisite: Alex's mistakes in English and his undisguised anti-Semitism, homophobia and numerous other prejudices manage to achieve the almost impossible feat of being simultaneously toe-curling and extremely amusing. Most entertaining for me, though, is Alex's dog, the superbly named 'Sammy Davis, Jr, Jr'.

Till total £253.50
23 customers

AUGUST

The influence of dealing in books may and should be all for good in helping people to ennoble the character of the bookseller. It is invariably the best kind of people who buy books and who have them to sell. Holding converse day by day with men and women of a literary temperament, habitually handling, thinking about, talking about, and dipping into books must help to mould one's character in the highest and best sense.

A bookseller, who was far from being 'ideal' named Don Vincente, had a shop in Barcelona fifty years ago. His love for books became madness of a most extraordinary and terrible kind. When he sold a rare manuscript or book, he followed his customer and secretly stabbed him to death. He never took any money from his victims, but murdered them for the sole purpose of regaining the books he had so recently sold.

R. M. Williamson, *Bits from an Old Bookshop*

It probably won't come as a huge surprise to anyone to discover that Don Vincente was a creature of fiction, although I can't help but admire him. At the time of the publication of Williamson's book, the legend of Vincente had yet to be disproved and Williamson clearly fell for it in much the same way that *The Protocols of the Elders of Zion* (published in 1903 in the Russian newspaper *Znamya* – a year before *Bits from an Old Bookshop*) convinced the world that there was a Jewish conspiracy which controlled the media. Hitler, Goebbels and other anti-Semites including Henry Ford all bought into the myth of *The Protocols*, despite the London *Times* providing irrefutable evidence in 1921 that it was no more than a 'clumsy plagiarism'. Many people, including some whom I consider friends, still believe that the media is controlled by a Jewish cartel. Anna provided the most compelling argument that this is complete nonsense when she told me that, if you put two Jewish people in the same room with two seats and a table, they'll be arguing over who takes which seat within seconds. A global conspiracy organised by a people whose identity is forged on argument is highly unlikely.

Demonic behaviour in Barcelona bookshops has a more

contemporary association with Carlos Ruiz Zafón's extraordinary book *The Shadow of the Wind*, a copy of which I received as a gift from a friend, Finn, several years ago. It's a superb book.

It's hard to not warm to Williamson. His assertion that it is 'invariably the best kind of people who buy books and have them to sell' is patently untrue. Even George Orwell, who wrote *Bookshop Memories* in 1936 – a mere thirty-two years after Williamson was writing – conceded that 'Many of the people who came to us were of the kind who would be a nuisance anywhere but have special opportunities in a bookshop.' I would certainly agree with Williamson, though, that being surrounded by books is an edifying experience, and that – as a bookseller – one is afforded little more than the opportunity to dip into them, rather than read them. This is something I have grown to love. When the shop is open, I am constantly discovering things that I would never have known that I wanted to know: the gauge of the Ffestiniog Railway (1 ft 11½ in.), Harry Potter's middle name (James – how dull) or that the first high heels were originally worn by the Persian cavalry during the tenth century to make sure that their feet stayed in the stirrups. I don't think that any of this has moulded my character in the highest and best sense, though. I recently told some friends at supper about Napoleon's penis and was met with complete silence, broken only by my solitary laughter.

MONDAY, I AUGUST

Online orders: 1
Books found: 1

Granny was in the shop today. She and Lucy alphabetised the poetry section again which, along with sci-fi, seems to degenerate into chaos remarkably quickly.

Donna, an American woman who has lived in Wigtown for most of her life, came in to collect the key to the kirk. During the tourist season volunteers staff the church so that it is open for visitors to the town. It's a fine Scottish kirk, dating from the late nineteenth century, and somehow I have become the custodian of the key.

The latest shop video has been shared quite a few times, and has been viewed 6,000 times. One of the people who shared it is Chinese and has left a comment which Facebook translates as 'Although the shop long talk super venomous tongue, but this shop is really great! Want to go visit.'

Email from someone called Iain in Edinburgh with books to sell. Replied that, from the photos attached to the email, they look worth the trip.

Till total £263
16 customers

TUESDAY, 2 AUGUST

Online orders: 1
Books found: 1

Granny and Lucy were both in again today, and continued the seemingly endless ordeal of organising the poetry section.

Two book deals today, both in small villages about half an hour from Dumfries, on the Solway coast. I left the shop just before lunchtime, stopping at the Co-op briefly to pick up a sandwich. I've decided that the best way to select one of their sandwiches is to close my eyes and randomly pick one. They all taste the same – revolting.

Drove to the first of today's book deals, a house in Carsethorn, to look at books belonging to an elderly woman whose family was forcing her to move to sheltered accommodation in Edinburgh, very much against her wishes. I'd never been to Carsethorn before, and was pleasantly surprised to discover that it is a really beautiful coastal village. Struggled to find her house so I called her from the van. She gave me directions in a tone that suggested that I was a complete imbecile. It turned out to be the only house in the village without a sign or number on its gate to announce its presence.

It was a beautiful cottage in a row of other beautiful cottages, defended by a series of gates to keep an elderly, blind dog from straying onto the one road in the village. Inside, it was cluttered with an anomalous assortment of beautiful Georgian furniture and hideous, cheap ornaments which covered every available surface. Even the bookcases were littered with them, making removing books an exercise in rearranging the display of small plastic horses, snow globes and tacky souvenirs. The books were fairly average, a mix of hardbacks and paperbacks, predominantly fiction, and were in almost every room of the house. She showed me around at about half the pace of a retreating icecap, pointing her stick at the books she wanted to keep – Dick Francis ('I knew Dick') and Marjorie Allingham ('family friend') among others. This is deeply frustrating for book dealers and antique dealers alike, to be summoned – and in this case it most certainly was a case of being summoned – to a house by someone who has made not the slightest effort to decide what they want to keep and what they want to sell. It invariably ends, as this deal did, with me making an offer on the books I'd selected, the old woman muttering something equivocal in reply, then spending the next hour going through what I'd made an offer on and removing the best of it, but still expecting my offer to remain the same. Eventually we agreed on a price of £120 for a few boxes, and she sat down in her chair in the sitting room and smoked cigarettes, watching a television programme that appeared to be aimed at teenage girls, while I packed and removed the boxes of books, negotiating the maze of gates between the house and the van, tripping several times over the stinking dog. The whole process took about an hour longer than it ought to have done, in part due to her insistence on going through every shelf with me, stabbing her stick at books I'd already decided I didn't want and reading out the names of the authors, just in case I was unable to see them for myself, which meant that I was an hour late for the second deal, which was ten minutes away in a modern bungalow.

When I arrived I was met by a man in his seventies with a small dog and a strong Newcastle accent. The dog was considerably less smelly than the one in the previous house. Inside, the house was a blaze of bright colours and modern furniture. The books had belonged to his wife, who, I had been told by one of his friends who had telephoned to see whether I was interested in the books, had died recently and unexpectedly. In a spare bedroom on the floor were about a dozen plastic containers full of craft books. His wife had been an embroiderer and the books were almost exclusively on this subject. She had bought many of them in my shop, and had also contributed a few stitches to the Great Tapestry of Scotland. As I was sorting through them, he told me how he had come to be a widower. They'd been on holiday in Perthshire. One morning his wife woke up with dreadful toothache and decided to go to the dentist. Back at their holiday cottage, the day wore on and she became increasingly unwell. They assumed that the problem was the anaesthetic that she had been given during her dental treatment. By early evening she was in such pain that he called NHS 24 and was told to put her in bed with her feet higher than her head, and to call an ambulance if her condition worsened. It did, very quickly. He called an ambulance, and when – an hour later – there was no sign of it; he called 999 again. He was told that the ambulance had left some time ago. In a state of understandable agitation he had gone out onto the road in front of the house to look out for it. Eventually he saw the lights approaching from a small, single-track hill road, rather than the dual carriageway main road from Dundee. When he spoke to the driver about it, he explained that he'd simply followed the satnav, which had resulted in the journey taking at least twice as long as it ought to have done. He followed the ambulance from the cottage they were holidaying in to Ninewells Hospital in Dundee, where it rapidly became evident that the situation was extremely serious. They arrived at Ninewells at 10 p.m. and at 3 a.m. the doctor told him that his wife, who had seemed perfectly healthy that morning, was dead.

The poor man was close to tears as he recounted the story and was clearly devastated by his loss. He had driven back to the cottage to find the supper he had prepared for them still on the kitchen table. He went to bed, slept for a few hours and awoke at 6 a.m. in a state of complete disbelief, so he decided that the best thing he could do was to go home. He called the owner of the cottage and explained what had happened. She came straight over to see what she could do. He had begun packing his bags and those of his wife when he realised that there was no point in packing hers, so he put all of her clothes in bin bags and asked the landlady to take them to the nearest charity shop. By his account, she could not have been kinder, and told him not to worry about anything like cleaning the place or paying, so he drove home with his bags and left his wife's belongings there. He told me that he remembered nothing of the journey home, and when he arrived back at his house – their home – it struck him that there would be formalities to deal with, so he called the landlady in a state of confusion. She told him that she would deal with everything, then drove to the hospital and dealt with the inevitable paperwork. We chatted about the future. He used to be a keen cyclist and plans to get back on his bike, and find other ways to keep himself busy while he deals with his terrible loss. I told him that if he comes to Wigtown festival he should look in and we can have a cup of tea and catch up. He shut the dog in a bedroom so that it wouldn't be in the way, and helped me to load the van. Gave him £200 for the books and headed home.

Till total £297.47
30 customers

WEDNESDAY, 3 AUGUST

Online orders: 2
Books found: 2

Lucy in.

Today was Wigtown Show Day. When I was a child, this was the highlight of the calendar. It used to be known as Cattle Show Day, but in an effort to reinvent it, the organisers have re-branded it to appeal to a wider audience than farmers.

It used to take place in a field in the middle of the town that was supposedly bequeathed to the people of Wigtown by a bene-factor, but which has somehow fallen into the hands of a developer. There's a whiff of impropriety about the whole affair if you listen to some of the townsfolk, but I have no idea what really went on with the transaction, other than in the artist's impression of the

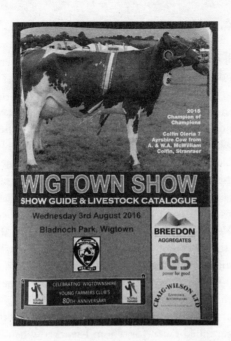

development all of the satellite dishes on the existing houses appear to have been airbrushed out, and enormous trees have been painted in. The show takes place on the rugby pitch, about half a mile out of town. It's always an entertaining day, and today was no exception; farmers – who lead solitary lives for the most part – get together and there's normally a considerable amount of drinking. Occasionally, an animal breaks loose and charges through the terrified crowd, and without exception there will be a group of children pointing and laughing hysterically at a cow having a shit.

The shop is always busy on Cattle Show day; it always brings people to the town.

Till total £484.48
46 customers

THURSDAY, 4 AUGUST

Online orders: 2
Books found: 2

Lucy was in today. Granny was working at The Pheasant. There was a lingering whiff of cow shit in the shop from the customers yesterday who had come in after a spell at the Cattle Show.

Bum-Bag Dave came in at eleven o'clock for no ostensible purpose other than to annoy me with his various bleeping devices. He appears to have acquired three digital watches, all of which make noises at different times. I'm pretty sure that he's got them timed to New York, London and Hong Kong in the deluded belief that the wheels of commerce will grind to a halt if he isn't constantly monitoring the world's most active stock markets.

A short American woman bought our entire Anne McCaffrey stock, roughly thirty titles.

Headed into Newton Stewart after lunch to visit the solicitor, a lovely man called Peter, for whom I worked when I was a law student, and who advised me to pursue a more interesting career, then went to the bank to have my annual Poverty Appraisal.

A woman came in just before closing with a collection of LGBT books, mainly academic works. They're not great sellers, but I gave her £40 for two boxes – it's a subject that I always like to have a stock of, partly because I like the shop to be representative of as diverse a number of people as possible.

Till total £399.50
24 customers

FRIDAY, 5 AUGUST

Online orders: 2
Books found: 2

Lucy in, Granny at The Pheasant. Facebook sidebar suggested this morning that I join the Apostrophe Protection Society. Must get out more.

A woman came in at 10 a.m. looking for a copy of *A Midsummer Night's Dream*. Lucy and I checked the Shakespeare section, but we appeared to have none in stock. Five minutes later, while the customer was browsing in the history section, the woman who sold me the LGBT collection yesterday came back in with five more boxes of books to sell, among which was an Arden Shakespeare copy of the *Dream*. I let the customer have it for nothing.

> Me: 'Lucy, if you're bored you can price up those books.'
> Lucy: 'How could I be bored when I've got this to read?'

She proudly held up a copy of a book called *Fashion Dog* which contained nothing but photographs of dogs wearing catwalk outfits.

Today was my father's seventy-fifth birthday. To mark the occasion, my mother booked several rooms in a hotel in Perthshire, and invited me and my sisters and cousins to spend a weekend together. We all get on well, so it was a most enjoyable time.

Till total £393.49
30 customers

SATURDAY, 6 AUGUST

Online orders: 2
Books found: 2

Mary covered the shop. She sent me a message at lunchtime to tell me that she'd bought a Danish pewter tankard in the Community Shop yesterday.

Spent most of the day drinking tea and catching up with sisters and cousins.

Till total £171.50
19 customers

MONDAY, 8 AUGUST

Online orders: 3
Books found: 1

Drove home from Perthshire yesterday afternoon. One of my chief delights, on the rare occasions on which I stay in fancy hotels, is to park the van next to the most expensive vehicle in the car park, particularly if I haven't cleaned it for a while. Normally whoever is on reception will give me a filthy look which suggests that they're thinking, 'This place is not for the likes of you.'

At 9.05 a.m. a man came into the shop. The lights were on, the sign read 'Open' and the door was wide open. He came to the counter and asked, 'Are you open?'

Sorting through books which a customer donated on Saturday, I discovered a signed copy of Heinrich Harrer's *Seven Years in Tibet* and what appears to be a tatty Penguin copy of *Rommel? Gunner Who?* (missing a cover), signed by Spike Milligan.

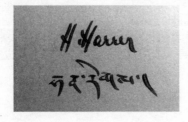

Stuart Babbington, stamp dealer and regular customer, dropped in at about two. He's always after copies of a book called *Wigtownshire Agriculturalists and Breeders*. I sold him a copy last year: it was published in about 1880 and contains photographs and one-page biographies of local farmers from that time. I can only assume that one of Stuart's progenitors features in it, which is why he's always so keen to snap up copies. We didn't have one in when he called in to the shop to say hello.

In the afternoon I began listing the embroidery collection on Monsoon, to upload to Amazon's FBA, the only platform from which I appear not to have been suspended.

Several years ago I bought a set of fairly flimsy Victorian library steps from the auction in Dumfries. They were only four steps high, and I painted on them:

Don't stand on
this if you
think
it
might
break

Today I found the bottom step split in two on the floor. I suppose it's a relief that it wasn't the top step.

TUESDAY, 9 AUGUST

Online orders: 3
Books found: 2

Granny came down in her turban and took over after I opened the shop. It's not actually a turban – it's a towel that she wraps around her head after she's washed her hair – but it looks remarkably like one. I had an appointment with the bank manager in Newton Stewart at eleven o'clock, a follow-up to my annual Poverty Appraisal. As I left the shop, Granny stuck her middle finger up at me and said, 'I hope he take your stupid fucking shop back off you.' Thankfully Sharon, the bank manager, is of a more generous disposition than Granny.

Found a book in a box about construction of geodesic domes written by a man called John Prenis. I had to re-read the cover several times.

Till total £350.93
38 customers

WEDNESDAY, 10 AUGUST

Online orders: 2
Books found: 1

Lucy opened the shop. I checked my emails and discovered one from Eliot asking if he can stay for a few days. I told him that he could, but that I'm off fishing in the Highlands. He arrives tonight and Granny will have to feed and entertain him. I waited until I was past Inverness before I pulled over and called her to let her know of his imminent arrival. I write these comments about Eliot with an enormous sense of guilt – I don't wish to portray him as a comic figure, nor to ridicule him – he's a close friend and extraordinarily good at his job, but he makes it remarkably easy to make light of his eccentricities.

Telephone call from someone wanting to sell his collection of golf books: 'Are you the tall one with gingery hair?'

Arrived at Lairg in time for supper.

Till total £588.70
46 customers

THURSDAY, 11 AUGUST

Online orders: 0
Books found: 0

Picked up a voicemail that Granny had left in a rage last night at 9 p.m. Apparently she'd tripped over Eliot's shoes, which he'd left on the middle landing. She had narrowly avoided falling down two flights of stairs. In fairness to Eliot, Granny's eyesight is so diabolical that she would probably have failed to notice a small elephant on the landing.

Till total £550.28
48 customers

FRIDAY, 12 AUGUST

Online orders: 4
Books found: 1

I took *Manners for Men* with me to Lairg as a source of anachronistic entertainment. Madge of Truth comments:

> It used to be the custom to tip the servants on leaving the house where one has dined as a guest, but this has fallen into disuse. There are many men who hand a silver coin to the butler, or footman, or waiting maid who helps them into their

coats, calls up their carriage, or hails a cab for them, seeing them into it, or rendering any other service of a similar kind.

Oddly, on fishing trips it is still expected that the guests will tip the ghillies. In fact, failure to do so tends to result in the guest being put on the poorest water if they are fortunate enough to be invited back.

Till total £146.50
18 customers

SATURDAY, 13 AUGUST

Online orders: 2
Books found: 1

Telephone call from Granny at 9 a.m. (I'd been fishing since 6.30, and plagued by midges) to let me know that the card machine wasn't working. She talked for about ten minutes, at the end of which I was beginning to think that the midges were considerably less annoying than they had been before she called. At the end of the conversation, she told me, 'Ah, the stupid fucking machine working again.'

Till total £591.49
33 customers

MONDAY, 15 AUGUST

Online orders: 2
Books found: 2

Daisy, my friend Frederick's daughter, arrived. There had been no rain over the weekend so the fishing was off. We all had lunch on the riverbank, then went for a swim in one of the deeper pools on the Oykel. I've been fortunate enough – for several years now

– to have been invited to fish on the Oykel and the Shin, two fine and beautiful rivers, by my friends Fenella and Frederick. Every year there are different guests, and we stay in a cottage just outside Lairg. I've now been going for long enough that I know the other guests quite well. I've also known Frederick's children from his first marriage since they were very young. They love to torment me.

I left at about two o'clock, taking Daisy with me – she wants to work in the shop. We stopped to look at books that one of the other fishermen, Patrick, wished to sell. His house was a beautiful place near Aberfeldy. There was some interesting material, including a copy of John Ross's *Narrative of a Second Voyage in Search of a North-West Passage*, published in 1835. It's a beautiful folio book bound in blue buckram, and illustrated with thirty plates, several of which were absent, reducing its value considerably. For me, though, there was an added interest. Ross was a Galloway man, and not only that, a west Galloway man. Although he met with limited success in his (arguably) ironically named ship *Victory* as an explorer and pioneer, on 1 June 1831 he succeeded in becoming the first European to reach the North Magnetic Pole. I admire him greatly for his combination of towering ambition and apparent lack of competence. On his return to dry land, he was noted for his failed attempt at a reconciliation with his wife and his constant beleaguering of the Admiralty for the inadequacy of its maps.

Home at 8 p.m.

Till total £564.35
34 customers

TUESDAY, 16 AUGUST

Online orders: 1
Books found: 1

Lucy and I opened the shop. An elderly man dropped off a box of books about heraldry yesterday, many of which contained heraldic bookplates.

Start every day off with a smile
and get it over with.

W. C. Fields

I'm planning to write to Debrett's to request my own crest. I've suggested a cross-hatched arrowhead piercing a customer who is wearing a pair of Crocs and a duffel coat.

Today's order was for a reprint of Newton's *Opticks* from the scientific instrument collection near Stirling.

Left the shop at 10 a.m. for a book deal in Dunscore (an hour away). The house belonged to a woman who had inherited her brother's books. It was full of dogs (I lost count after seven). The books were in a predictably filthy state, and their content was even more unsavoury than their condition – Holocaust denial, extreme religious right, anti-abortion. After a while I discovered that these were her books, rather than her brother's. She had decided to keep her brother's books because she 'didn't want that kind of liberal nonsense to be read by anyone' and to sell some of her own. She was a member of Opus Dei, and while he was alive she would regularly send her poor brother cuttings from the *Daily Telegraph*; he was a *Guardian* reader. I managed to salvage a handful of the slightly more palatable titles.

Home at 2 p.m. Daisy and Lucy spent the day gossiping. I have no idea what they were talking about, but it sounded like a foreign language.

Till total £153.18
17 customers

Online orders: 0
Books found: 0

Glorious sunny day. Today's first customer brought a mint paperback copy of Harper Lee's *Go Set a Watchman*, under a year old, original price £8.99 and asked, 'Is that really £2.50?' Initially I thought he was incredulous that it was so cheap, but it rapidly became evident that he thought that it was so overpriced that he threatened to involve Trading Standards.

Telephone call from a man with a Yorkshire accent: 'You've got a book advertised online. It's a racing calendar from 1817. It's £200 and I can't afford it so I'm not going to buy it.' As pointless telephone calls go, this must rank fairly high.

Daisy spent the morning cleaning dog hair from the books that I bought yesterday from the racist pensioner, then she and Lucy packed and labelled them for the Random Book Club.

Closed the shop and headed over to the pub for an AWB meeting. Carl, who has a guest house in Wigtown, is taking over the lease of Craft from Ben and Katie. They're leaving because, despite the excellent food and drink, they've found it hard to make money. They're going to move to France. Not much other news to discuss so the meeting was mercifully brief. Home just after six, then had a barbecue in the garden with Carol-Ann, Daisy and Granny, after which we had a game of badminton. There was a considerable amount of swearing and shouting from Granny's corner of the garden. We played until the bats came out at about 9.30.

Till total £200.50
23 customers

THURSDAY, 18 AUGUST

Online orders: 1
Books found: 1

Another beautiful Scottish summer's day. Lucy and Daisy in.

Just after the shop opened I went upstairs to make everyone a cup of tea. Lucy shouted up that a man had come in with a bag of King Penguins. I came down, armed with tea, and offered him £2 for each of them, to which he replied, 'It's not worth my while.' Lord knows what is worth his while.

Today's solitary order was for a book from the Beith collection – a paperback copy of *Orkney and the Land*, a book of old photographs and text by Kate Towsey and Helga Tulloch, priced at £25.

German woman asked for a book by an American man about a quest for silence near a lake but she couldn't remember the title or author.

Found another travel guide to France: how often do you wish you knew the French for 'O fy, for shame!' or 'I was very much affected by his tears'?

Till total £287.50
22 customers

FRIDAY, 19 AUGUST

Online orders: 4
Books found: 3

Petra arrived at 10 a.m. for her belly-dancing class. Nobody turned up, but when I mentioned to Daisy that Petra was teaching belly-dancing, she exploded with excitement and asked if she could go. While the noisy pounding went on upstairs, a customer bought a copy of *The Royal Artillery War Commemoration Book* (published on behalf of the R. A. War Commemoration Fund in 1920) to the counter. It's a rare and handsome book, bound in royal blue buckram and with the regimental crest stamped in gilt on the front board. The front paste-down endpaper is printed with the words 'This book commemorates the service in the Great War of' and a name written in a hand which I have yet to decipher. It looks very much as though it was produced by the artillery as an act of remembrance and gratitude, and issued to everyone who served and survived the horror of the First World War. This is printed on the page following the title page:

WE WHO ARE LEFT
OF THE
ROYAL REGIMENT OF ARTILLERY
INSCRIBE THIS BOOK IN PROUD REMEMBRANCE OF
FORTY-EIGHT THOUSAND NINE HUNDRED
AND FORTY-NINE OF OUR COMRADES,
WHO, CHERISHING OUR BROTHERHOOD,
GLORYING IN OUR GOOD NAME,
WHEN THE CALL CAME IN THE GREAT WAR
FOLLOWED THE PATH OF DUTY AND SELF-SACRIFICE
AND LAID DOWN THEIR LIVES FOR
THEIR KING AND COUNTRY
IN MANY STRANGE LANDS
FAITHFUL UNTO DEATH
IN THE SERVICE OF
THE GUNS

The customer had the whiff of a disgruntled colonel who had aspired to a higher staff rank. He reluctantly paid the £200 for the book, and then complained bitterly that he'd been here on Tuesday and that our copy of *The Official Army List, 1884* (published by the War Office) which he'd seen then had subsequently been sold.

Granny covered the shop while I drove to Dumfries with Daisy to look at a collection of golf books, then drop her off at the railway station. On the drive to the golfer's house, I asked Daisy what she expected from someone selling six boxes of books about golf. She told me that she very much hoped that it would be a man in a Pringle tank-top who lived in a very well-maintained bungalow and washed his car every Sunday. Her wish was granted. We were in and out in under ten minutes, including a cup of tea. Six boxes, £180. The seller, for all our stereotyping, was remarkably kind and hospitable.

Dropped Daisy off at the station then headed home. Arrived back to discover that a copy of this year's festival programme had been posted through my letterbox. Among the speakers on the opening day are former foreign secretary Sir Malcolm Rifkind and ex-*Blue Peter* presenter Janet Ellis.

Comedian Susan Calman, long-distance cyclist Mark Beaumont, journalist Sian Williams and chef and broadcaster Prue Leith pop up in the packed programme of nearly 200 events over ten days at the end of September.

Till total £223
29 customers

SATURDAY, 20 AUGUST

Online orders: 0
Books found: 0

The house is remarkably quiet without Daisy.

Telephone call from Mrs Heaton at eleven o'clock. She is now ninety-six and wants to buy her great-granddaughter a set of the complete works of Beatrix Potter. These come in from time to time, often in boxed sets. We don't have one in at the moment, but I'll keep a lookout.

In the early afternoon a young man dropped off three boxes of books from the library of John Junor, a journalist who died a few years ago. I'm ashamed to admit that, while I know his name, I know nothing about him. He stood as a Liberal, although his claim that he would 'rather admit to being a pig than be Irish' hardly chimes with the idea of a progressive, open mind. I suspect that I've taken it out of context, and it fails to represent him fairly. His grandson the journalist Sam Leith is highly respected, and was one of the judges of the Man Booker Prize last year.

The collection includes books signed by Harold Wilson and Dick Francis, neither of whom is in great demand these days. I listed them on eBay.

Till total £444.44
29 customers

MONDAY, 22 AUGUST

Online orders: 2
Books found: 2

Slept in. Granny opened the shop. When I shuffled down the stairs at 9.20, she made a theatrical look at her wrist (she wasn't wearing a watch) and commented, 'Oh, you finally decide to come to work in your bloody shop? I heard you snorking upstairs, lazy bastard.' She stuck a Post-it note on the counter about an inquiry from a man wishing to buy a book called *Edinburgh's Water Supply*. I called him and took down his details, processed the order and packed up the book while Granny stomped around for a while then left to work at The Pheasant.

The Gang of Four over-familiar Yorkshire people came in and spent an hour telling me stories about how many books they have in their house, and how they came to acquire them. Again.

Merce and her family dropped in just before closing. Merce and her sister Carme ran The Open Book in February, and Merce was making a return visit for a holiday with her family. It was a delight to see her again, and to witness her enthusiasm for the area once more. She clearly adores the place. We went for a drink in the pub.

Till total £322
28 customers

Online orders: 0
Books found: 0

Lucy was in, so I spent most of the day in the snug, editing the Cattle Show film. The first year I was asked to produce the film I looked at the previous offerings, which were about three hours long and completely unedited. There were lengthy spells of shots of the cameraman's muddy boots as he walked between sheep pens and cattle pens, obviously having forgotten to press 'Pause'. I decided to cut my version down to about twenty minutes, and interviewed the judges, asking what the criteria were for winning livestock. When I gave the edited copy to the secretary, she returned it to me and said that the committee would rather have something more like the previous years, so I removed most of my edits, made it about two hours long, unfathomably dull and re-submitted it. They liked it much better. I do this as a favour: I worked out last year that my hourly rate when I account for filming and editing is under £1 an hour.

While Lucy was on her lunch break and I was in the shop, a woman wearing a top hat came in, tutted her way through the fiction section then came to the counter and complained loudly that we didn't have a copy of *The Handmaid's Tale* in stock. It's a book I was given by a friend shortly after it came out, and I loved it. The same friend – Fenella – gave me the first paperback edition of *Trainspotting*. I still have it.

Sorted OS maps. Running low now that the rep from Nicholson Maps doesn't visit any more, since their insolvency.

Refunded an ABE order from a customer in Canada for a copy of George Gilbert's *Cathedral Cities of England*, vellum-bound and published in 1905 by Heinemann (£175), which hadn't arrived two weeks after we'd posted it out. Five minutes after I'd issued the refund I received a message from the buyer to say that it had just arrived. There's no way to reverse the refund, so I emailed the customer and asked if they could order it again if I re-listed it. There are decent people out there – just before I closed the shop, the money was in my ABE account.

Till total £426.47
44 customers

WEDNESDAY, 24 AUGUST

Online orders: 1
Books found: 0

Lucy was in this morning, so I took Merce and her family on a tour of the area, and picked up Granny in Sorbie. We all went for a swim in Rigg Bay. I don't think the Spanish had anticipated quite how cold the Scottish coastal waters would be, but they braved them anyway.

Back in the shop just after 3 p.m. to receive telephone call from a man in Essex who had found a copy of *The Encyclopedia of Unusual Sex Practices* on ABE and wanted to buy it directly from us. You'd think that if someone found a book online, then taken the trouble to telephone a bookshop to order it, that it would least have occurred to them that at some point during the conversation they might need to have their credit card to hand, but apparently not. After ten minutes of 'Hang on, I'll just check my jacket – no, not there. Just wait while I check my wife's bag. No, not there either,' he eventually managed to locate a card and we completed the transaction.

Till total £171.16
13 customers

THURSDAY, 25 AUGUST

Online orders: 1
Books found: 1

Left the shop just after Lucy arrived and drove to Glasgow to look at a book collection. Arrived in Pollok (a suburb south of the city) at eleven o'clock and met a woman who was disposing of her late father's books in a pretty Victorian villa – he'd had severe dementia and in a paranoid state had marked his initials on the edges of almost every book in felt-tip. It was an interesting and varied collection: mainly polar exploration titles, hillwalking, Scottish history and woodturning. I worked through it, picked out what I was interested in and offered her £350 for it. She told me that her father had become very difficult towards the end of his life, and was convinced that he was fine but that everyone else had gone mad.

Just before I left I asked if I could use the loo. She looked a bit nervous and reluctantly told me where it was, pre-emptively warning me that it had been pretty unpleasant in there during his final days as she tentatively unlocked the door. It was clean, although it had clearly undergone a deep clean. I suspect that his dementia had manifested itself in this room in a bit of an H-Block way.

Home at four o'clock.

Till total £242
21 customers

FRIDAY, 26 AUGUST

Online orders: 2
Books found: 0

Old man brought in a three-volume leather-bound set of Waverley novels. They were in appalling condition, and worth practically nothing. He wasn't too delighted when I told him that I didn't want them, and insisted – at considerable length – that they were extremely valuable. He left in a mild rage, but politely told me that he'd 'rather be buried with them' than give them to me for nothing, which was a fairly good outcome since I hadn't the least inclination to take them anyway.

At ten o'clock another elderly man brought in a rucksack of books about real ale: CAMRA guides from the 1990s. I suspect that he'll be taking them to his grave too.

There must have been some sort of planetary alignment which has motivated men with yellowing beards to bring the contents of their sheds to the shop today. Almost immediately after he left, another man, who could have been his twin (in fact, it has just occurred to me that he may have been the same man in a different cardigan – they smelled the same), came in:

Him: 'I've got four boxes of books, are you buying?'
Me: 'Depends what you've got.'
Him: 'They're really good books, I'll leave them with you
and come back in an hour.'

I'm not sure that I'd consider a spring 2013 Screwfix catalogue a 'good book', but that was about the best of them. He returned an hour later – smelling of soup – and told me that he was 'disappointed' that a town whose economy was based on books wasn't interested in the incalculable literary wealth contained within the pages of an out-of-date Screwfix catalogue.

After dozens of emails over the past year, I received one today from Amazon's impenetrable Seller Performance Team to advise me that my account has been reinstated. Ten minutes later I received another from them telling me that my Marketplace seller account had been permanently closed and would not be reviewed.

For some reason they haven't closed my FBA account. I no longer care.

Till total £434
37 customers

SATURDAY, 27 AUGUST

Online orders: 1
Books found: 1

Today was Lucy's final day in the shop. She's been reliable, honest and surly. I could scarcely ask for more from an employee.

Order for a biography of an animal artist, *Life of Joseph Wolf*, from Donald Watson's collection. It's going to Hong Kong. I bought Donald Watson's library – or what remained of it – a few years ago. He was a wildlife (predominantly bird) illustrator who lived about 40 minutes away, in Dalry. He'd been dead for a long time when I was called to clear his collection, the best of which had been bequeathed to the Dumfries Library. What was left was fairly poor and not in good condition, but it ticks over in the way that books about natural history tend to do, particularly if they're inscribed by someone well known in the field.

Anna came over to visit at lunchtime. She wanted to see my parents, so we dropped by their house to say hello – there was nobody there, so we went for a walk in the Wood of Cree, did some shopping, then dropped by on the way back to find that my father had just returned and was getting out of his car. I asked him where my mother was, to which he replied, 'She's in hospital.' Anna and I exchanged looks of shock, and my father explained that he had left me a voicemail message. I don't have voicemail activated, so the only explanation is that he dialled the wrong number and someone else now thinks that their mother is in hospital.

He explained that yesterday morning she had been rushed by ambulance to Dumfries Infirmary with a perforated stomach caused by an ulcer which had burst, causing her to lose one-third of her blood. Following surgery and a blood transfusion, she had stabilised and was apparently feeling better and making a slow recovery. Called her on her ward at 6 p.m. She told me that she'd been told to eat something and had thrown up, and was now feeling considerably worse. She told me not to tell my father. She doesn't want visitors.

Till total £180.48
22 customers

SUNDAY, 28 AUGUST

Online orders: 1
Books found: 1

Called my father first thing. Apparently my mother is stable and has started to eat again.

Anna came over in the afternoon to see how my mother is doing. I filled her in and we had some lunch.

At 6 p.m. there was a blackening. This is a local tradition when couples get married. For some inexplicable reason the bride and the groom are taken – instead of on a hen or stag night – down to the harbour, covered in mud by their friends, then dragged around on a trailer, sitting on a bale of hay, by a farm vehicle which trails them around every pub in the peninsula and honks the horn incessantly as it goes. It's a horribly fascinating thing to witness, and Anna, who was here for supper, hadn't seen one before. Both bride and groom were on the trailer on this occasion, bride covered in blue paint, groom covered in mud, oil and feathers. As they were going past the shop, a vintage tractor rally was passing in the opposite direction. God only knows what they made of the scene.

Online orders: 2
Books found: 0

Granny opened the shop. I drove to Dumfries. Went to the hospital. As I was parking, I spotted a friend of my parents who lives in Wigtown. He was walking from the car park towards the main entrance, so I wound down the window to say hello. He asked, 'So who are you visiting?'

I briefly explained and said I'd catch up with him when I'd parked, after which I found him sitting on a bench in the sun. I told him that my mother had been blue-lighted to the hospital. When I asked who he was visiting, he told me that he had been admitted on Friday with a heart problem. He and my mother must have been in Ward 7 (emergency ward) at just about the same time. We said goodbye and I went to Ward 10, to which my mother had been transferred as soon as she was out of the high-risk category. Found her and my father chatting. She was in much better form than when I'd spoken to her on Saturday, and was eating and drinking, although she looked and sounded utterly exhausted. Positive signs included her complaining about the woman in the neighbouring bed, who undoubtedly heard her. Apparently the neighbour had talked incessantly until about ten o'clock the previous night, after which she fell mercifully silent before a nurse came in and gave her some steroids. Moments later, once they'd kicked in, she renewed her soliloquy with invigorated energy.

Left the hospital at 2.40 and drove home. Had a brief chat with Granny before calling my sisters to fill them in on our mother's situation.

I hate to admit it, but Granny is a good person to have around in a situation like this – she was on top of everything in the shop, and for once didn't even insult me. Thankfully, she didn't offer to cook, though. I don't think I could have faced recycled cardboard and dried squash skins after a day like today.

Till total £302.79
21 customers

TUESDAY, 30 AUGUST

Online orders: 1
Books found: 1

I opened the shop, and Granny called The Pheasant to say that she couldn't come in.

Nicky dropped off a card for my mother. We briefly chatted about blood loss. I told her that if my mother had been a Jehovah's Witness then she would almost certainly have died. Predictable argument about blood transfusions and made-up religions followed.

Finn called to ask about my mother, and what was happening with Craft. He'd heard the rumour that it has changed hands. He was one of Ben and Katie's best customers, and was clearly devastated to hear that they're leaving.

Granny headed off to the bank to sort out her account in the morning once it was obvious that things were no longer in emergency status. She returned at lunchtime.

Customer asked where the Irish section was. Couldn't be bothered to show him, so sat in the chair saying, 'Forward three paces. Left 90 degrees. Two paces forward. Left again.'

Drove to Dumfries to visit my mother in the afternoon. I left the hospital at 3.30 to look at books in a house near the garden centre – conveniently on the way home. It must have been the shortest book deal I've ever done: fussy bungalow, fussy man with Midlands accent who showed me to the books, about 100 of them, piled on his dining table. Very little of interest. I took about fifteen out and made a pile, offered him a rather generous £50 for them, which – considering I'd made a 100-mile round trip to view them – I imagined he would be delighted with as they were probably all available for a penny on Amazon. He simply replied, 'No way,' to which I replied, 'Right, well I'll leave you in peace, thanks for getting in touch,' and left. The whole process took under five minutes.

Dropped into another house on the way home, just outside Castle Douglas. Completely different experience – elderly couple who had clearly both been keen mountaineers but had decided that their hillwalking days were probably over. They brought me tea, biscuits and even offered me a gin and tonic. There were roughly 500 books, all in good, clean condition, and about 100 more on polar exploration. I offered them £1,000 for them, to which they responded by saying that they'd only expected about £50 for them. Boxed them up and loaded them into the van.

Called my father at 8 p.m.; apparently my mother is doing much better.

Till total £319.99
24 customers

WEDNESDAY, 31 AUGUST

Online orders: 1
Books found: 1

Order for book about the history of microscopes from the scientific instrument deal from near Stirling in April. £45.

Telephone call from Christian, one of the festival trustees. He wants to borrow the van to shift some things for the festival. This is the time of year when you think you have plenty of time to prepare but quickly realise that you haven't.

Carol Crawford, the rep who visits every few months to sell new books, turned up at eleven o'clock with all the latest Scottish book releases on her iPad. As we were going through them, Sandy the tattooed pagan arrived with six sticks and they got chatting about where she's from – Sandy turns on the charm when there's a woman in the shop. It turned out that Sandy had done a residential course run by the National Coal Board in Strathaven (pronounced Straven), where Carol lives, when he was sixteen years old – before a brief stint in the coal mines and then a short spell in prison. It's not the done thing to ask someone who tells you they spent time in prison what they were in for, and Sandy has never volunteered this information.

A very annoying woman was in the shop when her phone rang. She went outside and stood in the doorway: 'I'm in a bookshop in

God-knows-where in Scotland and I've found a book I think you'll like. Do you want me to take a picture of the cover so you can get it on Amazon?'

A middle-aged woman with long grey hair and a lot of shawls bought £50 worth of books on mysticism.

Cut the grass and tidied the garden in preparation for the festival, and started to organise the front room for the Writers' Retreat.

My father called at 8 p.m. to tell me that my mother has had a mini-stroke, but with no damage to the brain. She'll go for a scan tomorrow to find out more, and hopefully come home. He sounded quite calm about it, but apparently she is not. My sister telephoned to discuss it – it turns out that our mother has had a few of these since being admitted to hospital.

Till total £219.50
20 customers

SEPTEMBER

The people who are drawn by their love of learning to patronise a book shop should be of a superior type. It is not needful that they be wealthy or be poor, be famous or unknown, for there is a delightful sense of social equality within the precincts of an old book shop which can be found nowhere else. The little barriers of class and creed disappear in the presence of immortality. Quietly and silently but irresistibly the books exert their influence over men's minds.

What an interesting medley of customers are drawn to a book shop. The callow youth entering his little circle of society enquires blushingly for a 'Manual of Etiquette'.

R. M. Williamson, *Bits from an Old Bookshop*

Williamson might well have saved the callow youth his blushes by selling him a copy of Madge of Truth's *Manners for Men*, published in 1897, just seven years before Williamson's own book. I hope that my slightly mocking observations of the formal conventions to which Madge advises such youths to adhere are not misinterpreted as mocking Madge: she was merely reflecting the preposterous social rules of her time. Madge of Truth (Charlotte Eliza Humphry) was a pioneer, and is widely recognised as one of the first female journalists in the UK. From 1873 she wrote a regular column for the magazine *Truth* (a typically sanctimonious title for a Victorian publication). It's far too easy to dismiss her work in the context of the work of today's journalists, but she was undoubtedly a groundbreaking figure, most of whose work was devoted to the previously largely overlooked subject of the interests of women. As she commented during an interview with *Women's Life* in the 1890s:

> The scope of women's work in the journalistic world is much greater now. When I first became a journalist only a few papers published ladies' letters, and these dealt principally with domestic servants, the management of babies, and similar subjects. Now women go in for golf, bicycling, and other games; in fact, the athletic girl is a new development, and as woman's world is widened, so is the field for women writers.

The social equality of bookshops is a point on which I whole-heartedly agree with Williamson: like libraries, bookshops are spaces that people mostly enter for the purpose of quiet reflection. The largely subconscious social signals by which many of us judge our fellows – the way we dress and speak, and even the cars we drive – matter for nothing when you're immersed in a book. Your companions in the shop are others with whom you share a love of the written word, even if theirs is a 1609 George Eld edition of *Shakespeare's Sonnets* and yours is a 1971 Haynes *Morris Minor 1000 Owner's Workshop Manual*. It doesn't matter. It's like being in a sauna – we're all denuded of pretence, and quietly and silently in the thrall of books whose writers know, or knew, far more than we do, and united in a love of learning. People whose paths may never have otherwise crossed become friends in the shop, possibly only for a few minutes, but it is a levelling space, and one that I love to be in, despite my remarks about some of those who I encounter. It's only when the vulgar issue of money is raised that hostility often follows.

THURSDAY, 1 SEPTEMBER

Online orders: 0
Books found: 0

This morning I sold a book signed by William Dalrymple for £2.50. Whoever priced it up (not me – probably Meredith) clearly didn't spot the signature. Not sure if it would have increased or decreased its value.

Putting books out after lunch and spotted two volumes of *Campbell's Tour* (1810) in different parts of the Scottish room which had clearly been listed separately and put in different places, despite being from the same set, the same owner and with the same bookplate in each. I removed them from our online catalogue and re-listed them as a set. Now that she's been gone for long enough not to come back and punch me, I blamed Meredith again.

A woman in a very badly home-knitted cardigan came to the

counter with ten books on embroidery. The total cost was £36.50. When I totalled them up and told her, she replied, 'What? I'm not paying that. I'll have to put one back.' She returned a paperback priced at £2.50 and came back with a smug look of satisfaction.

While she was putting her book back, an old man in checked trousers put a book priced at £3.50 on the counter and asked, 'Is there room for negotiation on this book?'

THREE POUNDS FIFTY.

Unloaded the eighteen boxes of books on mountaineering and polar exploration from the van. Straight away, a customer started rooting through them and complained that I don't have a first edition of Shackleton's *South* among them.

Girl in a school uniform came in and asked if we had a copy of *Kidnapped*. Showed her to the Stevenson collection but she couldn't find one. Pretty unusual – we have a good Stevenson section, and *Kidnapped* is usually in there somewhere.

Ran down from an emergency break to the loo to answer the telephone. It was an old woman who was keen to sell a set of Waverley novels. I asked if they were in leather bindings. She replied, 'How do I know if they're leather?' I found it surprisingly difficult to explain.

Granny cooked supper. It was pretty foul – under-boiled rice and some raw vegetables. She's been very kind recently, so I pretended I'd enjoyed it.

Telephone call from my father to let me know that my mother is now back home, and doing well.

Till total £175.16
15 customers

FRIDAY, 2 SEPTEMBER

Online orders: 1
Books found: 1

Extremely large woman asked me to get two Khaled Hosseini

books from a shelf because she didn't 'trust herself' to use a ladder. She spent several minutes looking at them, then asked me what the price was despite it being clearly written on the first page of each book. They were both £2.50. On being informed of this she replied, 'Oh, I won't take them then, if they're that expensive.'

Still sorting through the last of the books from the Beith collection. Pretty depressing to discover how much Scottish antiquarian material has dropped in value. I based my price on experience, having previously sold many of the titles in the collection for £50 and upwards. Checking them today, most of them have dropped to around £20, and so few of them have gone in the other direction that I'm quite astonished in the rare event that I discover one that exceeds my expectations. I paid about 30 per cent too much for that library. I did come across a fairly early copy of *Kidnapped* – perhaps that schoolgirl who was in yesterday will return.

In the afternoon – I forget when (I lose track of time when I'm on my own in the shop and don't have to tut in a passive-aggressive way at staff coming in late) – a customer came to the counter with two books on aviation, total £11. He asked for a discount then complained that he is finding it increasingly difficult to find books on Spitfires because 'bookshops seem to be closing down all over the country'. No discount. No slap is big enough for this particular flavour of fool.

Boy of about ten asked if I'd read all the books in the shop, then asked if I had 'the first-born'. After much confusion it emerged that he was looking for the first book in Robert Ludlum's *Bourne* series.

American group came in at 4.30. One of them, a man with a grey beard, came to the counter with two books about the clan Campbell. He didn't reply when I asked him for £11.50, then removed a £20 note from his tartan wallet (Macdonald clan) and tossed it disdainfully onto the counter. He was equally uncommunicative when I gave him his change. By contrast, a young Irish woman came to the counter five minutes later with a biography of the Scottish artist S. J. Peploe and was utterly charming, telling me how delighted she was with the book, and how she thought it would have been far more expensive, and thanking me profusely.

Closed the shop a bit early and went to the pub with Granny, Tom and Willeke. They came back here for something to eat (I found a pizza in the freezer). We opened another bottle of wine, and they stayed for the night. Granny was less than complimentary about the authenticity of the Co-op's 'Authentic Italian Pizza': 'It taste like a fucking German pizza.'

Till total £309.49
18 customers

Online orders: 1
Books found: 1

Regular customers – a woman with her teenage daughter (short pink hair and short blue skirt every time they visit) – came in and bought several books. They're probably my favourite customers, now that Mr Deacon has died. They're both friendly, and they're clearly passionate readers – they always buy books that I'm ashamed that I haven't read. I sometimes wonder if they do it on purpose. Today's haul consisted of *Ulysses*, *To the Lighthouse*, *Middlemarch* (which I have read), *Catch-22* and *The Quiet American* – all paperbacks.

Putting out books from the collection of the woman whose father had suffered from dementia in Glasgow, I came across a biography of John Paul Jones, who is credited in the USA as having founded their navy and is discredited in the UK as a pirate. He was born near Kirkcudbright (30 miles from Wigtown) and set fire to and destroyed the Cumbrian town of Whitehaven. Priced it at £18 and put it on a shelf in the local section. Ten minutes later a man came to the counter and asked if we had anything about John Paul Jones, so I pointed him to the book and he bought it. He'd never heard of him until last night when, taking a break in the area for the weekend, he'd unwittingly booked into JPJ's old home and the owner had told him his story. There is a sort of strange serendipity with second-hand bookshops. This sort of coincidence is far from unusual.

After I shut the shop, I sanded and varnished the kitchen work surface, which had developed a black mould near the sink, just in case the woman from the environmental health department of the council decides to carry out a spot check before the festival. The kitchen needs to pass their standards for the catering during the book festival. Which reminds me, I've run out of programmes. Must go to the office and get some more.

Till total £361.47
27 customers

SUNDAY, 4 SEPTEMBER

Spent the day in the garden, cutting things back and trimming the hedge so that there's clear access between the shop and Amy's Wine Bar, which is in a building behind the shop during the festival.

MONDAY, 5 SEPTEMBER

Online orders: 2
Books found: 2

Granny opened the shop, so I had a lie-in. My back is in agony after spending yesterday in the garden.

Email from my friend Ian, a book dealer from Grimsby, asking if I wanted a pallet of books. With the festival coming up, it might be useful to fill any gaps on the shelves, so I said yes. He's promised to deliver them before the festival begins.

A couple who had recently moved here and were divesting themselves of books brought in a box of books at lunchtime. Nothing of interest – three copies of Tennyson's works, all missing spines, Everyman sets in poor condition. Even with gaps on the shelves, they weren't suitable for shop stock.

Left Granny in charge and headed off to a book deal in Crossmichael, about 35 miles away. Nothing much of interest, although there was a fairly decent leather-bound set of Smollett's *History of England* – only valuable for the binding – and a few local history books. Nice little four-volume set in a slip case dated 1877, with frequent references to the 'Grand Master'. Not about chess. Or hip-hop. Freemasonry books do sell quite well, though.

Home in time to go for a pint with Callum and Granny at 7.30.

Till total £357.08
32 customers

TUESDAY, 6 SEPTEMBER

Online orders: 2
Books found: 1

At eleven o'clock I called the insurance company to put Norrie and Christian on the van's insurance policy. They both use it to ferry things around during the festival, rather than hire one. Discovered that I hadn't bothered to remove them after last year's festival, and they're still covered.

Someone parked a car full of yapping dogs right outside the front door of the shop. Captain spent an hour taunting them by sitting smugly on the doorway. The noise was appalling, but not quite as bad as the monstrous regiment of screeching children in the shop who poured out of the same vehicle.

Four packages arrive for Granny: clothes and shoes. She tried them all on and asked me what I thought. In an attempt to return her generosity when my mother was ill, I told her that they were lovely, but when she was trying them on, she looked down at her feet and said, 'No, I look like a pig with shoes on.'

Till total £224
21 customers

Online orders: 0
Books found: 0

First sale of the day was a book on Scottish place-names from the Beith collection, sold to a Canadian customer who told me that his family used to own Glasgow. I don't imagine for a second that this could possibly be true, but I suspect that *émigrés* often tell their children embellished stories about the land they left which, over time, become exaggerated to the point of being ridiculous.

I telephoned Majestic Wine and ordered thirty-six bottles of wine. I always have a full house during the ten days of the event, and feel guilty about drinking the wine that the Festival Company provides for use in the Writers' Retreat. Besides which, after one mouthful of the stuff, your taste buds are deactivated for at least a week.

Online inquiry about a first edition of *The Third Policeman*. While I was looking for it in the Irish section, I stumbled across a first edition of Oscar Wilde's *De Profundis*, priced (not by me) at £6 and published in blue buckram by Methuen in 1905, thanks to the efforts of his friend the journalist Robert Ross. It's a book that has featured in the culture pages of most newspapers recently as Reading Gaol, where Wilde was incarcerated, has recently been opened to the public. During his time there, Wilde was treated appallingly until a sympathetic governor – Major Nelson – took charge of the prison and circumvented the rules about prisoners being forbidden to write during their detention by permitting him the luxury of a pen, some ink and a sheet of paper every day on the 'understanding' that he was writing a letter. The result is an extraordinarily beautiful study of betrayal, loss and grief. Wilde (Prisoner C33) – broken by his time in prison, and largely abandoned by the hypocritical echelons of a society that once feted him – left England for France, where he died in November 1900, damned by the words of John Sholto Douglas, the ninth marquess of Queensberry – a man who couldn't even spell the word 'sodomite', with which he condemned the greatest wit of his age to a cruel and unjust end. I took our copy off the shelf and began to read it after the shop closed.

A woman with long, sandy hair bought three books on folklore and told me that I have the best job in the world.

Granny has managed to change the keyboard settings to Arabic. I can't work out how to change them back.

Till total £156.50
19 customers

THURSDAY, 8 SEPTEMBER

Online orders: 3
Books found: 2

Awoke to the sound of heavy rain and a howling wind which made the fireplace in the spare bedroom sound like the cry of some unearthly creature.

Delivery of ninety sacks of wood pellets arrived at 10.30. By the time I'd taken them to the hopper, I was completely soaked.

> Customer with an umbrella, which he decided to keep up in the shop, hitting several other people in the head and dripping water everywhere: 'Is there a café here?'
> Me: 'No.'
> Customer: 'So, no refreshments at all?'
> Me: 'No. It's a bookshop.'

We continued staring at one another in silence for another thirty seconds, just in case I might have forgotten that I have a café.

Very friendly man complimented me on the Spinoza collection in the philosophy section, but told me that he couldn't afford any of them. I explained that they had been given to me by Margie, and that they had belonged to her husband, the logician Richard Mason. The next customer – the one who asked if we have a café – came to the counter ten minutes later with a book about Welsh history, a hardback in a dust jacket. When I opened it to see the price I noticed the name on the endpaper: Richard Mason.

Sandy the tattooed pagan came in with five sticks, and spent £20 on books. I gave him £10 credit. The fab four over-familiar Yorkshire pensioners who have a house in Gatehouse came in. Two of them have written books which they've self-published. To my enormous amusement, they bored poor Sandy about their literary endeavours. He reacted with typical good humour, but made repeated and obvious signals to me to enable his escape. I ignored him.

Granny covered the shop so that I could go to the bank in Newton Stewart. On my way home I stopped in at my parents' house with a chicken pie from Owens, the butcher. My mother was in bed, so I chatted to my father for a while, then headed home. At least that means that he doesn't have to cook.

After I shut the shop, I went to the pub with Callum and Granny. While we were chatting, a remarkably tall woman came in. She's the current resident of The Open Book. All came back here at 9 p.m. and had some food and more to drink.

Bed at midnight.

Till total £284.93
23 customers

FRIDAY, 9 SEPTEMBER

Online orders: 2
Books found: 2

Found the missing book from yesterday's orders. It was a copy of Douglas Adams's *So Long and Thanks for All the Fish*, with the hologram on the black dust jacket. It was in the fishing section. I don't know whether to blame Meredith, Granny or myself.

Mary appeared at 10 a.m. with two boxes of books, mainly local history. I gave her £100 for them. In a copy of *Harpoon at a Venture*, by Gavin Maxwell, there was part of a handwritten letter from Maxwell to someone called J. M. McKeand, sent from Skye and dated 6 May 1960, the text of which intriguingly reads:

Many thanks for your letter and apologies for delay in reply, I was in hospital for an examination, but it was all a scare and there's nothing wrong with me.

Alas our dates don't fit, I shall be in Wigtownshire from May 17-22, but I must be back here by the latter date. Perhaps you would pay a visit here?

The scene you describe might be called bizarre, but in the course

and there the letter ends. I have no idea where the final page is, or what it revealed.

A young woman came to the counter as I was attempting to administer a worming tablet to Captain. This is never a pleasant experience for either of us, and my early efforts to conceal it in a piece of chicken (he always ate the chicken and spat the pill out) have been superseded by consistently unsuccessful attempts to force the pill down his throat. This requires the use of a welding gauntlet and a considerable amount of swearing and scratching, and inevitably ends in victory for the little bastard, and me contemplating the pill on the floor and thinking that it would probably be simpler if I ate the bloody thing myself.

Email from Nicky: 'Do you want me to send you a photo of the dead, bloated cow outside my window?'

My sister Vikki and her daughter Ella arrived mid-afternoon. They're planning to visit my mother tomorrow, and are staying with me rather than adding to my parents' burdens.

Till total £64.55
9 customers

Online orders: 3
Books found: 3

Vikki and Ella left at 10.30 to call in at my parents' and then head home to Fife. Willeke called in to say hello just as they were leaving. While she was here, Emma, the woman who is in The Open Book, dropped in to say hello. She was off exploring, so I gave her a map with some stickers highlighting interesting places.

At lunchtime a small boy asked if it was OK to talk in the shop, then spent ten minutes telling his father all about Roald Dahl. I didn't have the heart to tell him that Dahl was unapologetically anti-Semitic. When he'd finished, he asked his mother, 'Mum, is there a McDonald's near here?' The nearest one is in Belfast.

Man brought in a box of books about art. They had belonged to his recently deceased mother-in-law. Offered him £45 for them. He refused, saying that they were worth more. He came back three hours later, clearly having been offered less for them in every other bookshop.

Australian woman came in at about 3.30 and spent an hour wandering about. She bought a pile of paperbacks, and while she was paying I asked her what brought her to Wigtown. She pointed at a copy of *Rockets* and said it was because Anna's description of the place made her want to come here. She told me that the shop is just as she had imagined it, and that she and her husband had come to Wigtown via Culzean, just as Anna had on her first trip. She asked me to sign her copy, so I told her that if she left me her address and her copy, I'd get Anna to sign it and post it out to her. She looked utterly delighted.

Surprisingly windy for the time of year. Leaves starting to blow off the trees.

Till total £284.49
18 customers

SUNDAY, 11 SEPTEMBER

Online orders:
Books found:

Drove to Edinburgh for a book deal with a man, Iain, who had emailed last month. I didn't have time to look at the books today, so I spent the night at a hotel near Holyrood. I'll go to look at the books in the morning.

Had a conversation at the bar with two coach drivers, Robbie and Mike, tour guides. It didn't take long before we all began to complain about camper vans and caravans being driven by pensioners who had no idea how to drive large vehicles. The narrow road at the head of Loch Lomond – we all agreed – was the bottleneck that caused us the most problems. It's a strange problem: all three of us depend on tourists for our jobs, and we discussed at length the fact that the Scots are hopeless at promoting our history – Covenanters particularly. We began chatting because Robbie spotted that I was reading *De Profundis*. Normally, reading a book in a bar is a pretty clear indicator that you're not that keen on conversation, but Robbie had read Wilde, and it proved to be an opening to an interesting conversation, rather than a barrier to one, which was how I had originally intended it.

MONDAY, 12 SEPTEMBER

Online orders: 2
Books found: 2

Drove to Bilston, south-west of Edinburgh, and met Iain at 10.30. He was moving into a smaller house following the death of his wife, and had to dispose of most of their library. There was some interesting material, including a book of fairly early Dürer copperplate prints (although not quite early enough to be worth a huge amount). Most of it, though, wasn't great, but he wanted me to take everything. Ten boxes' worth; gave him £400 and left for home.

Made it home by three o'clock and chatted with Granny about the deal, and how the shop had been today. She told me that a woman had complained about Nicky's 'No Whistling' sign in the shop. Apparently it's a 'lost art'. Professional whistlers are known as *siffleurs*, and we've been advised that they should be encouraged rather than forbidden.

Till total £146.50
18 customers

TUESDAY, 13 SEPTEMBER

Online orders: 0
Books found: 0

Granny opened the shop so that I could carry on working in the garden to tidy up in time for the festival.

Emptied the books from Bilston from the van and began to work through them – quite a lot of rubbish (*Reader's Digest*s etc.) – then filled van with building materials from the garden, sacks of aggregate and cement left over from when Willie put the edging for the path in, offcuts of timber from various jobs and empty bags of wood pellets. Drove to Callum's and dropped them off there.

Incredibly smelly Australian man came in and told me that he'd been directed here by Emma from The Open Book. She told him that we have a good military history section. Australians rarely buy books because of weight limits for baggage on flights.

The annoying man who'd made such a fuss about his mother-in-law's art books last week made an unwelcome return with a box of books in fairly poor condition, then started going through them one at a time explaining what each book was, making a particular fuss over a signed copy of Sally Magnusson's biography of Eric Liddell, *The Flying Scotsman*. He pointed several times at the box, just to ram it home that they weren't to be confused with the other boxes which had come from the Bilston deal, before eventually leaving to go for a cup of coffee. He returned half an hour later.

Offered him £12 for about seven books. He started going through them and fussing about how they must be worth more than that, then went to have a conference about it with his wife in the car, as though they were selling a fine set of Chippendale dining chairs. He eventually came in and accepted the £12.

The smelly Australian man, having mauled the military history section, came uncomfortably close to the counter and said, 'Your British class system has been causing mayhem for you people for years. Have you got any books on that subject?' The tone of the first sentence seemed to suggest that the British class system was somehow my fault.

A friend of my parents came in with a box of his books. As he was leaving, he announced that he'd just been out hunting and they'd killed three foxes, to the horror of the six other people in the shop at the time, particularly since fox-hunting has been outlawed since the Protection of Wild Mammals (Scotland) Act 2002.

Till total £366.99
21 customers

WEDNESDAY, 14 SEPTEMBER

Online orders: 2
Books found: 2

Jeff Meade, Church of Scotland minister for Kirkinner, came in for a chat. Over the years Jeff has become a friend, and during that time he's revealed an irreverent side which has turned out to be rather a surprise for a man of God and a pillar of the community.

Rosie, a well-known local gossip (only about 20 per cent of whose conversation makes even the slightest sense to me), came in to tell me that a retired local bookseller had been at the bus stop telling people that my shop was 'full of nothing but dust'. Despite running a fairly unsuccessful book business in Wigtown – unless you consider a crumbling Georgian house with books piled every-where and cat shit in piles on the stairs a success – he considers himself an authority on the trade. I have never, in over twenty years of knowing him, heard him say a kind word about anyone. I banned him from the shop fourteen years ago because he and his wife came into the shop during the book festival and started telling my customers that my stock was poor and overpriced, and that they should all leave and go to his shop instead. I am long past caring what he has to say. He's a tall, thin man in his seventies, with a beard which looks as though it should be condemned by the government as a biohazard.

Daisy, who did her work experience in the shop earlier in the year, sent her personal statement for me to check over. In the dim and distant days when I had a CV, there was no such thing as a personal statement.

The couple who bring books from the library at Samye Ling appeared with five boxes of rotated stock.

My friend and fellow book dealer Ian's pallet of books arrived and was left by the courier on the pavement in front of the shop. As it was beginning to rain, Granny and I hastily hauled the books into the shop. The shop has rapidly become so full of piles of boxes and books that there's barely enough space to swing Captain, although, as cats go, he's a pretty large one.

Ran out of £5 notes, so I gave Granny £100 in £20 notes to go to the bank and exchange it for £5 notes. The moment she had the money in her hand, she said, 'Oh, so you finally pay the Granny? Fucking bastard.' I warned her that because I closed my Bank of Scotland account a couple of years ago, the staff at the bank usually complain when I do this. They did, but they reluctantly gave her the money.

The retired bookseller came in at two o'clock to collect the church key (his ban is temporarily suspended for visits of no more than thirty seconds if he's coming to collect the key). I mentioned that Rosie had been in the shop this morning to tell me that he had been making derogatory comments about my shop at the bus stop. He unconvincingly feigned ignorance, to the point of pretending that he didn't know who Rosie was. Everybody in Wigtown knows Rosie.

Finished going through the books from the Bilston deal on Monday. At least 80 per cent of it was rubbish, so I packed it into boxes and drove it to the dump in Whithorn (Newton Stewart dump is closed on Tuesday and Wednesday). Whenever I go to the Whithorn dump I stick my head round the door of the Porta-kabin just out of courtesy, before driving to the appropriate skip. Today the person in charge was a young man of about twenty, and he and his friend were sitting inside blowing bubbles of washing-up liquid. I explained that I didn't have time to recycle each book through the tiny slots of the paper recycling units, and asked if I could just throw the boxes in the household waste skip. He was fine about it. I suspect his relaxed approach to recycling may have had something to do with the eye-watering smell of herbal cigarettes.

Emma from The Open Book came in to say that she's having a day out in Kirkcudbright. I suggested that she visit Hornel's house, the Tolbooth and as many galleries as she can, and possibly a stop at Cardoness Castle on the way home. She complained about the frequency with which the retired bookseller comes into the shop and annoys her while she's trying to work. I explained that this is the nature of working in a bookshop, but agreed that he is a particularly difficult character.

Drove to Newton Stewart to go to the bank. Bought thirty-six loo rolls from Sainsbury's. We seem to go through a lot during the festival. Perhaps impoverished authors steal them.

Spent the evening, until darkness at around 8.15 in the garden, making the final preparations for the festival: bleaching the algae off the concrete surfaces, mowing the lawns. The garden is used during the festival both as a thoroughfare between the shop and the wine bar and – if the weather is nice – as somewhere for visitors to sit and relax.

Till total £244.95
19 customers

Online orders: 0
Books found: 0

Local man in his thirties with a bushy beard came in and bought three Patrick O'Brian novels. His wife works in the Co-op, and he's a keen reader. His little girl, about four, is obsessed with the stuffed badger in the shop and spent – as she always does – about five minutes just staring at it.

Moved the twenty-five large boxes of books from Ian's pallet to the back of the fiction section to open up a little bit of space.

Our credit card machine is getting a bit old and temperamental, much as I am, so I telephoned my supplier and asked them to replace it with a contactless one.

Email from Norrie asking for the use of the van on Sunday, to move some things for the festival.

Going through the books that a customer dropped in yesterday and came across a copy of *Through Masai Land* containing three handwritten letters between the book's author, Joseph Thomson, and Joseph Hooker, the famous nineteenth-century plant hunter and one of the key figures in the history of Kew Gardens.

Telephone interview about the festival at one o'clock with a man from the BBC called Nick for *The Culture Programme*, to be broadcast on Radio Scotland on Monday.

After lunch went to the dump in Newton Stewart with a cargo of broken cardboard boxes to recycle, then to the bank to lodge two cheques. It seems like a charming remnant from the past when someone decides to pay for books by cheque, although I settle most of my bills that way. On my way back to the shop, I dropped in on my parents with half a dozen apples from the garden. My mother was having an afternoon nap. Such is the luxury of retirement.

At four o'clock my father appeared in the shop with my mother in the car. It's the first time she's left the house since returning from hospital. They didn't get out, but had decided that it was probably a good idea for her to leave the house.

Carol-Ann, Callum and Granny and I went to Craft after

work. Bumped into Emma from The Open Book there. We all came back here. Late night.

Till total £228.99
21 customers

FRIDAY, 16 SEPTEMBER

Online orders: 2
Books found: 2

Customer – an old man with a yellowing white beard – came to the counter and said, 'Hello, I'm in the trade. Patrick O'Brian.' Assuming that he was introducing himself, I extended my hand and introduced myself. He gave me a puzzled look before explaining that he was looking for books by Patrick O'Brian. He looked furious when I told him that I'd sold a few yesterday, and even more so when I charged him 5p for a bag.

Man brought in four boxes of early twentieth century books with beautifully illustrated spines and front boards to sell: authors such as Bessie Marchant, Percy F. Westerman and W. H. G. Kingston. He'd bought them purely for decoration. Unfortunately they are almost impossible to sell, so – hoping that he'd say no – I offered him £50 for them. He decided to keep them, but was very gracious and polite in declining my offer.

Emailed Anne (who together with Eliot runs the festival) to let her know that Richard Demarco had been in touch to say that he wants to come to the festival and do an event. Might be handy in the event that an author has pulled out.

Spent the evening in the garden again, clearing the path between the shop and Emily's studio which will become Amy's pop-up wine bar this time next week for the first half of the festival. Staked up the apple tree which had fallen over in the winds last weekend. Granny spent the evening packing books for the Random Book Club.

Till total £126.49
14 customers

SATURDAY, 17 SEPTEMBER

Online orders: 1
Books found: 1

Customer spent an hour in the shop and came to the counter with a pile of books.

> Me: 'That's £88, but I'll let you have them for £80.'
> Customer: 'Can't I have a discount?'

Spent the day sorting through Ian's boxes from the pallet that arrived on Wednesday. Mostly sci-fi and cinema, both of which are good subjects in the shop.

At noon a couple brought in five boxes. The shop was so full of boxes of books now that they had to leave them in the doorway. Two boxes contained an incomplete ninth-edition *Britannica*; the others were copies of the *Proceedings of the Society of Antiquaries of Scotland*, or PSAS as they're known in the trade. All impossible to sell. They left them and disappeared before I could tell them to take them away with them, so for the rest of the day customers wishing to enter or leave the shop had to squeeze past them.

A customer came in with two chihuahuas on a leash. Another customer – a local woman who I dislike intensely – came in and went over to pet one of them, at which point it began growling and barking aggressively. Rather than apologise and leave with the yapping dog, the woman stood in front of the counter and started chatting to the annoying local woman while the thing continued to bark (surprisingly loudly for such a tiny creature) for about a further five minutes.

Painted the garden shed in the evening, Carol-Ann came round for supper. She's a stalwart during the festival and always comes over for it if she can – she mucks in whenever a pair of hands is required. She also takes great delight in meeting authors and shocking them by cursing and talking about bodily functions. She and Stuart Kelly get along famously.

Till total £219.66
7 customers

SUNDAY, 18 SEPTEMBER

Today was my sister Lulu's fortieth birthday. We've all hit middle age now.

Spent much of the afternoon painting the garden shed again, and fixing solar lights around the garden so that the pathway to Amy's pop-up wine bar is relatively safely illuminated.

My friend Ruaridh turned up at 6.30 and we went to Craft. Carl takes over soon, so Ben and Katie – the king and queen of burgers – were having a final thank-you party for all of their loyal customers: Finn, Tom, Granny, Sean Williams and a great crowd of others were there. Ben, rather than thanking us for turning up, spent much of the night complaining about the people he'd invited who hadn't turned up.

MONDAY, 19 SEPTEMBER

Online orders: 2
Books found: 2

Awoke at 7 a.m. to the metallic crashing of the marquee being unloaded from the lorries in the square. By eleven o'clock the frame was up. Granny was remarkably impressed. The moment the marquee goes up, there's a buzz about the town. Until that happens, the festival seems like a nebulous, distant idea, but it becomes a slightly stomach-knotting reality as soon as the huge, white structure appears in the middle of the town.

Christian and Norrie turned up to borrow the van to shift the chairs and other props for the Festival Cinema from his house to the county buildings.

At twelve noon Isabel and her husband George arrived with a sheep trailer containing George's uncle's (also called George) mahogany dining table, which I've bought from them. George and I struggled, but eventually got it up the stairs and into the drawing room (which will be used as the Writers' Retreat). It looks fantastic. Ever since the dining table collapsed during a formal dinner during the festival a few years ago I've been on the lookout for a replacement.

Sandy the tattooed pagan and his friend Lizzie came in. Sandy brought two boxes of books that he'd picked up during his regular trawls of the charity shops of Stranraer. Gave him £35 credit for them. He always makes great theatre about how he's a 'poor old man' being underpaid for his lifetime's collection of fine literature, particularly if there's an audience, and even more so if he's just got them for practically nothing from the charity shop.

Went to the butcher to pick up some stewing steak which I'll use for a casserole tomorrow. Usual chat with Steven (the butcher) about fishing.

Petra dropped in to steal some Galloway Pippins from the garden. The Galloway Pippin is a native apple of which there were only a handful of specimens known still to exist. Thanks to the concerted efforts of a few enthusiasts, it has been brought back from the edge of extinction. I don't know what Petra wanted them for, but I caught her filling a bag with them from one of my trees.

Granny did the postage for the RBC. Postman turned up at 5.15 p.m. to pick up the bags (five). As soon as the postman left, Granny managed to stab herself in the knee with the scissors while opening one of the boxes from Ian's pallet.

Painted the garden shed for the third and (hopefully) final time.

AWB meeting at 5.30 p.m. here, attended by Carl, Jayne and Sarah. Since so few people had turned up, I opened a bottle of wine and we just sat around the kitchen table and chatted. We've decided to have a small festival after the Book Festival, based on the theme of Fire and Light, since it's the time of year when Diwali, Hanukkah, Halloween and other festivals of light are celebrated.

Painted trestles in the garden afterwards to make some temporary tables.

Eliot arrived at 6 p.m. and kicked off his shoes in the doorway between the kitchen and the landing. I tripped over them at 6.05. By 6.10 his glasses were on the dishwasher, his wallet on the dresser, and by 6.15 he'd managed to distribute the contents of his luggage throughout the entire kitchen.

Cooked a casserole for supper tomorrow.

Till total £264.19
19 customers

TUESDAY, 20 SEPTEMBER

Online orders: 0
Books found: 0

Norrie appeared at 9 a.m. to pick up the van. Granny gave him the key and told him that she was looking forward to going to the Festival Cinema – she's a bit of a film buff, and has introduced me to some films that I would never otherwise have discovered.

Eliot managed to break the switch for the kettle when he was making a cup of tea in the kitchen. In the absence of boiling water he then announced that he was going to the Glaisnock Café for breakfast before facing the staff in the office. Shortly after he'd left, I stood on a teaspoon that he had dropped on the floor after abandoning his attempt to make tea.

Very annoying elderly Australian book dealer asked if I could post books to her in Queensland. The shop was busy, and we were clearly preparing for the festival, but she persisted in treating me as though she was our only customer and I had nothing else to do.

Granny and I have filled every spare moment recently listing books on FBA in a desperate attempt to clear some of the boxes from the shop before the festival begins. I've filled in the tortuous uplift form so that hopefully they'll be gone soon, and off to the Amazon warehouse in Dunfermline.

New card machine arrived. Granny was very upset about it. She told me that she'd become quite sentimentally attached to the old one, which had been there since she first worked in the shop. The new machine came with packaging and labels to return the old machine. Apparently the postman will pick it up in a few days.

After we'd shut the shop, I heated up the casserole. Eliot arrived just as it was ready. He'd bought steak for his supper, but decided to eat the meal I'd cooked for Granny and me instead. He made much capital of the fact that he'd bought a bottle of wine, which he presented to me, then proceeded to drink himself.

Till total £139.18
16 customers

WEDNESDAY, 21 SEPTEMBER

Online orders: 0
Books found: 0

Eliot got up and started clattering about at 9.30. At ten o'clock a film crew making a news feature for Border TV arrived and filmed in various locations in the shop all morning. Eliot hadn't mentioned that they were coming, but I rarely say no to publicity, and this was great exposure for the festival and for the business.

Email from Claire in the festival office asking if I could make the golden pencil, the prize for Wigtown's Got Talent. I agreed to, as I do every year. This involves driving to the sawmill and picking up a small, round fence post and a tin of gold spray paint and a tin of black paint. It's surprisingly simple, and effective.

Drove to the dump in Whithorn to empty the van and drop off the old dining table. Sadly the young men weren't blowing bubbles this time, although the smell of their unusual brand of cigarette still lingered in the air around their hut.

Maria turned up at four o'clock with all the wine, soft drinks, plates, cutlery etc. for the Retreat. This is very much an all-hands-on-deck affair, with everyone passing by on the street being roped in to help.

Eliot asked if he could use the table I bought from Isabel for one of his new ideas for the festival this year, The Living Room, as he needed a 'grown-up piece of furniture' to give it a bit of style.

Eliot was back and forth all day. He's decided to stay here for three nights, although Anne is a bit cross because she has booked him a flat for three weeks in Wigtown. I do enjoy having Eliot to stay – he brings with him a tide of creativity that sits narrowly on the safe side of chaos.

Supper in Craft with Eliot, Granny, Kate – this year's artist in residence – and Becca and Rose, the festival interns this year.

Till total £312.99
29 customers

THURSDAY, 22 SEPTEMBER

Online orders: 1
Books found: 1

Awoke at 8 a.m. to the familiar sound of stamping and crashing from downstairs.

Janet Howie arrived at nine o'clock – she's the mother of a former employee, and incredibly level-headed. She offered to help out at the festival on a couple of occasions when we were short-staffed and this year has offered to cover the shop for the whole ten days. It frees me up to deal with the inevitable unexpected crises which arise during the festival, and allows Granny to go to work at The Pheasant when they need her most. The festival brings so many people to the area that they are doing dozens of covers every day, although she wasn't required until four o'clock today, so was around in the shop until the 3.15 bus showed up.

At eleven o'clock Christian turned up to borrow the van at the same time as Eliot arrived to tell me that two men from Scottish Power would be coming to pick up the table later. Rebecca, one of the festival staff, arrived half an hour later with two slightly confused men who had clearly been sent to Wigtown on another job, and whom Eliot had enlisted to shift furniture.

At 12.15 a driver from UPS came to uplift the FBA boxes. Finally there's a little bit of space in the front of the shop.

At 12.30 the postman came to uplift the old credit card machine. I thought Granny was going to burst into tears at its departure, so I distracted her with a series of questions about her health. This tactic never fails, and before I knew it I was giving the thumbs-up to the postman as he scanned the package and left, while Granny continued to give me chapter and verse about her knee and her failing eyesight. I suspect it won't be long before the latter becomes so bad that she isn't able to see her knee to worry about it.

The over-friendly Yorkshire pensioners came in and pestered me for a while as the two men from Scottish Power wrestled with the table which, only a few days earlier, George and I had struggled up the stairs with. I was clearly attempting to sort out a problem with the internet router, but that was no obstacle to a barrage of questions along the lines of 'Are you busy? You must be busy with the festival starting tomorrow.' They managed to get in the way of the Scottish Power men at every conceivable point but didn't hold back with plentiful offers of helpful advice.

Email from Nicky: 'Are you all excited??? Homebrew, gladrags and Portaloo are packed and ready for sharing!' This can only mean that she's planning to spend the festival in the car park (the old cattle show ground) in her revolting van, Bluebottle. I miss her terribly, and told her that she was welcome to sleep here, but would need to bunk up on a sofa because we have a full house.

Phoned Majestic, from whom I had ordered thirty-six bottles of red wine for the festival on 7 September. Still no sign of them and no replies to two emails. They assured me that the delivery would arrive in the next day or two.

At 1.30 Maria arrived with a fridge. We always need an extra fridge to cope with the volume of food consumed in the Retreat during the festival. We struggled but managed to get it upstairs eventually, apologising to customers on the staircase who tutted disapprovingly when we asked them if they'd mind moving so we could pass.

Stuart Kelly arrived with his parents at 1.45 and made his way up to his usual room in the house. Stuart is a fine writer, literary critic and a good friend. Eliot ropes him into the festival every year to chair events. Stuart has the extraordinary capacity to devour a 600-page book in under two hours, and to be able to chair an event at incredibly short notice if one of the other chairs can't manage. From Eliot's point of view, this is a remarkably valuable asset.

At two o'clock I dropped the mail over at the post office. No sign of William, thankfully. I normally wait until two because it means that Wilma will almost certainly have returned from her lunch break. On my way across the road I bumped into Sharon (bank manager), who was sitting on the steps of the Mercat Cross enjoying the sun. She and her friends were in town to help set up the school in preparation for the children's festival. The children's festival takes place in various venues around the town, but the school is the obvious choice for many of them.

I met Adrian Sykes in the shop at three o'clock. Adrian is the father of an ex-girlfriend and a tremendously intelligent and successful man. He's here to take part in the festival and is giving a talk on his book *Made in Britain*, a historical biography of 8,000 people who he believes made the country what it is today.

The rep from Majestic called back to say that there had been an IT problem and my order hadn't come through to the warehouse, so he took the order again, over the phone this time, and promised that it would be here tomorrow.

We'd finished setting up the Writers' Retreat by four o'clock. Janette, who normally cleans the shop, came and tidied everything up.

Till total £159
12 customers

FRIDAY, 23 SEPTEMBER

Online orders: 3
Books found: 1

Laurie arrived at nine o'clock to make sure everything was in place
for the Retreat to open at ten. Maria arrived shortly afterwards.
Laurie is a former employee and someone who I consider a good
friend, although from her comments about me on social media
anyone might wonder whether this is reciprocated. Every year she
manages the Writers' Retreat, and does a superb job. On paper,
she's there to introduce people to one another, and make sure
that visiting authors make it to their events on time when they're
having too good a time, and to make sure that, when volunteer
drivers arrive to collect them, they're ready to go. In reality, on top
of this, she helps Maria – makes sure that there's always hot water
in the urn, waitresses when the Retreat is too busy for Maria's staff
to reasonably be expected to manage and a number of other things.
If things are really bad, she occasionally asks me to help out. She
rarely gets that desperate though.

Peggy and Colin turned up at the Retreat at 11 a.m.

Another Colin (the photographer) arrived at three o'clock.
He's here in his official capacity as the festival photographer. He's
been coming for years, and is as much a part of the fabric of the
festival as anything. Much as I despise being kind about anyone,
I'm very fond of Colin – he's charming, and a greatly welcomed
face every year.

Bumped into Enna, ex-girlfriend, in the shop. She was here for
her father Adrian's talk.

Lee Randall turned up at four. She's become a good friend
over the years, and chairs events during the festival. She and Stuart
Kelly were once colleagues at *The Scotsman*.

The wine delivery from Majestic arrived.

Maria turned up with the food for the Retreat. Although
delicious, there was a distinct lack of meat – I think she's mainly
gone for a vegan menu this year.

Polly Pullar arrived in the evening. She came over for
something to eat and we discovered that her son had gone to the

same school as me, although several decades later. Neither of us had particularly enjoyed the experience.

Filled up the log basket and lit the fire.

Nicki arrived with a hamper full of food (mostly from the Morrisons skip) and some home-brewed beer at three o'clock.

Alastair McIntosh and Malcolm Rifkind both appeared at 6 p.m. Twigger arrived at 6.30. By 6.45 all of the food in the Retreat had been eaten.

Amy spent the afternoon setting up the wine bar and putting laminated signs in the garden directing people towards it.

Hardeep Singh Kohli arrived at 7 and went to the Retreat to discover Eliot there, complaining that there was no more food, so I went to the Co-op and bought a few bags of crisps, some dips and olives. We had a few drinks in the Retreat then headed down the hill for the fireworks, followed by the opening party in the big marquee. A dozen or so of us headed back here afterwards. Bed at 2 a.m. It's always the same at the start of the festival: the good intentions for an early night go out of the window immediately, and things slide rapidly downhill from there.

Till total £385.40
36 customers

SATURDAY, 24 SEPTEMBER

Online orders: 1
Books found: 1

The weather was diabolical when I opened the shop, so I lit the fire and burned the last few logs in the basket. Slightly concerned that the marquees might not last the day because of the wind. Janet arrived – as always – in irritatingly good humour.

My old friend Richard dropped in at three o'clock with his friend Ryan. They were off to see Malcolm Rifkind's event, but we managed to squeeze in a cup of tea.

At the weekend during the festival we have a far more packed schedule than during the week, and the Writers' Retreat serves lobsters at lunchtime. For me, this means that my house stinks of slowly decomposing marine crustaceans for a few days. This might sound like a bourgeois complaint, but if you think it is, then try it out, particularly if you're not the person who has eaten the lobsters.

After lunch I took four bin bags and six boxes of glass recycling from the kitchen, loaded it all into the van and drove to the dump at Newton Stewart.

Tonight was the evening of Wigtown's Got Talent. It is always an excruciating combination of terrible singing, unsuccessful magic tricks and awkward stand-up spattered with a light dusting of actual talent. Anna's friend Annie Stone arrived during the interval and pulled up in her car outside the shop just as I was opening up to race in with other audience members for a pee. There's no loo in the marquee, so anyone requiring the use of one generally tends to befriend me and take the key to the shop. After the talent show ended (I forget who won – it's usually a local bagpiper or teenage girl) a large group of people (including my sister and her husband) returned to the Retreat and drank most of the wine, which was meant to last the entire week. The last guests left at 3 a.m.

Charlotte, who is doing the publicity this year, and I tidied up the Retreat. She left at 3.30 a.m. I went to bed at 3.45.

Till total £885.07
97 customers

Online orders: 1
Books found: 0

Woke up at 7 a.m.

Weather much better than yesterday: sunny but chilly. Marquees are still standing, thankfully. Janette arrived just as I was wandering back from the big marquee with my sister's handbag (she left it under her seat after Wigtown's Got Talent) and cleaned the Retreat.

Maria and Laurie arrived at 9 a.m. and set up the Writers' Retreat. Janet helped them, in the absence of any customers.

Jason Webster arrived at lunchtime. He's a friend of Twigger's and has been coming to the festival for years – like Twigger, he's almost a fixture of the festival and can be relied on to muck in with everything. I asked him to fill the log basket so that I could take the bags from the Retreat to the recycling in Newton Stewart.

Polly Pullar appeared after Jason and introduced me to Angus MacDonald. I'd never met him, but we have many shared interests, and chatted for some time. Ruaridh and Naomi – friends from nearby Gatehouse – arrived at the same time and we had lunch together. Ruaridh (though I would never say this to him) is someone of whom I am deeply fond. I've known him since he was born, and he relentlessly mocks me.

The fire was dwindling by about two o'clock, so I put some logs on, which involved asking Susan Calman to move out of the way while she was prepping for her event with Lee Randall. I hadn't realised that she has a bit of a public speaking anxiety, something I share with her.

Once the fire was roaring, and Laurie was back in charge, I went for a drink with Claudia at the wine bar. Claudia – like Jason, Twigger and Stuart – has become a fixture of the festival over the last ten years. If anything needs to be done – chairing events, moving furniture, cooking – she can be relied on to get her hands dirty, although she's mainly here to promote and publicise Wigtown for the week.

Anna and Tom arrived at 7.30. Jason cooked a pork risotto

for ten of the writers who refused to leave the Retreat. Eliot had organised a 'Fuck-Up' event at 7.30 in the garden, where people talked about things which they'd made a complete mess of. It seemed entirely appropriate for the festival, so I kept the shop open until eight o'clock. Went upstairs and joined the refuseniks for supper. We all stayed up until 1 a.m. Ben and Beth (Bookshop Band) joined us at 9 p.m. Beth, it turns out, is pregnant. Laurie, who normally goes home every night, had a few G&Ts and decided to stay over. She slept in the bookshop bed.

Dumped the remains of the day's food in the van. Six bags, mainly of lobsters, and several leaking.

Till total £546.95
49 customers

MONDAY, 26 SEPTEMBER

Online orders: 2
Books found: 1

Opened the shop with a fire in my head following last night's excesses. Janette had been in since 7 a.m. and cleaned the kitchen and the Retreat. Laurie emerged at 9.15 looking pretty shattered. Granny arrived at 9.20, and between us we managed to salvage a semblance of civilisation after the weekend. Janet arrived at ten.

Angus MacDonald arrived at ten, and Maria treated him to some coffee and brownies at the Retreat. Laurie joined him, and by about eleven was back to her usual self.

Drove to the Martyr's Stake at eleven o'clock to pick up Anna, who had gone there for a walk, then drove to my parents' house so that she could see my convalescing mother. They're very close, and Anna hadn't seen my mother since she was discharged from the hospital. We stayed for half an hour, which I think was about as much as my mother could take. Drove to the dump at Newton Stewart afterwards to drop off 185 empty wine bottles and about a dozen bags of food waste from the Retreat. The woman who is in charge of the dump at Newton is a far cry from the stoners at the Whithorn dump. She and I get on, but we have an understanding that can only be comparable to a camp commandant and a prisoner of war. Normally she comes to the van to make sure that I'm not depositing nuclear waste or anything else which I shouldn't be dropping off, but today the stench when I opened the back of the van was eye-watering and she kept well away. Even the cold nights of September don't halt the decay of decomposing shellfish. If mercies can be small, this one must have been microscopic, and the foul stink of the bags of weeping, leaking lobsters were clearly too much for her.

Rebecca, one of the festival employees, turned up at two o'clock and asked if I could give her a hand shifting four tables to the venue – someone's house – for the festival dinner later, so I left Janet in charge and between us we managed to move the furniture. The festival, if you're an author, is a thing of glamour and celebrity. If you're a resident of Wigtown, it's like working for Pickfords.

The internet stopped working in the shop (and the Retreat) at three o'clock, leaving lots of frustrated authors unable to go online and catch up with their emails. Spent an hour fixing it. It was working again by four.

Several customers attempted to get into the Writers' Retreat, which is far from unusual during the festival. Laurie turned one away: he marched indignantly downstairs and complained to Granny that he was 'bitterly disappointed' that he couldn't have something to eat, and all that he wanted was a free bowl of soup, which he didn't think was too much to ask for a loyal customer. When Granny asked him how many times he'd visited the shop, he told her that this was his first time in Wigtown.

Went to Adrian Sykes's event in the County Buildings. He was superb, very entertaining, and Stuart, as always, was a great chair.

Janet left at six o'clock but I kept the shop open until eight to allow people access to Rab Wilson's poetry event. Louise Gray, author of *The Ethical Carnivore*, called in at about seven o'clock. We chatted about her book, which she told me was inspired by Jonathan Safran Foer. She decided to only eat meat that she had killed and prepared herself for a year. She's lapsed now.

Retreat (and house) was empty apart from Granny and me for

two hours because Eliot, Twigger, Stuart and Jason went to the pub. At ten o'clock Becky and one of the volunteers – Malcolm – came back. Strange chat from Malcolm about how he couldn't get a job (he's trying to start a business that revolves around lucid dreaming). Stuart was deeply suspicious of him and insisted on walking Becky back to her flat rather than leave her accompanied by Malcolm and his lucid dreams.

Bed at 2 a.m.

Till total £669.27
48 customers

TUESDAY, 27 SEPTEMBER

Online orders: 2
Books found: 2

Opened the shop at 9 a.m. to find a writer waiting outside, demanding to be let into the Retreat. I explained that it doesn't open until ten, but this seemed to have little or no impact on his determination. I reluctantly let him in and lit the fire while he complained about his disappointment that a full English breakfast wasn't awaiting him on his arrival. Once he'd got that out of his system he started telling me about the book he'd written and was here to talk about. I'm afraid I completely tuned him out, although I vaguely remember that he'd written a biography of a scientist I'd never heard of. I have to admit I was quite taken by his sense of self-importance, and almost started to believe his propaganda that the subject of his biography (although I suspect that I heard him say 'autobiography' on one occasion) was possibly the most important man who ever lived.

Granny had gone to visit her favourite tourist attraction, the doctor's surgery, and missed the whole affair.

Maria and Laurie arrived at 9.15 with Holly, Maria's assistant for the rest of the week. She's a photographer, and Anna is a massive fan of her work.

Lee Randall appeared at ten o'clock, and we chatted over a muffin and a cup of tea in the Retreat while the biographer busied himself with what sounded like remarkably important telephone calls but were – I suspect – nothing more than him paying a gas bill.

Becky (intern) arrived at 10.10 a.m. with the children's author Tracey Corderoy, who was utterly charming.

Sandy the tattooed pagan appeared at 10.30 with four sticks. I suspect he times his visits to coincide with when he thinks there might be interesting people in the Retreat.

Man brought in two boxes of books. I picked out about twenty and gave him £40 for them. Among them were a book called *The Humanure Handbook: A Guide to Composting Human Manure* and another called *Marriage Technique* – a brilliantly anachronistic book from the 1930s. I put it on the shelf, priced at £6.50. In under five minutes a Portuguese woman spotted it and bought it. One of the boxes contained a Scottish dictionary from 1827 and two Jasper Fforde novels, one of which, *First among Sequels*, a woman bought for £6 at four o'clock.

Late in the afternoon, when the Retreat was quiet, Laurie covered the shop while I drove to Michele's house with Becky to pick up the tables that Rebecca and I had dropped off yesterday. When I came back I discovered Laurie immersed in the Scottish dictionary. She was chuckling over the entry for 'Trump', which reads 'to deceive, to cheat'.

T R O—T U M   227

Trowth, *s.* the truth, troth.
Truff, *v. n.* to steal.
Truff, *s.* a turf.
Trugs, *interj.* troth, a petty oath.
Trummle, *v. v.* to tremble.
Trump, *v. a.* to deceive, to cheat.
Trump, *s.* a Jew's harp.
Trump, *v. n.* to go off in consequence of disgrace, or necessity.
Trumph, *s.* a trifle.
Trumph, *s.* trump, a winning card.
Truncher, *s.* a trencher.
Tryst, *v. a.* to appoint one, to meet a person.
Tryst, *v. n.* (to make a) to make an appointment.

Woman with a very nasal voice asked, 'Do you have any books on the old railways of Dumfries and Galloway?' I showed her to the new books section and pointed out five different titles on the subject, which, considering most of the railways in the area were removed in the 1950s, is quite a few. She replied, 'Is that all I've got to choose from?' She bought two of them.

We'd run out of wine for the Retreat, so a couple of volunteers appeared at three o'clock with four boxes of red and four of white.

Managed to grab a bowl of soup in the afternoon, otherwise ate nothing all day.

Short, moustachioed man, balding but with a few greasy long strands of hair from the side of his head tied into a tight, short ponytail, bought a copy of *The Joy of Sex*.

Woman came to the counter with a book carefully wrapped up in a bag and asked if we buy books. When I told her that we did, she replied, 'Well, I don't want to sell this.' And proceeded to unwrap an extremely tatty copy of *Medieval Costume in England and France*, a book worth about £3. I told her that I wouldn't buy it even if she was selling it. Not sure whether it was an elaborate ruse to make me think it was a valuable book.

Sandy the tattooed pagan exposed himself to Polly Pullar in the shop. She was delighted and took photographs of him stripped to the waist.

Bum-Bag Dave appeared with his usual assortment of luggage and shuffled about for a while, moaning loudly about how there's never anywhere to park during the festival because it's so busy. He doesn't drive.

Went to Amy's Wine Bar after closing the shop at 6 p.m. for a drink with Lee. Came back and started tidying up in the Retreat – Eliot was talking to the broadcaster Aasmah Mir. I tidied up around them. Eliot didn't introduce me.

It was Stuart's pub quiz this evening. I joined a team with the interns, neighbour Graeme Stewart and a woman who had written a biography of Josephine Tey. We came in with a resounding last place. Back here afterwards with Rose and Becky (the interns), Eliot, Charlotte and Granny. Bed at 2 a.m. Granny volunteered to stay up and lock up behind her once everyone had left. She fell asleep in the armchair by the fire and eventually kicked Eliot and

Charlotte out at just after 4 a.m. Eliot told Granny that she could just leave the house unlocked, but she refused.

Till total £263.85
34 customers

WEDNESDAY, 28 SEPTEMBER

Online orders: 1
Books found: 1

Granny appeared at 9.30. She'd missed her bus to work at The Pheasant because she slept in. Janet was busy today, so I was on my own in the shop all day. Lit the fire in the Retreat just as Laurie and Maria arrived with today's treats.

Amy's wine bar was closed today. I think it was a success, so hopefully she'll want to do it again next year.

Potty Dotty's son Gary dropped in with seven boxes of her books. She died last year. I hadn't heard. Dorothy had been a customer of the shop long before I took over and was interested in books about Korea. I'm not sure what her diagnosis was, but she clearly suffered from mental health problems. I inherited her rather cruel nickname from another business in the town whose doorstep she frequently darkened. She had paper-thin, almost translucent, skin and eyes that would have terrified the most fearless of people. Her appearance in the shop always made my heart sink – the hour following her arrival was invariably a question of sitting down and listening to conspiracy theories – but I'm sad to hear of her death. Customers who were regulars when I bought the shop are increasingly rare, and when I hear of the demise of any of them, no matter how difficult they may have been, it feels like a small milestone on the path to my own inevitable totter towards the tomb.

Charlotte and Eliot appeared at 9.15. Stuart told me that he'd heard raised voices from the Retreat last night at about 3.30 a.m. Charlotte told me that they'd left here at four, then gone back to

Eliot's flat to continue what was clearly a fairly lively argument about teamwork.

Processed orders and took them over to Wilma at the post office. She seemed in good spirits. I think it's because William has received an offer for the business.

The four over-friendly Yorkshire people showed up at 11 a.m. and insisted on telling me that their roof had been leaking but now isn't, and that a mouse had got into their garage and eaten a corner off a cardboard box. Every sentence was punctuated with a laugh as though the whole story was utterly hilarious.

After five days of dealing with interesting authors in my home, today I met the most obnoxious of the festival so far. I was wearing a T-shirt that my friend Colin had given me. He'd bought it in a market in Kuwait. The person who founded the Youth Orchestra of Iraq was in the Writers' Retreat and asked me what the Arabic text on it meant. I told him that I didn't really know, but that Colin had assured me that it meant 'God is great'. Five minutes later, another author who had eavesdropped on the conversation cornered me in the shop as I was putting books out, pointed his stubby finger at the T-shirt and said, 'Oh, no. No, no, no. That doesn't mean that at all. Ha ha! In fact it doesn't mean anything. It makes no sense. It's not even Arabic. You can't go around telling people that. You're completely wrong.'

Sara Maitland appeared at 11.30. We sat on the bench outside the shop while she smoked a cigarette, then came in and had a cup of tea in the Retreat.

Email inquiring about a two-volume set we're selling called *Horses of the British Empire*. It's by a man who is either blessed or cursed with the magnificent name of Sir Humphrey F. de Trafford. Ours is a rather fine set bound in red calf with a gilt cartouche on the front board of each volume. We've priced it at £300. The customer asked if we'd be prepared to sell it for £100 because apparently he's de Trafford's great-great-nephew. I told him that this wasn't really a legitimate reason for a discount.

Old man in a blue beret bought £20 worth of books and asked for a bag. I told him that we're legally obliged to charge 5p for bags. He refused to pay, then returned minutes later and bought the Blaeu map of Eskdale (roughly 350 years old) on the landing for £200.

Customer came to the counter with a paperback copy of Agatha Christie's *Third Girl* which had two pencil prices, one 12½p, the other £2.50, and demanded to know which was the correct price. The ½p coin was phased out in 1984. She must have recently been revived from a coma.

Went upstairs to make a cup of tea at four o'clock and came back down to discover a cat litter bag full of apples, a bucket of flowers, three plastic bottles of home brew and a bag of 'festival shoes' in the middle of the front of the shop. Only one explanation can exist for this: Nicky. I went back upstairs to discover her in the Retreat. She greeted me with her customary 'Helloooo!'

Closed the shop at 6 p.m. Beth and Rebecca turned up at seven for a supper of Co-op pizza, garlic bread and the leftovers from the Retreat. Stuart and Nicky had a fairly intense argument over religion so we abandoned them and moved into the kitchen.

Till total £656.95
46 customers

THURSDAY, 29 SEPTEMBER

Online orders: 1
Books found: 1

Janette came in at 7 a.m. to tidy the Writers' Retreat. I half expected to find Stuart and Nicky still there, arguing over some obscure point of theological dogma.

Stuart and Twigger were up when I came down to open the shop. Twigger had filled the log basket and lit the fire, and Stuart had emptied the dishwasher and cooked a fried breakfast. Looked out of the window of the Retreat to see Granny at the bus stop with a cigarette in one hand and a cup of coffee in the other. I knocked on the pane and she looked up, spotted me and did her daily salute of raising her middle finger, although on this occasion she was obliged to put her coffee on the bench.

Order for *Horses of the British Empire* from the de Trafford in South America who had asked for the £200 discount. Bloody chancer.

Nicky came in at ten, looking very much like a woman who had drunk a gallon of home-brewed beer, lost an argument about transubstantiation then slept in a van.

Twigger and I loaded the eight bags of waste from the Retreat, and 120 empty bottles (water and wine – didn't care to get into an argument with Nicky about one turning into the other) into the van and drove to the dump, then on to the bank to lodge the takings for the week. It looks very much as though the Newton Stewart branch of RBS will be closing in the fairly near future.

Ted Cowan and Ruaridh McNicol were the first to appear at the Retreat, at 9.15 a.m. Laurie and Maria had set up early today, probably expecting impatient authors to appear before ten. Which they did.

> Customer: 'I'm looking for books about a famous Galloway gypsy. His name's Billy somethingorother.'
>
> Me: 'He's called Billy Marshall, he was the self-styled King of the Scottish Gypsies. Andrew McCormick wrote about him in a book called *The Tinkler-Gypsies of Galloway*.'
>
> Customer: 'Billy, Billy, oh, if only I could remember his second name.'
>
> Me: 'It's Marshall. Billy Marshall.'
>
> Customer: 'Billy, Billy, Billy … it will come to me eventually…'
>
> Me: Sigh.
>
> Customer: 'MARSHALL! That's it, Billy Marshall. I knew it would come to me.'

Beth and Rebecca covered the shop between 6 and 7 p.m. so that I could go to the wine bar with Tom, Willeke, Michele, Lee, Granny, Twigger and Charlotte. They left at 7.30 to pick up their friend Mo from Barrhill railway station.

Closed the shop at 8 p.m. Bath at 9 p.m. We've run out of bubble bath and loo roll. Seven people staying in the house, mostly Stuart's fan club. They're a decent bunch and all mucked in to help tonight, which was a busy night at the Retreat: probably fifty people there between eight o'clock and midnight. Claudia arrived with friends. Once everyone had gone, we tidied up so that Janette isn't faced with a nightmare in the morning. I went to bed at 2 a.m. and left Beth in charge of locking up. Adrian, Charlotte, Stuart, Beth, Rebecca and Mo were all still up. Mo slept in the festival bed, Beth and Rebecca slept in the parrot room, one of the spare rooms, which has wallpaper decorated with parrots.

Most of the wine I bought from Majestic has now been drunk.

Till total £276.51
37 customers

FRIDAY, 30 SEPTEMBER

Online orders: 0
Books found: 0

Janette in at 7 a.m. to clear up the Retreat. It wasn't too bad, despite the crowds of last night. Stuart and Twigger were both up when she arrived, and gave her a hand.

My cousin Gerald appeared at 10 a.m. to see if there was anything he could do. He's clearly inherited the 'helpful' gene which has passed me by. He's visiting from Ireland, partly for the festival and partly to see my mother, his aunt.

Glorious sunny day, but I didn't crawl out of bed until 8.50. Stuart, Rebecca and Beth were in the kitchen when I sheepishly appeared. Holly and Laurie arrived at 9.10. Maria was off today. Eliot appeared at 9.20 and requested a bath, which meant that the bathroom was occupied until ten, so I was unable to brush my teeth. I could have lit the fire with my breath by the time Eliot emerged.

Janet was waiting outside when I opened the shop. I think she enjoys her time working in the shop. She's utterly unflappable and spends most of her time behind the counter, knitting.

Lit the fire in the Retreat at 9.30 a.m. Polly Pullar appeared at 9.45 a.m.

Colin (photographer) in at 9 a.m. There are some people who

take advantage of the Retreat and some who are always a pleasure to see. Colin falls firmly into the latter category – he's one of the hardest-working people at the festival, and always looks as though he feels he ought not to be taking advantage of the free food, but there are precious few people who deserve it more than he does, and plenty who don't deserve it at all.

Beth covered the shop during Janet's lunch break so that I could mow the lawns to tidy the garden up for the last weekend of the festival.

A customer asked, 'Do you have a section for books that are so damaged that you can't do anything with them?' I'm not quite sure what sort of business model he imagines that I operate for the shop.

Hughie from the distillery dropped in at about two o'clock for a chat about fishing. He reminded me that I'm supposed to be filming Steve Dowling's music event at Bladnoch Distillery this evening at 7 p.m. I had completely forgotten. It's a musical that he's been working on with Allison, a festival regular who normally produces puppet theatre.

At 3.15 a young French woman with pink braided hair appeared and asked if she could work in the shop for a couple of days. She's cycling around Scotland and free camping. She asked if I had anywhere that she could camp, so I showed her to the freshly mown lawn in the garden, where she pitched her tent.

Amy decided to open the wine bar again for the weekend, and came over for £1 coins. We (and she) always run out of them during the festival. After she'd gone, I went to the County Buildings for more bin bags. We're rationed in our use of bin space, and if we go over the designated number we have to pay for more. During the festival we use possibly a hundred or more, so I have to buy extras. It's always worth remembering to do this before the weekend, when we go through them at an incredible rate because the festival is busier on those days.

Man and woman in matching red fezzes arrived at 5.15 p.m. I think they're part of the festival. They certainly made themselves at home in the Retreat.

Pru (Eliot's wife) and their children arrived and went straight to the Retreat.

BBC turned up to do an interview with Scottish crime writer

Graeme Macrae Burnet, who has been shortlisted for the Booker Prize for his book *His Bloody Project*. Pru and the children chose the moment when he was in mid-flow to come down the staircase where the crew had set up and have a raucous chat. The crew had to stop filming.

Jenny Brown arrived at 6 p.m., just as I had to take Allison down to Steve Dowling's for the musical they've written. I was too busy to film it, so I set up the camera and showed Allison how to switch it on and press 'Record', then left and came back to the shop.

I filled the log basket in the Retreat at 6.30, although Prue Leith kept getting in the way. I was starting to think that she was doing it on purpose. Philip Ardagh arrived at about seven o'clock. Beth and Rebecca moved from the parrot room to the snug to make room for another writer.

Amy had booked local singer Gina for a live music event in the wine bar tonight, so I headed over to make sure everything was set up. Carol-Ann covered in the shop until 7.30.

Following a boozy night at Amy's wine bar, Anna decided that it would be a good idea to embark on a moonlit walk to the stone circle at Torhouse. She asked me how far it was, so I told her that it was about 2 miles. A group of about twenty set off at about 11 p.m. After they'd left, I checked and it turns out that it's 4 miles. They were pretty annoyed with me when they made it home at about 1.30 a.m.

I did a rough count of the number of dishwasher cycles we've done since the festival began. I think we're looking at about sixty, which is roughly eight a day.

Only three bottles of wine left from the thirty-six delivered by Majestic.

Bed at 3 a.m.

Till total £487.39
45 customers

OCTOBER

How happy I felt on that Saturday night after closing. I had drawn
nearly four pounds, and thought that I was going to be a second
Nelson or Chambers. I think the beginnings of things are always the
most interesting. The early struggles, the overcoming of difficulties,
the first blows in the battle of life, are in books of biography the most
fascinating pages. One looks back to the first day's experience in a
new enterprise as to a red-letter day which can never be forgotten.
There is the uncertainty, the alternating hopes and fears, of it all, and
the day crowned with the promise of future success.

R. M. Williamson, *Bits from an Old Bookshop*

Closing on a Saturday night is always a delight, particularly when
you work for yourself and Sunday is your only day off. And £4
must have seemed like a fortune in 1904, but sometimes, over 100
years later, it can still seem like rich pickings when compared with
a day when the till hasn't troubled you in the slightest. I don't know
whether it's sentiment, human nature or the arrogance of youth,
but Williamson's assertion that beginnings are the most interesting,
exciting times most certainly chimes with me. Not that I don't still
adore what I do – I wouldn't swap it for anything – but there is
something about starting out on a new adventure which thrills;
sometimes knowing nothing about what you're doing is considerably more exciting than the vaguely drudgerous sense of repetition
that comes with experience.

Part of the excitement that Williamson refers to as a second-
hand bookseller comes from not knowing what you'll discover
every day – whether it is Napoleon's penis or, as in my first week
in the trade, a copy of *The Coventrian*. An elderly man brought in
what appeared to be (and was) a cheaply produced school magazine
from the early twentieth century. He asked me how much I was
prepared to offer him for it. At first glance I thought it might be
handy for lighting the fire, but he told me to flick through it, and
when I did, he stuck his finger on one of the pages and said, 'Do
you recognise that name?' At the end of a poem (school magazines
tend to be full of them) was the name Philip Larkin. This man had
been at King Henry VIII School in Coventry with Larkin, and this

was the poet's first poem to be printed. I gave him £500 for it and sold it the following day for £800.

Williamson makes reference to a number of men – and they're all men – who have made significant fortunes from bookselling, although he qualifies this by explaining that in his time the term 'bookselling' also included publishing, and this is largely where the fortunes to which he refers were made. Samuel Richardson (born in 1689 and the author of *Pamela*) was, I discovered thanks to Williamson, a bookseller. Dr Johnson, who Williamson describes as 'the ponderous and prosy lexicographer' (Scots tend to dislike Johnson, in part because he defined oats in his dictionary as 'A grain which in England is generally given to horses, but in Scotland supports the people'), was the son of a bookseller. Jacob Tonson, a bookseller (born in 1656), published Dryden, Milton and many others, and founded the Kit-Cat Club (not the one in Berlin). Thomas Guy (born in 1644) was a philanthropic bookseller who founded Guy's Hospital from profits from sales of copies of the Bible. Thomas Nelson, William Blackwood and the brothers William and Robert Chambers are but a handful of the litany of literary booksellers who, according to Williamson, amassed enormous wealth and all lived to a grand age. Williamson comments: 'If Jacob Tonson and William Chambers are average representatives of the trade, then let all poor men make their sons booksellers, for the leading facts in these two men's lives are alike. They began life poor, lived far beyond the allotted span of years in the sheath of this flesh, and died wealthy.'

SATURDAY, I OCTOBER

Online orders: 0
Books found: 0

Opened the shop at 9 a.m.

Marlene, the French cyclist, was up and about when I opened the shop. I'm amazed that anyone can emerge from a cold autumn night camping in Scotland and look quite so glamorous. I took one look in the mirror and decided that I looked as though I'd spent a month in a Siberian Gulag. Granny wasn't working in The Pheasant today, so she and Marlene tidied up the shop while Janet covered the counter, and I went upstairs. I was in the kitchen when a tall man came in, introduced himself as Max and said that Dan from Buzzfeed sent his regards. We chatted for a while, and eventually I told him to piss off, which Pru overheard and got in a state about, clearly failing to differentiate banter from a genuine insult. She works for Granta and Max is one of her (extremely successful) authors.

Colin, the photographer, turned up early at the Retreat and told me that he'd been in the Galloway Inn (opposite the shop) last night. The police turned up at about ten o'clock while he was standing outside with the smokers, looking for one of the authors. A female police officer parked up and emerged from the car, at which point one of the smokers spotted her and said, 'Kirsty, can you give us a lift up the road?', to which she replied, 'See what's written on the side of that car; it says Police, not Taxi.' Apparently he went on to complain at great length that, since she had caught him drink-driving and he had subsequently lost his driving licence, he felt that it was incumbent on her to get him home from the pub.

Carol-Ann appeared at 10 a.m. looking very rough after spending the evening in Amy's Wine Bar. The Retreat was heaving from the moment we opened. Laurie was beginning to look stressed, which is quite remarkable for someone I've never really seen show any signs of emotion. Or even humanity, for that matter. Cyber-ethicists could do far worse than to experiment with her to model robot behaviour.

Picked up Claudia and Allison for a swim in Rigg Bay. Slightly chilly birthday swim, but at least the sun shone on us. Back home soon afterwards to discover that the fire had gone out, so I relit it and bumped into my cousin Ros, Gerald's sister, on the stairs. Prue Leith was in the Retreat again. She has a remarkable, almost admirable, ability to always be in the way. Whether it's putting logs on the fire, clearing tables or filling up glasses of wine, she manages, with GPS precision, to be in exactly the spot you would hope her not to be.

Katie, a former employee who has now – to my astonishment

and horror – qualified as a doctor, appeared at 3.30. Carol-Ann and the girls banned me from the kitchen so that they could create a vile birthday cake. I retreated to the Retreat, where Jenny, Lee, Philip Ardagh, Twigger and other friends were loitering. Jenny produced a contract from Profile, which I signed to much clapping and ceremony at three o'clock. Eliot, who I hadn't told about the book, looked confused and asked what was happening, so I explained that I'd been keeping a diary and that Jenny had found me a publisher, to which he replied, 'Oh, that's what it is. I was in your office and noticed a pile of papers, so I picked them up and started reading them.' This is typical of Eliot. Even the words 'Private and Confidential' are more of an invitation than a deterrent to him. It's hard to be annoyed by it, though – he has a curiosity that would have eliminated the whole of Scotland's cat population.

Rory Stewart was in the Retreat for a while, and Philip Ardagh left at four o'clock, just as Carol-Ann and Laurie appeared with my birthday cake. It was in the shape of an erect penis. I'm not entirely sure that the country's culturati are at one with Carol-Ann's sense of humour.

Closed the shop at six. Laurie made a curry for around twenty of us, including my cousins. Gerald was, unsurprisingly, helpful, chopping, peeling and slicing things for Laurie, then we all went over to the big marquee for the ceilidh. Danced with Marlene (the French cyclist), Granny and Polly. We all came back here after the last dance. Siobhan – who runs the Young Adult part of the book festival and with whom I have a long-running and pointless feud, the origins of which neither of us can remember – came back with her parents and we all chatted into the small hours.

Till total £985.95
65 customers

SUNDAY, 2 OCTOBER

Online orders: 0
Books found: 0

Beautiful sunny day. Opened the shop at 9.10 a.m. with a diabolical hangover. Spotted a glass which appeared to contain Coke on the kitchen table and swiftly swallowed it in the hope that it would assuage my raging thirst. It was red wine, and cheap stuff too.

Mercifully Marlene appeared from her tent shortly after I'd opened up and took over the 'public-facing duties', as apparently working in a shop is now euphemistically described. I'm starting to wonder a bit about Marlene – in spite of her interesting appearance and equally interesting decision to cycle from Denmark to Spain at an age when most of her peers are probably becoming lawyers or accountants, she is starting to strike me as a bit dull.

Beth, Rebecca and Mo were all up and in the Retreat at 9.15 when I went up to light the fire. Laurie and Holly were in the kitchen laughing at the empty bottles everywhere when Maria arrived at 9.30.

Bathroom was occupied when I got up. Managed eventually to get the chance to brush my teeth at 10 a.m. I still have no idea who was in there.

Customer at 2 p.m.: 'You'll have to move your art section. The lighting's atrocious, you have to move all the time because of people going past, and the stock's not as good as it used to be.' When I sarcastically thanked him for his kind words, he told me that it was 'constructive criticism'. Tempted to constructively criticise him for his greasy moustache, short trousers and strange, soup-like odour.

Ben and Beth, the Bookshop Band, arrived at 3.30 and set up for an event in the shop at four o'clock. Callum and his children turned up, as did a good crowd. I handed out free glasses of the remaining festival wine. Colin came along to take some photographs. He'd managed to bash his head when he was walking into his bedroom at his B&B last night. Apparently it's a very low door. He had a small cut on his forehead, a relatively minor scar to bear from ten days of the festival.

My cousins, Ros and Ger, left at 3 p.m. to catch the ferry back to Ireland. Amy closed the wine bar at four o'clock, the same time that Claudia, Peggy and Colin and Jenny all left.

Went for a walk round Lovers' Lane at 5.30 with Twigger and Anna, then home to eat the remains of Maria's vegan food and some lobsters followed by a viewing of *Superbad* – we always watch a film in the Retreat on the final evening of the festival. Stuart, Twigger, Lee, Anna, Granny, Eliot and Marlene were all there, and most of them fell asleep shortly after I switched the projector on.

Till total £534.98
49 customers

MONDAY, 3 OCTOBER

Online orders: 0
Books found: 0

Granny and Marlene in the shop. Marlene slept in her tent in the garden again last night. Between them they managed to sort through all of the boxes that Potty Dotty's son had brought in, price them up and put them on the shelves.

Amy came in at lunchtime to clear out the wine bar. I spent the day tidying up the Retreat and attempting to return the house to normal.

Eliot came for supper and cooked a Thai green curry, which

involved the use of almost every kitchen implement, not one of which he washed up. Stuart, Twigger, Anna, Eliot and Marlene watched *The Princess Bride*. I fell asleep about five minutes after it started.

Bed at 2 a.m.

Till total £139.99
9 customers

TUESDAY, 4 OCTOBER

Online orders: 0
Books found: 0

Opened the shop at 9 a.m. – Granny and Marlene took over so that I could drive Stuart Kelly back home. Eliot gave Twigger a lift back to London. They left at 7 a.m. He's not the best of drivers. At least Twigger is pretty fearless.

At ten o'clock Stuart and I left for the Borders. He'd lined up a couple of book deals near Town Yetholm, where he's currently living with his parents. During the drive Stuart commented that the landscape and air had a decidedly autumnal feel about them which hadn't been there on the journey twelve days previously, when his father had driven him to Wigtown. It's the same every year, as if the festival's end is the harbinger of the seasonal change.

We arrived at Yetholm at about 1.30 and had lunch with Stuart's parents. His mother had made a delicious Scotch broth. After lunch we walked to his neighbour's house, where he'd laid the books out on some tables. It was a modern bungalow but with fine antique furniture. Stuart's neighbours were a retired couple, and very kind – cups of tea and biscuits appeared seconds after we arrived. The books included Rackhams, Dulacs and others from the Golden Age of illustration. I gave them £450 for two boxes of books. I fear that I may have overpaid. We chatted about the provenance of the books while I was looking at them. They had belonged to one of Scotland's first female vets. She had been born in 1910 – the same year as my grandfather – which means that they must have been at the Dick Vet (Scotland's veterinary university) in Edinburgh at the same time.

At 3 p.m. I jumped in the van and followed Stuart's father's car up a winding country road to a house on top of a hill where we were met by a remarkably unfriendly old woman. The main reason for me agreeing to drive Stuart home was that she'd told him that she wanted to sell her late husband's aviation collection. As soon as we arrived she pointed at it and said, 'I'm not selling the aviation books, I want to sell the books on the stairs and', pointing at a small bookcase of probably 150 books, 'those over there.' I went over to look at the books, and she told me that people were quite wrong to look down on Book Club editions. All of her books were Book Club titles. I told her that we don't sell them, and very few bookshops do. She sneered at me, so I went over to the other bookcase. Stuart meanwhile was flapping uncomfortably around at the awkwardness of the situation. It wasn't awkward for me, but I could sense his discomfort at the woman's general rudeness. I picked out about thirty books on military history and offered her £80. She told me that she was 'very disappointed' by my offer and began counting them, telling me how good they were, shaking her head, then counting them again. This carried on for about five minutes, and with every passing second my instinct to offer her more drained away until eventually I told her that it was my final offer and I would rather leave empty-handed than pay above the odds for them. I left empty-handed and delighted to be out of her house. Stuart looked embarrassed. He had no need to be. He wasn't the one who had been rude. We said goodbye and I drove home.

Came back to find Isabel's uncle George's table had been returned and was in the big room.

The big marquee had been taken down by the time I made it home at 7.30. Granny and Marlene were chatting in the kitchen. Granny was threatening to cook, so I staged an intervention and went to the Co-op and bought steaks and potatoes. Now that the house is empty, I told Marlene that she could have a bed in one of the spare rooms for the night.

Till total £119.48
7 customers

WEDNESDAY, 5 OCTOBER

Online orders: 0
Books found: 0

Opened at nine o'clock; no sign of Marlene until ten. I think the luxury of a bed was too much for her.

Stuart called to say that he'd left his phone and iPad chargers behind, so I told him that I'd send them on.

Anna left at lunchtime for a week in Edinburgh. Marlene left at four o'clock to cycle to the Isle of Whithorn, via Garlieston. She's going to camp in the woods at Cruggleton Church and come back tomorrow.

Intern Becky came round for supper. Granny was keen to cook again, but I managed to distract her by suggesting that she choose a film for us to watch later. Made sushi and stir-fry. Becky is off to South Africa to count baboons for an environmental project in December. Granny chose *Elevator to the Gallows* to round off a cheery evening.

Till total £123.97
7 customers

THURSDAY, 6 OCTOBER

Online orders: 0
Books found: 0

Opened the shop at 9.10. Granny appeared shortly afterwards with her turban and octogenarian slippers on, and told me that she's 'not fucking working today, you fucking bastard'.

Telephone call from an ABE customer in Edinburgh who had ordered a copy of *John Thomson of Duddingston* and been sent the wrong (unsigned) copy. I spent twenty minutes looking for the signed copy but failed to locate it, so I called him back and suggested that he return the copy for a full refund, with grovelling apologies. He wasn't happy with that: it involved him having to re-package the book and then walk to the post office. When I asked what he had in mind as an alternative (having explained that I'd had to pack the book and walk to the post office to send it to him in the first place, and that it hadn't been that much of an ordeal), he repeated his initial complaint that it wasn't as described in our ABE listing and that he was unhappy with it. It didn't take long before negotiations were reduced to him demanding a refund which was of equivalent value to the time and inconvenience that would have been involved in him having to walk to the post office. When I told him that the standard procedure in these circumstances was for the customer to return the item, and that we would refund him on receipt, he kept returning to his initial complaint until, out of frustration, I asked him if he wanted me to drive to Edinburgh to collect it. After initially replying, 'Yes, that would save me a walk', he finally agreed to return it for a refund.

At 9.45 a woman brought in six bin bags full of books. Entirely Catherine Cookson paperbacks, apart from one Ellis Peters omnibus and a Nigel Tranter novel. I gave her £4 for the Peterses and Tranters, and offered her another £4 to take the rest away. She declined the second offer.

Sold £85 worth of books about antiques and collectibles to a man who does the jewellery and weapons appraisals for an auction house.

German man came in at 4 p.m. with two boxes of books about the Peninsular War. Gave him £40 for them.

Marlene got back from her cycling tour of the Machars. She camped in Cruggleton churchyard last night. No ghosts, apparently. She had a shower and I managed to convince Granny not to cook again. We had pasta and finished off the final jar of the wild garlic pesto that I made in May.

Bed at midnight, after watching *Rear Window*.

Till total £126.90
6 customers

FRIDAY, 7 OCTOBER

Online orders: 2
Books found: 2

Opened the shop a little late, at 9.15. Marlene appeared at 10.30 and took over. She appears to have recovered from her cycling trip. I went back to bed and slept until one o'clock.

Callum came round at 2 p.m. with a trailer of logs for the fire.

The unsigned copy of *John Thomson of Duddingston* was returned in today's post, accompanied by a reasonably confrontational letter demanding a refund including the extra £11 for postage, followed by this less than conciliatory paragraph:

> Unless I have confirmation from you one way or another that you have complied with this requirement within 7 days I shall have no option but to bring this whole matter to the attention of ABE Books. I have bought books through the ABE Books website on a number of occasions in the past through various book dealers, but I have to say I have never experienced this great inconvenience and disappointment previously.

Emailed him to say that I have now located the signed copy and am happy to exchange it and refund his extra postage, or issue a full refund instead.

Went to the bank after lunch, then dropped in on my parents to see how my mother is getting on. She seems to be making a remarkable recovery.

Closed the shop and went to the pub with Callum, Marlene, Granny, Paul and Anna, and Willeke. Callum convinced Marlene to sail with him from Stranraer to Portpatrick tomorrow.

Till total £152.98
11 customers

SATURDAY, 8 OCTOBER

Online orders: 3
Books found: 3

Breakfast at 8.15 with Marlene. Callum arrived at 8.30 to pick her up for their sailing trip. Granny appeared at 8.45.

Telephone call at 9.30 from the police. I have a friend who suffers from occasional mental health problems. He was arrested in a local pub last night, and asked the police to let me know. In the past I've done my best to look out for him when trouble arises.

Processed the orders – amazingly, found all of them. Dropped them off at the post office. Thankfully William was having his morning nap.

No market in Wigtown this week. Everything seems decidedly dreary and autumnal now that the festival is over and the leaves are starting to fall from the trees.

My friend's father came in to tell me that he had been picked up by the police, who'd taken him home. He hadn't heard that he was in the cells in Stranraer, so I reluctantly broke the news to him. Both agreed that it was probably the best place for him in the short term, until the health service can help him back to his usual self. He

has disappeared in the past when he hasn't been well. At least we know where he is, and with luck the effect of the drink and weed will have worn off by Monday and he'll be better, but, having seen this process before, I suspect that the psychosis has gone too far to reverse without a section and enforced course of anti-psychotics.

Sold a three-volume set of Robert Gould's *History of Free-masonry* (1883) for £110, half red morocco, to a couple with a baby. The books must have been on the shelves for ten years. Gould was blessed with the middle name Freke by his parents.

Callum dropped Marlene back at the shop at 6 p.m. We had a chat about a property that has come on the market. When I was a child, it was a pub – The Red Lion – and it is on the same street as the shop. It's a large property but needs a great deal of work. Callum agreed to come and have a look at it.

Gave Marlene a copy of *Black's Economical Tourist of Scotland* from about 1880. She'll need it if she's travelling with Callum.

Till total £232.49
11 customers

MONDAY, 10 OCTOBER

Online orders: 1
Books found: 1

Opened the shop early to let the cat out. No customers until lunchtime. Another beautifully sunny day. My friend who had been picked up by the police was in court this morning, but I couldn't go because I was on my own in the shop. I know how much he values a friendly face when he's struggling with his mental health.

Yesterday, following a walk on the beach in the afternoon, Granny and I stopped in Port William to pick up something to drink. As we were parking, Granny became quite agitated at the sight of a man wearing a hoodie using a public phone box, and decided that the only possible explanation was that he was a drug dealer and didn't want the call to be traced.

Fire extinguisher service man appeared at 10 a.m. and replaced one of the fire extinguishers. Granny returned from a trip to the doctor at the same time, so I went to the bank in Newton Stewart and stopped at Vincent's to replace windscreen wipers on the van. Philip (the mechanic) laughed when he saw the state of them. They must have been several years old, and were about as effective as colliding with a pigeon once every hundred miles.

A customer looking for a book about the seashore told Granny that she 'hadn't been very helpful'. At the time Granny had been taking a telephone call from someone who wanted to know our opening hours, but the woman talked over her, demanding books about shells or something, then – clearly considering herself a priority over whoever Granny was on the phone to – flounced off in a huff.

Marlene worked in the shop all afternoon, then cooked crêpes for supper. Apart from Granny's 'pizza', which consisted largely of butternut squash skin and burned carrots, I can barely remember a less fulfilling meal. I'm starting to question the myth of the Mediterranean diet. Before going to bed, Marlene washed all her clothes and put them up to dry on the aerial drying rack in the kitchen.

Till total £38.98
5 customers

TUESDAY, 11 OCTOBER

Online orders: 1
Books found: 1

Granny opened the shop so I went back to bed for an hour. Still pretty tired following the festival; with every passing year my recovery time extends by several days.

Awoke at 11 a.m. and said goodbye to Marlene before I left. She had several devices – camera, iPad, phone etc. – all plugged into some sort of fancy adapter in the kitchen for one final charge before her trip to Ireland en route to Spain. She was planning to cycle to

Cairnryan, camp overnight, then catch an early ferry tomorrow morning, before cycling to Callum's brother's house for the night. Nick, Callum's brother, lives in Newtownards, south of Belfast.

Maria came to collect the fridge at 11 a.m. In previous years her spare fridge (usually brought to the kitchen by her husband, Mike) has occupied a corner of the kitchen for up to six months following the end of the festival.

In this morning's post was a returned copy of Cowper's poetry that had been erroneously listed as being in 'like new' condition, which was highly unlikely, considering that it is 150 years old. The customer was not happy with it and returned it demanding a refund. It's tricky to imagine what someone's expectations were for a £15 book that was a century and a half old. Although admittedly 'like new' may have been a little misleading.

Loaded the van with empty boxes and left for Helensburgh at 11 a.m. Arrived at a large Victorian villa with a magnificent view across the Clyde just after two o'clock. The house had been split into two flats in the 1960s, and the couple who met me there were around retirement age, and very kind, producing tea and biscuits on my arrival. The house had belonged to her parents. Her mother died last year, and they'd recently had to put her father into a home, as he'd reached a level of dementia that meant that he was unable to carry on living independently. The books were mainly on UK topography, with an emphasis on the Lake District, the north-east of Scotland and Wales, as well as some railway and aviation books. No fiction. Took thirteen boxes and gave them £400. They very kindly helped me shift the boxes to the van. It's surprising how rarely this happens, but it makes things considerably easier and I always appreciate it.

Dreadful journey home over the hills – wild and windy. Finally made it back at 8.30 p.m.

Till total £236.70
12 customers

WEDNESDAY, 12 OCTOBER

Online orders: 2
Books found: 2

My friend Nick, a picture restorer, popped in for a chat with Callum, who was fixing a loose skirting board. Jeff Mead, the minister, appeared at 10 a.m. and told me that he has to bury one of his closest friends on Friday. He refers to God as his 'invisible friend'. Jeff, as I'm sure I've said before, is a good man, and – I suspect – one of many silently atheist men of the cloth.

Sandy the tattooed pagan came in at 12.15 and demanded a cup of tea. I told him that I was too busy, but he spotted Granny loitering near the history section and said, 'Dinnae worry, Francesca can make me one.' Despite my protestations, Granny went upstairs and returned with a cup of Lady Grey. 'What's this muck?' was all the thanks she received. Sandy clearly prefers a less floral brew.

Email from Jean Brittain, local writer, to say that she has a private library to sell on behalf of her late friend's family. Have arranged to go and see them on the 21st.

Another returned ABE book, this time Katharine Cameron's *The Flowers I Love*. It was exactly in the condition described in our listing, but the customer decided to return it in any case. This will drop our ABE performance below their acceptable level and may well result in another suspension.

Two young women giggling in the erotica section at 3 p.m.

Parents appeared at 4 p.m. and complained that they had to park four spaces away from the door of the shop. My father, who has an almost pathological dislike of shopping, and consequently is oblivious to the fact that it has been illegal to smoke in shops, pubs and restaurants since 2006, immediately loaded and lit his pipe, and proceeded to share his opinions on various subjects about which we disagree, encased in a cloud of smoke of his own making. Thankfully, the shop was fairly quiet.

At 4.30 I drove to Dumfries to pick up Anna from the bus station on the sands. Stopped at Newton Stewart on the way home to get her a pizza from the chip shop to break the fast of Yom

Kippur. Dropped her off at Finn and Ella's, where she's staying for a while, at seven o'clock. Back home at 7.30.

Till total £241.66
22 customers

THURSDAY, 13 OCTOBER

Online orders: 0
Books found: 0

Amy in at 11.30 a.m. to pick up the last of the wreckage from the wine bar.

William, the Irish antique dealer from Newton Stewart, showed up at 11.45 with a van full of thirty boxes of books. He put the best of them nearest the door so that I'd see them first. He wanted £1,200 for them. Told him that my top offer would be £500. He wasn't happy, and left.

Email from Marlene to say that she's staying with Callum's brother and has sent me a folder with photos which she'd like me to organise into a film for her website. She clearly imagines that I have nothing else to do.

Telephone call from an RBC member who had called on Monday to cancel his subscription. When he phoned today to complain that I hadn't done it, he said, 'I spoke to one of your colleagues, a Taiwanese lady, on Monday.' It must have been Granny.

Quite a few younger (this becomes more flexible as I become older) people in the shop today. One of them was a woman who spent half an hour stroking Captain while her boyfriend trawled the sci-fi section and bought a paperback copy of *The Hitchhiker's Guide to the Galaxy*.

Till total £88.44
10 customers

Online orders: 0
Books found: 0

Sunny day again. That's almost ten days in succession.

David, a Mancunian man who moved to Wigtown in 2000, came in looking for a copy of *The Merrick and the Neighbouring Hills*. Found a paperback reprint for £8. The hardback, published by a small publisher in Ayr in 1929, is a rather attractive book, bound in blue buckram with gilt titles. It used to sell for about £40. Now it has dropped to about half of that, like so many books.

Customer came to the counter with £15 which she'd found on one of the seats by the fire. It must have fallen out of someone's pocket.

Digby, the local tractor dealer, came in at lunchtime. He was looking for a book called *The Parting of Ways*, by Shiela Grant Duff. We had a long chat about the book festival. He complained that his questions to visiting speakers were dismissed during events. He wasn't very happy. Also talked about his approaching retirement, and the complications of passing on a family business to the next generation, particularly when they don't want to inherit it. Selling tractors is not everyone's cup of tea.

Checking through the books from Stuart's friend in the Borders, I came across one called *Townsend's Monthly Selection of Parisian Costume*, an (obviously) monthly periodical from 1831, each month of which contains four pages of hand-coloured illustrations of the dress of the day. This copy was leather-bound and contained two years' worth of the periodical. The only copy I could find online was for just one of the monthly issues, and was £25, so I priced it at £400. It won't sell for that, although my maths briefly convinced me that it ought to.

Ninety years ago today *Winnie the Pooh* was first published by Methuen, illustrated by E. H. Shepard – and with a relatively rare thing for its time, an illustrated dust jacket.

Till total £166
16 customers

SATURDAY, 15 OCTOBER

Online orders: 1
Books found: 1

Slept in – opened the shop at 9.10. Granny staggered down the stairs at ten and told me that she wasn't feeling well, so I suggested that she go back to bed.

Sold a copy of *The House at Pooh Corner* that came from the deal with Stuart's neighbours for £70. The anniversary yesterday has clearly generated a little interest in A. A. Milne.

My friend Stephanie dropped in at lunchtime and invited Anna and me to supper tonight. Stephanie teaches at Stranraer Academy, and is one of the best mimics I've ever met. Mercifully, I've never heard her imitating me, but I'm quite certain that it would be both very funny and completely accurate. Her husband, Matthew, is an exceptionally good cook, so the combination of entertaining company and delicious food make it an invitation that only a fool would decline.

In the inbox this morning:

> My name is Sarah. It is my opinion that the-bookshop.com
> is well done and it is apparent you are a leader in your
> industry or will be one quickly.
>
> I am reaching out to you today...

Due diligence and Sarah are clearly complete strangers. And if any two words are guaranteed to consign an email to the junk folder, they are 'reaching out'.

Rain started at noon and didn't stop until midnight.

Drove to Matthew and Stephanie's for supper. Anna drove there from Finn and Ella's. Most of Matthew's meals involve wild animals which he has shot, and tonight's venison casserole was utterly delicious.

Till total £113.50
11 customers

MONDAY, 17 OCTOBER

Online orders: 3
Books found: 3

Orders for *Theatrum Scotiae* (£200), *Rambles in Galloway* (£40) and *Clyde Passenger Steamers* (£7). *Theatrum Scotiae* is an expensively produced reprint of a book originally published in 1693. It's full of copperplate engravings. This edition was published by Heritage Press in 1979 and limited to 500 copies, only available by subscription, folio-sized and bound in quarter calf. Looking at it as I packed it up, I couldn't help thinking that at £200 it was vastly underpriced.

Granny appeared at 10.30, following a weekend of sickness and vomiting. She has been given the week off from The Pheasant, so is planning to work in the shop every day.

One of my neighbours, Ian the archaeologist, came in at 4 p.m. looking for a book of psalms. His mother (who lived four doors up the street) died on Saturday. I hadn't heard.

Callum and I had a look at The Red Lion. He pointed out all of the work that's required, and estimated the cost. I think it's worth making an offer.

Till total £261.38
18 customers

TUESDAY, 18 OCTOBER

Online orders: 1
Books found: 1

No sign of Granny when I opened the shop, so I shouted upstairs. A feeble reply told me that she's really ill, worse than yesterday. Offered to make her some soup: 'Oh Gad, no. Please, no.' I think she may have a respiratory illness – there's a good deal of coughing and wheezing.

Order for *Glasgow Sonnets* by Edwin Morgan, a 16-page paperback, £35.

A woman came into the shop, spotted Nicky's Bookseller's Code and read the entire thing aloud. This has started to become an alarmingly regular occurrence. When she was about halfway through, a young couple with a baby in a pram came in. The baby started screaming, so they left. I suspect it may have been because of the woman reading Nicky's rules, rather than the baby screaming.

One of my friends, who I ought not to name, appeared at two o'clock, bedraggled and damp. He told me that he'd been trapped in a farmhouse for two days because he was visiting his friend Jeff, who'd promised to drive him to Wigtown, but they'd decided instead to take magic mushrooms and fell asleep. Jeff was in no state to drive, so he'd walked the 6 miles.

All afternoon customers had been making comments about free marrows, and it was only when one woman became quite upset that I hadn't given her a free marrow that I asked what she was talking about. She suggested that I look outside, so I followed her advice and discovered that there was a huge marrow on the bench in front of the shop, with a sign that read 'Special Offer – free deformed marrow with every book purchased'. No idea who put it there.

Final customers of the day were a young couple who bought three books, including a copy of *The Rucksack Man* that Twigger had given to me years ago. We had a chat about it, and other exploration books.

Went for a walk with Anna down by the River Bladnoch and back up the old railway line. Saw a dying lamb next to an abandoned, rusting tractor on the railway line. Called the farmer to let him know.

Once more there should have been a story here about one of my friends, but he's asked me to remove all references to him. In this case, it's probably a mercy – it was a remarkably dull anecdote about his efforts to rebuild an old farmhouse.

Till total £232.46
25 customers

Online orders: 0
Books found: 0

No sign of Granny again today. Messaged her to make sure she's OK. She replied that she's feeling very weak. For once, I think that a visit to the doctor is probably a necessity rather than a luxury. She thinks that she may have had pneumonia.

Sunny day. Email from someone with the wonderful name of Annette Corker, wanting to sell books:

> There is a number of books, mainly hardback, from authors such as Peter James, Kathy Reichs, James Patterson, Lee Child, Ian Rankin, Jack Higgins, Frederick Forsyth and John Le Carré.
>
> There is also a collection (4 books) named *The National Burns* by George Gilfillan, a collection of Shakespeare books (6 books) and a collection of books called The Waverley Novels. Not all of these are in a great condition though I'm afraid.

I replied that we're not really in the market for that sort of material at the moment.

Dropped the orders for the past few days off at the post office at 11 a.m. I've worked out the best time to go there to avoid William. On the way back I passed a group of three elderly women at the market cross discussing whose funerals they're planning to attend this week.

Every day is an education: a young man bought £50 of music books and commented that the music on the radio in the shop was *Hiawatha's Wedding Feast* by Samuel Coleridge-Taylor. Pompously assuming that I knew better, I commented that – as far as I was aware – Longfellow, not Coleridge, had written *The Song of Hiawatha*. He politely informed me that he had, but that Coleridge-Taylor was a composer who was named after Samuel Taylor Coleridge, and that he had set the words to music at the turn of the twentieth century.

Today we had our first contactless payment. I had expected

it to be a young person buying contemporary fiction, but it was a retired man with a beard who bought a book about road-building.

Woman came in with three boxes of books about psychology which she didn't want any money for. I didn't really want the books, and wouldn't have given her any money, but she was so kind that I thanked her and took them.

Spent much of the day packing the random books.

AWB meeting at Craft at 5.30 p.m. Andrew spent much of it challenging Anna about her new job working for the festival in a marketing capacity. He told her that as an American she couldn't possibly understand Wigtown, and that she should expand her 'group of friends'. This is far from unusual: I have no idea why, but Andrew dislikes me, Anna and almost everyone I know, but in a small community there's not much for it other than to smile and nod in silent fury. We briefly discussed the Fire and Light festival. Nobody has had much time to organise anything.

Granny appeared at 7 p.m. and I made her some chicken soup. She had the shadowy appearance of someone who has been unwell and has only just emerged from her sick bed and hasn't made a full recovery. Although it clearly took considerable effort, she still managed to smoke a few cigarettes before retiring to her room to fill the stale air with the sound of rattling coughs.

Till total £194.97
15 customers

THURSDAY, 20 OCTOBER

Online orders: 1
Books found: 1

Sun shining, cloudless sky.

Granny shuffled in at 1 p.m. after a visit to the doctor. Apparently she had a severe case of bronchitis. The doctor asked her if she'd taken any medication, to which she replied, 'Yes, but just cigarettes.' Apparently he gave her a stern rebuke and warned her about the risks of trying to smoke her way out of a chest infection. He wrote on her medical notes, 'Stop smoking!!!!!'

Carried on packing and labelling the random books for this month's mail-out.

Three ABE inquiries for books, all demanding discounts.

The woman who donated the boxes of psychology books came back with three bags of non-academic books, including seven brand new Tintins, all of which will sell quickly.

Granny worked behind the counter while I sorted through boxes.

Till total £162.19
19 customers

FRIDAY, 21 OCTOBER

Online orders: 1
Books found: 1

At 9.30 a.m. Sheila came in to pick up the overseas orders – five to go out, four of them from the Random Book Club. We ship our overseas orders with a local business – Historic Newspapers – which has a contract with a courier. Circumvents the need for customs forms.

Kate the postie mistakenly delivered a letter addressed to a neighbour in this morning's post. As I was taking it to the correct address, I spotted a small gnome on the bench in front of the shop with a card which read, 'Well, you obviously didn't appreciate the veg anyway.'

A woman with very similar hair to mine (I'm sure she'd be furious to be described as such) came to the shop at 10 a.m. and bought a couple of books from the crime section. She introduced herself as Caroline – she's from Vancouver and is running The Open Book.

Man telephoned at 10.30 and asked, 'Hello, is that Anne?' Now, I can understand how a myopic octogenarian can mistake me (from a distance, sitting down and with my back turned) for a woman, but my voice is unmistakably male.

My friend with mental health problems telephoned at eleven o'clock to tell me that he has been sectioned. Drove to Dumfries to see him in the psychiatric unit. The journey took twenty minutes longer than usual because of roadworks and tractors. Picked up 50 g of tobacco, a jar of Carte Noire coffee, some apples, oranges and a £20 voucher for his mobile phone for him. Had to wait ten minutes at an empty desk in reception because the receptionist wasn't there. He was deeply unhappy about the section – chatted to him for about ten minutes then left to look at the book collection in Straiton.

Arrived at Jean's house at 3 p.m. Straiton is a beautiful village high up in the Galloway Hills. She had about 800 books from her late friend's library which she was selling on behalf of his family. The books were mainly modern history with a few other subjects, but in good condition. I offered £450 for them which she thought that the family would consider reasonable. Quite a lot will do for the Random Book Club. They were in boxes in the spare bedroom and in stacks on every step of the stairs. Jean and I loaded the van. It's always a huge relief to have someone who is prepared to give you a hand, whether it's boxing books or shifting them to the van which was so full that I had to put two boxes in the cab to accommodate all of them. Jean is a freelance writer who I really only know because she interviewed me a while ago for a piece she was writing about children's books for a magazine. She's currently working on a book about the ritual stones of Scotland.

Back home at 5.30 p.m.

Callum called around at seven, so Anna came over and ordered a Chinese meal from The Unicorn in Newton Stewart and we all drank wine and caught up. Went to bed at 1 a.m. Anna and Callum stayed up until 3 a.m.

Till total £132
6 customers

SATURDAY, 22 OCTOBER

Online orders: 1
Books found: 1

Granny in at 10.30 a.m. She appears considerably further from her deathbed than she was on Thursday.

As I was unloading the sixty-seven boxes of books from the van, Sarah from Craigard Gallery (three doors up the street) appeared and asked if I could give them a hand shifting a cabinet which they had needed during the festival, and which the marquee people had delivered for them from the County Buildings. It was too big to fit in their car, so I said I'd go round with the van later.

Granny told me that a customer with a young boy (probably eight years old) came in and the boy found an expensive book in the Games section (mainly chess and bridge). He clearly wanted it, but his mother wasn't prepared to pay for it. When they left, she told Granny that every time she gives him his pocket money, he saves it all up and always spends it on books, as though this was something to be condemned rather than encouraged.

Katie, former employee and now doctor, appeared at 1.30 p.m. She, Anna and Carol-Ann went for a walk while Graeme and I wrestled with the heavy and awkward glass cabinet that Sarah had asked us to move earlier. Eventually we managed to get it into the van and down to the County Buildings, where Grace gave us a hand moving it back into the hall.

Till total £204.95
18 customers

SUNDAY, 23 OCTOBER

Online orders: 1
Books found: 1

Opened the shop at 2 p.m. for our AWB Fire and Light Festival, which we had sketchily prepared at the last meeting.

Steve Dowling, local stove maker, came to give a demonstration of his latest stove technology – only Graeme from Craigard Gallery turned up.

Two women with English accents spent ten minutes poring over two massive Victorian Brown's Bibles which were unpriced, and probably destined for the dump. Told them that they were £10 each. One (in tartan leggings) bought the better of the two.

Margie appeared at 4.50 for her talk about the role of fire and light in religion, which had an audience of seven. Not bad, considering the time of year, and how little marketing we did.

Heard geese overhead as I was locking up for the first time since they left in spring.

Till total £45
7 customers

MONDAY, 24 OCTOBER

Online orders: 0
Books found: 0

Opened the shop at 9 a.m. on a beautiful sunny autumn day.

Granny appeared at about 10.30, still coughing, and still smoking. She's moved out of the house and is staying with a friend in Wigtown.

Family of four appeared at noon. A middle-aged man came to the counter and said, 'I called three weeks ago about bringing in some books. We've got them with us.' His son quipped, with a hint of sarcasm, 'Yes, it's only fourteen boxes,' as though I would go weak at the knees at the prospect of having to deal with so many books. He clearly hadn't noticed the sixty-seven boxes behind him from Jean's house in Straiton which I picked up on Friday. He took the sack barrow and brought the boxes in, then piled them inconveniently in a doorway, blocking access to the rest of the shop. I told them to come back in half an hour and I'd go through them. From about 300 books, I managed to pick 60 that were worthy of gracing the shelves: mainly heraldry and regimental histories. Offered them £100 when they returned – the woman (whose father the books had belonged to) was delighted and said that she'd spend the money on treats for her children. When I asked them if they could take the unwanted boxes of books away, they declined and swiftly left the shop.

With the sixty-seven boxes from Jean and now a further fourteen the shop was looking pretty untidy. Granny and I loaded the van with anything we could dump, and I drove to the recycling in Whithorn, only to be told by the officious Yorkshireman at the gates, proudly sporting a fluorescent vest which he had clearly bought himself, that the boxes of books were classed as 'commercial waste' and as such he couldn't take them. If only the bubble-blowing stoner boys had been on duty. Drove back to Wigtown and stopped at The Open Book, where Carolyn, the current resident – the woman from Vancouver – delightedly said that she would be happy to have the twenty or so boxes of books that I'd hoped to divest myself of. I unloaded them just as Bum-Bag Dave arrived and bumbled about the shop.

When we were at the van, I said to Carolyn, 'So, you've met Dave then?', at which she dropped her head, looked disconsolately at the pavement and sighed, 'Yes, every single day since I've been here.'

I cooked a leg of lamb for Granny and Anna.

Till total £201.50
11 customers

TUESDAY, 25 OCTOBER

Online orders: 1
Books found: 1

Another gorgeous sunny day. Granny was late: she was getting her hair cut in Newton Stewart this morning. I told her that I hadn't realised that Margaret Thatcher's hairstyle had come back into fashion. She pointed at me and replied that she was unaware that the homeless look was back in style, then proceeded to give a scathing indictment of everything about my appearance.

Order for a book this morning: *The 6th Battalion Royal Scots Fusiliers 1939–46*, a small, unprepossessing hardback published in 1946. It sold online for £200.

Sandy the tattooed pagan dropped in at 11.40 with a box of books, to add to the sixty-seven other boxes from Jean and the pile on the table from the fourteen brought in yesterday.

Customer (aged about seventy) and his wife came to the counter at 2 p.m. He had two dictionaries – one Brewer and one biographical. As he was paying he told me, 'I'm the sort of person who reads dictionaries.' Just one of the many conversation-killing sentences to which I'm subjected on a daily basis.

Till total £219.27
23 customers

WEDNESDAY, 26 OCTOBER

Online orders: 3
Books found: 3

Opened the shop at 9.05 a.m. Granny appeared at 9.45 a.m. I left her sorting through the sixty-seven boxes of books and headed up to Kilmacolm at 11 a.m. to the address that Emily P-B had given me. Emily is someone with whom I have mutual friends, but I've never met. She is carving out a career helping people with large houses dispose of their contents when they decide to move. The house in this case was a very large eighteenth-century house, and home to Lord Maclay. Arrived as they were sitting down to lunch with Andy, an ex-SAS serviceman who was sweeping the chimneys in the house. Joe (Lord Maclay), Emily, Andy and I sat around the large kitchen table, which was festooned with trays of cold meats, hard-boiled eggs, bread rolls and cheeses. During lunch, Joe asked Andy, 'What's the name of that thing you do, with the wings?' It turns out that Andy has a wingsuit and regularly goes to Switzerland to jump off cliffs and fly through crags and ravines before pulling the cord on his 'chute. Emily had never heard of this activity, so he showed her a terrifying video he'd shot on his GoPro last year. He's the only person I've ever met (that I'm aware of) who has done this.

Both Joe and his wife know Galloway well: a rare thing. Joe told me a story about a time he was shooting at Lochinch, the home of the earl of Stair. The previous incumbent, John Stair, had invited him, and by lunch he'd barely hit a single pheasant. During lunch Joe overheard Lord Stair talking to someone else about his shooting skills. Apparently he'd said, 'I have no idea why he hasn't shot anything; after all, it's just poultry.'

After lunch, Emily and Joe showed me around the enormous house. The books were in various rooms, and at first glance appeared to be far from what I expected from an eighteenth-century country house. Spent a couple of hours looking through them, and picked out about ten boxes' worth – probably less than 5 per cent of the total. Offered him £430 for them, including a Pont map. As I was leaving, Joe spotted my fishing rod in the van and asked me if I was a fisherman. I confirmed that I enjoy salmon fishing and there followed an impassioned conversation. Joe had fished all over the world, but his favourite place was the Falklands, where the sea trout are bounteous and large. He invited me to join his team next year, which I eagerly accepted.

Left at 5 p.m. and got home just before 8 p.m.

Till total £173.95
8 customers

THURSDAY, 27 OCTOBER

Online orders: 1
Books found: 1

Granny in at 11 a.m. She looked me up and down and said, 'Pfft, the *clochard* look again.'

I was showing Granny how to list antiquarian and rare books online – the opaque terminology and things to look for – when a customer brought in three plastic crates of books that had belonged to an elderly friend of his who had died recently. Mainly books published by the BBC based on TV series, which never sell second-hand, and things about the 2012 Olympics. Nothing of interest.

Screaming children came tearing through the shop at three o'clock, followed by exhausted-looking parents.

My mother sent me some old family photographs, including one of my great-grandmother from about 1880.

Till total £288.55
20 customers

FRIDAY, 28 OCTOBER

Online orders: 1
Books found: 0

Mary came in with three boxes of old veterinary books that she'd found in the Community Shop. She looked slightly crestfallen when I told her that they weren't worth anything.

An old man came in at eleven o'clock with four biographies of long-forgotten jockeys. I offered him £1 each for them, to which he replied, 'Is that all? After all the money I've spent buying Maurice Walsh books in here?' I'd never seen him before, and wondered quite how he thought I was morally obliged to pay him for books that I didn't want just because he'd bought books from me that he did want.

Woman wearing what appeared to be pyjamas came to the counter with five books and two OS maps. She started making a fuss about the condition of the dust jacket of a hardback priced at £4.50 and demanding a discount. I tried to explain to her that when I'd priced the book originally I had taken the condition of the jacket into account, and that was why it wasn't £8. She reluctantly coughed up the £4.50 for it, then put the OS maps back on the shelf in what appeared to be some kind of protest.

Till total £97.98
7 customers

SATURDAY, 29 OCTOBER

Online orders: 0
Books found: 0

Slept in – opened the shop at 10 a.m.

Sold two copies of the same book to two different customers: a book called *English Maps: A History*, by Catherine Delano-Smith. They came from Jean's house.

Sold a copy of *Ring of Bright Water*, hardback in a good jacket, to a Northern Irish man for £6.50. Fifteen years ago that would have been a £20 book. Gavin Maxwell, the book's author, grew up near Wigtown, and his books (on the whole) sell well. *Ring of Bright Water* sells better than his other books, probably because it was made into a film in 1969.

Shop started filling up at 2 p.m. but we had barely any sales all day.

Granny turned up at 3.30 and offered to work in the shop for the last hour and a half, by which time everyone had left. Even if there had been any customers, I imagine that her hacking cough would probably have sent them fleeing for fear of catching the bubonic plague, Spanish 'flu and bronchitis.

Till total £222.48
16 customers

MONDAY, 31 OCTOBER

Online orders: 0
Books found: 0

Slept very badly last night – sciatica has returned to my left leg. Hobbled down to open the shop at 9 a.m.

Email this morning from a man who needs to sell his late father's books, 1,500 in total, so that he can put the house on the market. Mix of railway and topography. I replied saying that we'd be interested but would need to see them, and asked roughly what he was expecting to get for them. He told me that he would be happy with £4 per book, which – after an exchange of messages – I estimated would make me a net loss of about £1,500.

Granny in at 11 a.m. She's definitely getting better, but still looks and sounds like someone you'd cross the street to avoid. Arguably, this isn't significantly different from when she's in good health. She didn't respond particularly well to me pointing this out, and – between wheezes and rattling coughs – managed to squeeze out the words, 'You shitty fucking bastard.'

Man came in and asked if he could cut up a tree that Scottish Power had felled on the land at East Kirkland, my father's farm. I told him that he'd need to speak to my father as it's really not within my power to give someone permission for anyone to do anything on anyone else's land, even my father's. He looked fairly confused.

Quiet day in the shop; even the cat looked bored.

Till total £22
3 customers

NOVEMBER

As an advocate for the very widest possible distribution of books,
I am in favour of public libraries. Their existence is in the long
run a benefit to the bookseller. A man may get his taste for books
originally at a public library, and afterwards purchase a library for
himself. The more books the better, the easier access to books the
better. One would draw the line, however, at lending novels free
at the expense of the taxpayer. It is, I suppose, better to read novels
than to read nothing, but the pity of it is that exclusive novel reading
seems to destroy the victim's taste for any other class of literature.

A long-continued spell of novel reading makes its own peculiar
mark on a man's character. His eyes have a dreamy, far-away look,
he takes little interest in passing events, he is comparatively careless
as to the opinions of men and women he meets, he forgets names and
faces, he neglects social duties, and his dearest delight is to lie in bed
all Sunday reading his novel.

R. M. Williamson, *Bits from an Old Bookshop*

Fiction appears to have been something that it has long been
fashionable to sneer at, with the possible exception of Virgil,
Homer, Chaucer, Willie Shakespeare, Walter Scott or Jane
Austen. Following his casual rebuke of the male readers of fiction,
Williamson continues with an assault on female readers:

> If the excessive novel reader be a woman, she neglects her
> home duties, is careless and dowdy in her attire. She is seen
> as regularly at the circulating library as the tippler is at the
> public house. If she be a married woman, pity her husband;
> when she should be dusting the house or cooking his dinner
> she is engrossed with the doings of some lofty Lord with a
> wicked past, who has fallen in love with a lowly but virtuous
> maiden. How can a woman cook her husband's potatoes
> properly when her mind is filled with romance?

In the history of the printed word, fiction probably occupies little
more than a small, dark corner – overshadowed by pompous
theology and biased accounts of history. Even Orwell, a writer

of both fiction and non-fiction, observed in *Bookshop Memories*, that Ethel M. Dell's novels, 'of course, are read solely by women, but by women of all kinds and ages and not, as one might expect, merely by wistful spinsters and the fat wives of tobacconists'. There appears to have been a stodgy myth in the lofty world of literary criticism that fiction was for the feeble-minded. Thankfully, the twentieth century seems to have dispelled that myth, and most of the inky giants of the past hundred years have been those who have penned novels, rather than concordances. Who knows what Williamson or Orwell would have made of Project Gutenberg – a plan to make every work of literature out of print ever published free online to the world. Perhaps they would have approved: a part of me does, but another part wishes that the author and publisher would receive some sort of reward for their effort. How else do words reach the world?

Even so, fiction is still a slow seller in my shop, most likely because it dates more rapidly than any other genre. I've mentioned this in previous books, and I don't wish to deepen this path by treading it again, but fiction is (generally) of its time and, even then, of its immediate time. Farewell, Ethel M. Dell. I suspect that we in the second-hand book trade are the only souls who are aware that you ever wrote best-selling books, or even that you ever lived. Perhaps the wistful spinsters and the fat wives of tobacconists may return and demand that the printing presses once more roll to the tune of your novels on which Orwell poured such scorn. Let's hope that they don't neglect those potatoes, though.

TUESDAY, 1 NOVEMBER

Online orders: 1
Books found: 1

Bob, a retired local farmer, appeared at about 10 a.m. with a box of eggs. Since retiring from cows and sheep, he's maintained his agricultural interest by rearing hens in his garden, and always appears to have more eggs than he can manage, so I end up with a box every week during the laying season. Today's dozen were blue. Not sure what variety of hens squeezed them out.

Order today was for a book called *The History and Social Influence of the Potato*.

A man with a ponytail and wife with crutches (a far from unusual combination) bought eight David Eddings novels.

Carried on sorting through the piles of books all over the shop. Granny had organised three small mountain ranges of books piled across the floor into rejected stock (destined for The Open Book), Random Book Club stock and shop stock. Probably over a thousand books.

A young man with an eyepatch bought a biography of John Wayne (priced at £4) and asked if he could have it for free. I'm not quite sure why. I told him that I'd be prepared to do an exchange for the £5 note I could see poking out of his wallet.

Unloaded the Maclay collection from the van, then filled it with the reject stock from Jean's friend's library and drove it round to Lochancroft, the old warehouse which was full of Emily's canvases and brushes. She'd moved all her artist's equipment back in after Amy had taken the contents of the wine bar out. Spent half an hour moving things around and unloaded twenty-three boxes, which will hopefully go to The Open Book. The life of the second-hand bookseller mainly involves moving boxes from one place to another, and trying to make them fit into a small space, like some sort of awful game of Tetris.

My sectioned friend called from an unfamiliar number and accused me of blocking him on my phone. I haven't, of course. He's still under section, and sounded considerably more unwell than when I last saw him. Promised him that I'd call him in the morning. It's an awful thing to witness a friend – and such a kind, witty person – going through the torment of delusion, mistrust and captivity. What's particularly interesting is that he is so convinced (and convincing in his descriptions) of the narrative going on in his head that I start to question whether it is I who have lost my grip on reality rather than he.

Carolyn, who ran The Open Book last week, dropped by to buy some books. She's staying an extra week in the Glaisnock, a B&B in town. I invited her over for supper with Granny – she's fascinating; she works as a coroner in Vancouver. Granny was incredibly excited to discover this, with her morbid predisposition. Over roast lamb she told us about a case she's working on that involves a twenty-year-old woman who was found dead in her locked room four days earlier with her laptop in one hand and her mobile phone in the other, neither of which had been switched on at the time of her death. She had a friend who her three flatmates described as her 'boyfriend', which is something he denied when interviewed by the police. Granny is working on the case, and already has a number of extremely implausible theories.

Bed at 1 a.m.

Till total £84.50
7 customers

WEDNESDAY, 2 NOVEMBER

Online orders: 1
Books found: 1

Called my sectioned friend back on the number from which he called yesterday. I don't want to compromise our friendship by revealing his name, or for him to feel that I've exploited his situation by writing about it, but I suppose calling him 'my sectioned friend' almost defines him by the section, and he is so much more than that, so I'll call him Pete.

When I telephoned, my call went straight to voicemail so I left a message. Afterwards a charge nurse called me back from the ward he's being detained in. Apparently the phone is a ward phone – he said that he'd tell Pete that I'd called, and he would call me back.

A man in red trousers and one of those expensive tweed jackets only worn by people who believe that Harris is a tweed rather than a Hebridean island, came to the counter and bought two game cookery books. He had a bush of nose-hair, a single one of which appeared to have escaped the rest of the herd and reached almost down to his chin.

Booked a haircut for Friday.

Androgynous-looking customer bought two books about the French Revolution, total £14. They paid with a £20 note and as I was giving them their change I intended to say 'six change' but instead came out with 'sex change'.

Till total £147.99
12 customers

THURSDAY, 3 NOVEMBER

Online orders: 0
Books found: 0

Sheila appeared at 9.10 a.m., to collect the international mail.

A theatre director who appears about four times a year turned up at 11 a.m. She always buys about £100 worth of books from the antiquarian section.

Very cold day, the shop was freezing, even with the heating on. When the wind's from the north, it sucks what little warmth there is in the shop out. Or from the west. Or east, now that I think about it.

Called the mental health ward at 2.30. No reply, so left a message.

Put an offer in with the solicitor on The Red Lion. It's a vast property, and although it needs a good deal of work, it has a decent roof. It would give me very useful storage space for books, and possibly inspire me to start selling online through my own website.

Email from a man who is interested in *The Durbar*, by Dorothy Menpes – a stunning book bound in decorative buckram, limited edition, published by A. & C. Black in 1903. It came from the Kilmacolm collection and is priced at a ridiculously cheap £75. He wants it for £20.

Went to the pub, which has now reopened under Carl, who currently runs the Glaisnock. Burger Ben and Katie have left. Finn and his youngest child, Louis, were there, as was Carolyn from

The Open Book. Granny and I stayed for a couple of pints, then left. The place was heaving, as it always is for a few days after it changes hands and locals emerge from the woodwork out of curiosity, only to discover that little has changed other than that the new owner has employed different staff, who will shortly find themselves unemployed following the two-week surge in curiosity, after which the only customer is an old man nursing a pint for several hours. I once saw the retired bookseller sitting in there for two hours with a glass of tap water.

Till total £270
18 customers

FRIDAY, 4 NOVEMBER

Online orders: 0
Books found: 0

ABE orders have been pitiful for over a week now. I suspect that I may have been suspended again.

At 10 a.m. a man brought in a bag of shooting and fishing books, good titles in decent condition. In the early days I would have been sure of selling these quickly, but nowadays they seem to sit on the shelf gathering dust. Gave him £25 for them.

Sold a book on Scottish cooking to an American woman who, clutching the cash in her hand, insisted on telling me at considerable length that her mother had owned a similar book but had lent it to a friend who hadn't returned it and who denied ever having had it in her possession. She eventually handed over the £6 and wandered off, probably to repeat the story in another shop.

Went for a haircut at one o'clock. I look like Napoleon Dynamite. Then to the dump to drop off the cardboard boxes. Thankfully the security woman didn't spot me. She's got it in for me now that she thinks that I'm dumping 'commercial waste' because I've got a van.

Bum-Bag Dave in at 4.30 p.m. He bought a book on the F-86

Sabre from the aviation section, complained about the price then demanded to know when the bus to Newton Stewart left and – as always – complained bitterly when I told him that I had no idea.

Till total £58.50
4 customers

SATURDAY, 5 NOVEMBER

Online orders: 0
Books found: 0

Spent the day insulating the shed. Granny complained that the shop was freezing, and told me that she'd rather spend the day in the shed once I've finished insulating it. I told her that I'd be much happier if she was there so I didn't have to listen to her incessant moaning.

Till total £153.50
12 customers

MONDAY, 7 NOVEMBER

Online orders: 3
Books found: 2

One of today's orders was for a two-volume set, *The Mineralogy of Scotland* – which came from the house in Glasgow that had belonged to the man who had suffered from dementia. It sold for £500.

Went to Penkiln sawmill to pick up more timber for the shed.

Dropped off twenty boxes of books at The Open Book, which this week is being run by a woman called Lizzie. Compared notes about Bristol, where she lived for three years and I lived for five.

Took down the sign outside the shop directing people to Amy's Wine Bar, which has been up since the festival, and which has encouraged more people to come to the shop than the Bookshop sign. Perhaps I should have left it up.

Till total £73.99
8 customers

TUESDAY, 8 NOVEMBER

Online orders: 1
Books found: 1

Opened the shop just before 9 a.m. Kate, the postie, dropped off the mail shortly afterwards and told me that Captain had followed her all the way up the street. Granny appeared at about ten o'clock and complained that there had been a queue in the Co-op. She's developed a proprietorial sense of ownership over both the Co-op and the Community Shop which only comes with living here for a while. We spend the afternoon processing the books from Kilmacolm.

Peter (Ben Bookshop Band)'s father turned up at 5 p.m. I'd offered him a bed for the night.

Drove to Dumfries to see Pete in the mental health ward, but because I hadn't made an appointment they wouldn't let me see him.

I stayed up until midnight watching the US election coverage. Not looking great. Or looking great, depending on whether you think Trump is a disaster-in-waiting or the swamp-draining saviour of Washington.

Till total £101
6 customers

WEDNESDAY, 9 NOVEMBER

Online orders: 0
Books found: 0

Telephone call from Anna – in tears – at 7 a.m. to say that Trump has won the US presidential election.

Email from the man who's interested in the Menpes copy of *Durbar*. He's now prepared to pay £30, rather than the £20 he initially offered for it. I checked and discovered that the next cheapest copy online is currently £450.

Sandy the tattooed pagan came in to buy some books. He's written another book of short stories. He was keen to take Granny out for lunch, but as always completely forgot her name. 'Seamus, where have you hidden Esmeralda today?'

Till total £49.50
4 customers

THURSDAY, 10 NOVEMBER

Online orders: 3
Books found: 2

Awoke to a message from Carol-Ann to tell me that the gutter above the bothy door is leaking again and she's worried it will flood. Checked when I opened the shop: the downpipe is blocked and everything has backed up. Removed the pipe and cleared the gutter so that it's flowing and won't flood the bothy.

Eliot appeared at 1 p.m. and asked if he could stay for the night. It was good to see him – he's much less stressed outside the festival period.

Went to the pub after closing the shop. We bumped into most of the festival board; Finn, Simon, Edward and George, who were having a post-meeting drink. Came home at 6.30 and cooked for

Granny and Eliot. We all tripped over Eliot's shoes, even Eliot. He had left them between the table and the cooker, precisely the part of the kitchen guaranteed to get the most traffic.

Till total £102.50
10 customers

FRIDAY, 11 NOVEMBER

Online orders: 1
Books found: 1

Opened the shop a bit late. November and December are always a depressing time of year – it's fairly dark all day, and dawn creeps in later by the day. No customers by lunchtime, when Tracy and her cousin Diane arrived. Tracy asked me if they could stay here for a few days. I agreed readily – I welcome the company.

Till total £38
5 customers

SATURDAY, 12 NOVEMBER

Online orders: 0
Books found: 0

Breakfast with Tracy and Diane, then opened the shop – spent the morning tidying up because we had an event upstairs at 2 p.m. Chris Rollie, who works for the RSPB, found the diary of a local man called McHaffie Gordon who lived here about 100 years ago. It's a fascinating document which covers Gordon's natural history observations. Chris has done a superb job of reproducing it, with illustrations. The event was fully booked, and as well attended as any event outside the festival could hope for. I think the real reason for Tracy's visit was to go to Chris's event. They know one another from her time working for the RSPB, the year in which she was employed to work in the visitor centre of the Osprey Room and the same year in which the ospreys decided not to return to Wigtown.

Till total £121.50
8 customers

MONDAY, 14 NOVEMBER

Online orders: 2
Books found: 0

Tracy and Diane left at 9.30. Callum drove them to Ayr.

Granny came in at eleven and spent the day organising the poetry section, complaining about the cold. I put the central heating on a couple of weeks ago, but only for an hour a day. I'll buy Granny a thick coat.

Woman brought in two bags of books, one modern fiction and one full of books about the north-east of Scotland. Gave her £25.

Chris Rollie telephoned in a fluster about copyright library copies of his book about McHaffie Gordon. There are several libraries that are entitled to a free copy of each book published in the UK. The copyright libraries in the British Isles are the British Library, the Bodleian Library, Cambridge University Library, the National Library of Wales, the National Library of Scotland and, although not part of the UK, the library of Trinity College Dublin.

Woman brought in a bag of fifteen M. C. Beaton paperbacks at 3 p.m. Gave her £10 for them. M. C. Beaton is a Scottish writer (and former bookseller) who wrote the wonderful Hamish Macbeth series, and subsequently the Agatha Raisin books, which seem to have cornered the market that Agatha Christie once dominated. I can't think why.

Pete telephoned from hospital at 2.45 p.m. He's desperate to escape from his captivity. I wish I could orchestrate an escape, but it's clear from speaking to him that he still has demons to deal with, and I don't think they're going away any time soon.

Till total £54.50
6 customers

TUESDAY, 15 NOVEMBER

Online orders: 0
Books found: 0

Glorious sunny day. Granny stomped in at 11.15 a.m. in a foul mood, and spent the afternoon sorting the crime section again.

Came downstairs from making a cup of tea (Lady Grey) to find a man actively encouraging his young son to maul a copy of a rare and valuable book about Scottish costume in the antiquarian section: 'Oooh, look at that lovely picture, why don't you see if you can find one of a deer on a hill?' The cross hairs are trained on him.

David Lever, who runs a B&B with his wife in Wigtown, brought in two bags of climbing books, including one signed by Chris Bonington. Gave him £10 for them.

Till total £132.50
7 customers

WEDNESDAY, 16 NOVEMBER

Online orders: 1
Books found: 0

Telephone call this morning: 'What time does the bank open?' How the hell should I know?

Parents appeared at 4 p.m. after tea with their friends the

Pyms. Mother looked shattered. It's the first time she's been out socially since she came out of hospital.

Till total £35.50
3 customers

THURSDAY, 17 NOVEMBER

Online orders: 2
Books found: 1

Regular customer Alan came in at 9 a.m. and bought a dozen old OS maps. He always asks me questions like 'Does this one of Derbyshire have the old railway line that went through Ashover Butts station?'

Couple came in and bought five books. She'd been in twice earlier in the week and had brought her boyfriend because 'When I told him to imagine the best bookshop in the world, and then imagine one better, this is it.' She also described buying second-hand books as being of a similarly charitable nature to rehousing animals from a shelter. I was tempted to try to sell them the shop.

Two customers – a man and a woman – appeared to be having a sniffing competition. The man blew his nose, about five minutes after he'd arrived in the shop, which put him at a temporary disadvantage, but he was back in the game before too long, and the sound of wet snot filled the air once again.

Received a lengthy email inquiring about the condition of a paperback copy of James Robertson's superb book *And the Land Lay Still* which we're selling online for £3.50. I say 'superb book' because after I'd found our copy, I decided to start reading it and was immediately drawn in. I've told the customer that our copy has been sold and have taken it off ABE. I'm keeping it.

Till total £132.50
3 customers

Online orders: 0
Books found: 0

Quiet until noon, when Gerard (natural history book dealer) and Peter, one of his regular customers, appeared. Then a small rush of about six customers, one of whom knocked over a pile of boxes, then sneezed in my face as I was tidying them up. I had to clean my glasses.

Gerard spent £100 on natural history books, Peter £7 on a copy of Doughty's *Arabia Deserta* in fine condition with a dust jacket.

In today's post, a copy of *The Oldie Review of Books*, in which I've taken out an advert for the Random Book Club. Excellent two-page article by Tom Hodgkinson – the editor of *The Idler* magazine – entitled 'Bookselling Is Unpaid Social Work', essentially echoing Orwell's sentiments in *Bookshop Memories*: 'There are always plenty of not quite certifiable lunatics walking the streets, and they tend to gravitate towards bookshops, because a bookshop is one of the few places where you can hang about for a long time without spending any money.' While the language isn't particularly appropriate in today's context, and I hesitate to quote this passage with my old friend Pete banged up because he sees things that nobody else does, Orwell and Hodgkinson are in agreement about the role of bookshops in society.

A customer – a tall man I'd never seen before – told me that he'd had Marlene, the French cyclist, stay with him for a couple of days on her trip through Ireland. I salute her audacity when it comes to asking complete strangers for accommodation and food.

The new boiler appears to have stopped working, so I called the helpline of the company I bought it from. No reply. I suspect that they may have been cashing in on the grants for renewable energy and wound up the business once they dried up. Cold night – worried about pipes freezing. Granny came over to say hello and found me on my back with an arm under the boiler – 'Oh, the lazy fucking bastard finally do some fucking work.'

Till total £240.99
8 customers

Online orders: 2
Books found: 2

Both orders this morning were for books about Napoleon. I wonder how his penis is.

Man with a Bluetooth headset came to the counter as he was in the middle of a telephone call. He put two books about car number plates (£25 total) on the counter, and looking straight at me, said, 'Put your finger in the hole. No, in the hole, there's a little button, you need to push it down. No. The bridesmaids. You drop off the mother of the bride then pick up the bridesmaids.'

Old woman came in waving a £10 book voucher which I'd donated as a raffle prize for some fundraising thing. She came to the counter and told me that she'd won it at the bingo, but that she doesn't read books and could she have the £10 instead. I didn't bother trying to explain to her that if I did that, I'd be losing more money because £10 worth of books in the shop probably cost me £4. She wandered about the shop muttering, 'What's a £10 book worth?' I finally resolved the situation by asking her to find someone she knows who likes reading, finding out what they like to read, then coming back and that I would help her find £10 worth of books to suit that person.

Drove to Dumfries to pick up Anna. In her capacity as Cultural Tourism Development Officer for the book festival company, she's organised a creative writing course next week, to be run in the house. Jason and Twigger are running it. She's managed to find four people to take the course. It feels strange to see so much of her, particularly since we're no longer in a relationship, and haven't been for some time. I understand her emotional attachment to Wigtown, but I don't think I would have stayed around if I'd been in her situation.

Spent the evening trying to get the boiler working in the freezing cold. No luck. Hopefully I can find someone to repair it before everything freezes.

Till total £339
17 customers

SUNDAY, 20 NOVEMBER

Online orders: 0
Books found: 0

Spent the morning trying to fix the boiler, then drove Granny to Lockerbie to catch the train to Edinburgh. She's flying to Italy tomorrow morning for a week.

Got back to find Twigger and Jason in the kitchen chatting to Anna. Went to the pub for supper with them and the four people who are taking the course. One of them is a middle-aged woman with dyed blue hair which I suspect she thinks makes her look interesting.

MONDAY, 21 NOVEMBER

Online orders: 1
Books found: 1

Jason was up and about when I got up at 8 a.m. No sign of Twigger.

Freezing cold day made worse in the shop because the boiler still isn't working.

Telephone call from someone with a book collection to sell. After a few minutes of trying to establish subject and quantity, and making a vague arrangement for me to come and look at them, she asked me my name. I told her it is Shaun.

She replied, 'So is that spelled S H U N?'

It might as well be.

Lit the stove in the drawing room at 8.50 a.m.; course started at 9.45. It was warm enough to remove a coat, but not a jumper, by the time everyone arrived.

The woman with the dyed blue hair arrived at 9.30, as Jason and I were setting up tables, pencils etc., and demanded coffee. Apparently she 'can't function' without it, which makes me wonder how on earth she managed to get dressed and drive here.

Anna appeared at 9.35, closely followed by Adrian, one of the people on the course, who told me that the thermometer in his car had read minus four at its lowest on his journey over here from Portpatrick. The shop can scarcely be any warmer.

Phoned the company about the boiler. Very cold last night – concerned about pipes freezing in the loft of the bothy, as well as the comfort of the people doing the course.

Callum turned up with ten bags of logs which may prove very useful if I can't get the boiler repaired. Granny had told him that it was freezing in the shop, and he kindly dropped them off. He told me that the elderly woman who used to live two doors down the street from the shop has died. Pickings are rich for the Grim Reaper at this time of year.

Spent the day labelling and processing the random books. As I was sticking the labels onto a pile of parcels I happened to look out of the window onto the street, and noticed that large numbers of locals in dark suits were passing. Janette came in later to clean the shop and told me that it was the funeral of the woman who lived a couple of houses away. There's something quite sobering – and unusual – about seeing hundreds of people, formally dressed in black, walking down the street on a cold November day.

The writing course seemed to go well. Twigger and Jason were happy, and nobody got frostbite. They all went to The Open Book for supper, cooked by Anna (who's staying there), which is about as far removed from a treat as it's possible to imagine. Apart from a meal cooked by Granny.

At five o'clock the postman came and collected the random books (seven bags).

Till total £51.98
4 customers

TUESDAY 22 NOVEMBER

Online orders: 1
Books found: 1

Cold day, but not nearly as miserable as yesterday. Still, there was ice on the pond, and a heavy frost on the lawn. Lit the fire and the gas space heater in the big room. The woman with the dyed blue hair arrived fifteen minutes early and demanded coffee, again.

Adrian arrived five minutes late and told me that it was minus five in Kirkcowan when he was driving over. Kirkcowan is the highest – and consequently the coldest – point on his journey.

Callum in at 10 a.m. for a cup of tea. He and Twigger know each other fairly well – we've all been hillwalking together – so they caught up over a cup of tea in the kitchen.

Peter Thomson, who has a haulage business locally, arrived at four o'clock to check out the hopper for the new boiler. I'm sick of lugging sacks of pallets, so I'm hoping that Peter can blast them from his lorry into the hopper. Quite a bit of teeth-sucking, but he reckons he can manage it.

Two customers left the shop at 4.30 p.m. after spending just five minutes browsing, complaining about the cold.

Phone call from Vincent, who has found a car for Anna. It's a Honda Jazz and will doubtless be on its last legs. Will call the insurance company and put it on my policy tomorrow, as it is prohibitively expensive for Anna to insure a vehicle.

Boiler engineer finally came round, after numerous calls and emails to their office in which their replies suggested that the problem was down to my incompetence in operating the cursed machine. He finally conceded that a part of the ignition system had failed and needed to be replaced. Apparently the part needs to come from Austria and will cost several hundred pounds. When I told him that I'd only bought the boiler from him a year ago and that it was still under guarantee, he said that labour costs weren't covered.

Stayed up late with Twigger (Jason wisely went to bed at eleven). Chris with the dyed hair has been complaining about the cold in the house. Not much I can do other than light all the fires, since the central heating is still down.

Till total £36.49
4 customers

WEDNESDAY 23 NOVEMBER

Online orders: 2
Books found: 2

Ice on the pond again this morning, and on the inside of the kitchen windows.

Clear, sunny day. When it's like this, the low winter sun pours into the big room, so hopefully it will warm up and Chris with the dyed blue hair won't complain too much. Lit the fire and the gas space heater anyway, just to be on the safe side.

Blue-haired Chris from the course arrived early (9.15 a.m.), and as she marched officiously through the shop stopped and demanded, 'Is there any proper coffee upstairs?' clearly expecting – and hoping for – the answer to be 'no' so that she could add this to her litany of complaints. I had expected that this might happen, so I'd made a pot of filter coffee. When I told her that, yes, there was proper coffee upstairs, she looked bitterly disappointed.

Adrian arrived at 9.30 and told me that it was a balmy minus two in Kirkcowan. The two other people on the course – Ryan, an American firefighter who jumps out of planes to control wildfires, and Erich (German) – appeared a minute or so later. Callum was shortly behind them to finish insulating the shed.

Lit the fire in the shop to offer at least one warm corner for the handful of customers who dare to venture into Wigtown at this time of year.

Jeff Mead, minister of Kirkinner church, appeared at 10 a.m. and bought a book of Rupert Brooke's poetry. As he was paying, he told me that he'd found a poem within it that he hadn't read before;

one in which Brooke rages against God. He told me that it struck a chord with him.

Telephoned the insurance company at 11.30 and added the Honda Jazz to my policy for the sum of £390.

At 12.50 p.m. – the undoubted highlight of my week so far – had an argument with a cold caller about who my electricity supplier is. After about thirty seconds he ended the call with, 'Just fuck off, you bloody bastard,' then hung up.

Sandy the tattooed pagan came in this morning and browsed for a while in the Scottish room, but it was so cold in there without any heating that he gave up more quickly than usual and went off to cut wood for walking sticks after buying three books.

Supper with Twigger, Jason and Anna.

Till total £33.50
5 customers

THURSDAY 24 NOVEMBER

Online orders: 1
Books found: 1

Today's order was for a mountaineering book that Twigger had been talking about last night over supper. I sometimes wonder if there's someone listening in on us.

Adrian was the first of the writing group to arrive this morning, at 9.23 a.m. Apparently it was minus six in Kirkcowan on his way here. We all had tea in the kitchen – I could see everyone's breath.

Received the following inquiry for a copy of *Through Broadland in a Breydon Punt* (£75): 'Hello – could you possibly provide me with a photo or two of this copy? You describe its condition as "acceptable", but my experience has been that Scottish booksellers are honest to the point of severity in their descriptions, whereas English ones are often laughably optimistic in theirs.' I sent him two photographs of the book.

Parents dropped in at noon, mother looking tired with lipstick all over her teeth (as usual). They were off to Tarff Valley (agricultural stores) to buy birdseed.

Jason and Anna spent the afternoon cooking for a thanksgiving dinner. Ryan, Adrian, Erich, Twigger, Jason, Anna and I sat down around the table I bought from Isabel for the first meal eaten on it since I bought it in September. Mercifully, Jason took charge of the cooking.

Till total £97
8 customers

FRIDAY 25 NOVEMBER

Online orders: 1
Books found: 1

Order today was for the book the customer had emailed about yesterday: *Through Broadland in a Breydon Punt*. He ordered it and sent me a charming email about what good value the book is, and giving a potted biography of the author, Arthur Henry Patterson, a self-taught naturalist who spent much of his life exploring and documenting the natural history of Norfolk, particularly the Broads.

Black Friday – the day on which retail supposedly has its biggest takings before Christmas. By noon we hadn't seen a single customer.

The boiler company emailed about the faulty part. It's going to take two more weeks to arrive.

Man came in at 1 p.m. and told me that his blind friend had been in a shop in town yesterday and seen some candlesticks for sale but couldn't remember which shop. Quite how a blind man saw candlesticks is nothing short of miraculous.

Twigger and Jason left at 1.30 p.m. after lunch. They both live in Dorset, so shared a lift up, and home. I think the week went well, although there will unquestionably be complaints from one of the participants, and not just about the coffee.

Slim German woman arrived at two o'clock with six bags of

books, mainly about homoeopathy, dogs and acupuncture. It turns out that we have mutual friends, and that she specialises in treating people with bad backs, so I managed to convince her to do an acupressure session, although I'm not entirely convinced of its efficacy.

Bought an iPad for my father, as his seems, according to my mother, to have reached 'terminal velocity'.

Went to the switching on of the Wigtown Christmas lights. Petra's daughters did the honours – they all flew back from Austria for the occasion.

Till total £28.99
2 customers

SATURDAY 26 NOVEMBER

Online orders: 3
Books found: 3

Day 8 with no heating or hot water. I'm now entirely dependent on whisky for warmth and Tesco Value Baby Wipes for sanitation. I smell like a drunk baby.

Email from Kerri at the boiler company telling me that, even though they can replace the faulty part for free, I'll have to pay for the labour. Her father had told me that it would be in the region of £200.

Woman brought in a box of books, mainly encyclopaedias and that sort of thing, but there was one biography of Beethoven with very unusual wooden boards. I gave her £10 for it.

At 10 a.m. Erich and Ryan from the writing course appeared. Erich is going back to Germany and asked for directions that wouldn't take him back to Glasgow airport on the same route by which he arrived – a single-track road over the hills, in darkness and sub-zero temperatures. Checked online and the Stranraer road is currently closed, so I gave him directions to go via Dumfries. It's probably the longest route, but also the one least like the road in *An American Werewolf in London*.

Found a copy of Twigger's *Big Snake* in a box of books, next to a copy of a book about enemas.

Till total £279.47
19 customers

MONDAY 28 NOVEMBER

Online orders: 2
Books found: 2

One of today's orders was for a Folio box set of P. G. Wodehouse: £65 in the shop, £120 online. It still baffles me that people think that everything is cheaper online. If you're as incompetent as I am, it's more than likely that things will be cheaper in the shop, and there's no postage to pay.

Latest dull boiler news – the engineer will be here on Thursday, hopefully. The defective part will be replaced for free, but I have to pay the cost of fitting it, which has risen to £280. Oh, and I also have to pay the costs of the man who sold me the boiler with the faulty part coming out to tell me that the boiler has stopped working because he sold me a boiler with a faulty part.

Ryan from the writing course appeared at 9.30 to say goodbye before heading back to Glasgow to catch his flight home to America. He's keen to buy a house in Wigtown.

Emailed the boiler company twice. This is the tenth day without heating or hot water. Eventually they replied to tell me that the faulty part will be replaced for free, but with Rob the knob's call-out and the additional costs it now appears that it will cost me £336 to get a boiler that cost a fortune to finally heat the water and the house.

Man with beard and duffel coat appeared at 10 a.m. and produced a list with a lot of numbers – he was a Penguin collector, and even though we probably have more Penguins than any bookshop in Scotland, he tutted and asked, 'Is that all of them?' when he paid for the thirteen he bought (£25).

Granny appeared at lunchtime, dressed in a camel overcoat and a black trilby. She's back from her trip to Italy and for some reason has decided to dress like a private detective from a cheap 1950s film.

Called Trading Standards about the boiler company. Case log 13986123.

Till total £146
8 customers

TUESDAY 29 NOVEMBER

Online orders: 2
Books found: 0

Sold the Beethoven biography with the wooden boards for £18 to Mole-Man, who seems to have developed an interest in classical music.

Sandy the tattooed pagan dropped off a pile of sticks. I was upstairs making a sandwich when he arrived and was – as is often the case – alerted to his presence by a shout of 'Seamus! Where are you?' from the bottom of the stairs.

Granny covered the shop for the afternoon while I tidied up the garden before winter fully sets in. Cut back the buddleia and took the dead flowers out.

A woman came in wearing muddy wellies and asked if I'd like to buy copies of a book which she has produced: *300 Farmers of Scotland*. Took ten copies. Local customers will buy it as Christmas presents.

Email from a woman in Canada who found a set of *The Complete Works of Gerrard Winstanley* that we're selling on ABE, and asked me to put it aside until she can scrape the cash together for it. I removed it from the website so that nobody else can buy it. Probably won't hear from her again.

Till total £46.50
6 customers

WEDNESDAY 30 NOVEMBER

Online orders: 1
Books found: 1

Norrie appeared at 9.30 a.m. to let me know that he's starting work
on 11 North Main Street – a property which my parents own and
which, for the past fifteen years has been home to Historic Newspapers, a business that has the world's largest archive of old newspapers. The enterprise has expanded, and they've recently built a
warehouse in Bladnoch on the site of the old creamery. The festival
company has – after much wrangling – taken on the lease of the
vacant property at Number 11.

Telephone call from a woman in Somerset who ordered three
copies of *Tripe Advisor*, a book that I produced a few years ago with
spoof reviews of the shop submitted by Facebook followers. Shortly
afterwards a woman came in looking for signed S. R. Crockett
novels. Crockett was a local author who wrote historical fiction set
largely in Galloway. He lived here in the late nineteenth century
and his first editions were limited in number, and all signed. To
my surprise, I have come across very few of them, but we had a
copy of *The Grey Man*, at £85. She bought it. So, despite only three
people entering the shop all day, four people's Christmas presents
were bought from us.

Till total £126.50
2 customers

DECEMBER

A home is a sacred place; the pictures on the walls may not be of much monetary value, but they are hallowed by the memories of those dear ones who placed them there; the books may be old and shabby, they may not be first editions, but were they not treasured and read and re-read by our fathers? Every little knick-knack in a home twines itself around one's heart as one remembers some incident which connects it with the past.

The pleasure derived from collecting books is a pleasure that never palls; a joy for ever. Once a lover always a lover, is a true saying when applied to a lover of books. As old age draws near, the man who has found his delight in athletic sports is unable to indulge his taste, but the lover of books can find a solace and joy in the companionship of his silent friends which increase as the years go round.

R. M. Williamson, *Bits from an Old Bookshop*

Williamson, like most second-hand booksellers, was clearly aware of both the vital importance of living book collectors, and the uncomfortable element of buying back the books of the dead to whom he had sold books. Sentimentality seems to be the preserve of the living, when it comes to objects. It appears to belong exclusively to things that the living have acquired. Rarely, when clearing a house, do I encounter a son or daughter who cares much for the shabby old objects, or who feels that a knick-knack twines itself around their heart when they're desperate to sell the house of an aged (or dead) parent. The knick-knacks and books which they have bought, however, they prize far more highly than a grandfather's medal for service in the Boer War or a vase that was given as a wedding present to their parents by someone with whom one of them may have been having an affair.

It saddens me greatly when I'm clearing a house to see things that have obviously been of great importance to the former residents being so casually consigned to the rubbish bin, and it is so often black-and-white photographs of people who clearly meant a great deal to those who have died – or moved out – and took the trouble to frame the photographs. It never fails to make me think of Dylan Thomas: 'Only you can see in the blinded bedrooms, the combs and petticoats over the chairs, the jugs and basins, the glasses of teeth, Thou Shalt Not on the wall, and the yellowing, dickybird-watching pictures of the dead.'

Williamson is unquestionably correct, though, that a passion for books will last as long as your eyesight and your mind permit, while your love of pole-vaulting may not be quite so long-lived.

THURSDAY, I DECEMBER

Online orders: 2
Books found: 2

Anna left for Edinburgh in her new car, the Honda Jazz. Andrew from Beltie Books dropped in to extract £40 for next year's booktown brochure as Anna was leaving. I overheard her wish him a breezy 'good morning' which he completely ignored.

Callum called in at 9.30 to have a look at the back of Lochancroft, a property which I'm thinking of converting into a holiday let. Apparently it needs quite a lot of work. He has also offered to tidy up the area where the new boiler is.

George, the boiler engineer, appeared at ten o'clock and performed a repair that immediately tripped the main fuse for the shop and plunged everything into darkness for several hours so, as well as no heat, we also had no light or sound for most of the day. It's a good job that the boiler can't take away the sense of smell and touch, or there would be nothing left.

Till total £29.50
3 customers

FRIDAY, 2 DECEMBER

Online orders: 2
Books found: 1

Five minutes late opening the shop this morning. Callum was hammering and sawing out the back when I opened.

Man who looked like a fat Des Lynam brought in a box of Folio books, all in slip cases and in good condition. Sticking out of each one was a piece of paper with a price that he had decided was accurate from looking the titles up on ABE. This is never a good sign. I offered him £20 for them – about a quarter of the total that he'd totted up. Eventually we agreed on £25.

Local antique dealer Hugh appeared at lunchtime and asked if I'd bought any paintings recently, as he always does when he appears. I'm never quite sure with Hugh whether he knows a great deal about art or practically nothing. He talks a good game though.

I was writing a letter to a friend in the shop when a customer leaned over and commented, 'You've got lovely handwriting.' She started reading it out loud for anyone within earshot to hear. I'm struggling to decide what's worse – customers, or no customers at all.

Old woman brought in a carrier bag of mint paperback crime fiction, all by Carola Dunn, a writer I had never heard of. Gave her £10 for them. She's the same woman who last week brought in a set of M. C. Beaton Hamish Macbeth novels.

Till total £17
4 customers

SATURDAY, 3 DECEMBER

Online orders: 0
Books found: 0

Callum was busy out the back when I opened the shop. Isabel came in at noon and interrogated me about various invoices and expenses, as usual.

At 2 p.m. customer telephoned to order a book he'd found on ABE. He asked if we could waive the ABE commission because he was buying directly.

Carol-Ann came in at lunchtime to put a wash on. The bothy doesn't have a washing machine, so she has to use mine. It has – on more than one occasion – caused a problem with girlfriends who have discovered other ladies' undergarments left in the drum.

Customer wandered around the shop and eventually came to the counter, where I was listing books, and said, 'Oh, I didn't see you in the corner there.' Splendid. The wall of books is my cloak of invisibility.

Drove to a house in Auldgirth, near Dumfries, to conduct a probate valuation on a deceased estate. Granny covered the shop for the last hour. I left at 4 p.m. as the executor – the son of the late owner of the books – works in Edinburgh and could only get away on Saturday afternoon. Arrived at the cottage in darkness at 5.30 to find him boxing up the contents of the kitchen. He was about my age, possibly a few years older. The books were in the sitting room and spare bedroom, and the house was freezing cold – his father had died in July and they were only just getting round to winding up the estate. The heating, understandably, hadn't been on for months. Interesting collection of books, largely on art and photography. Gave a probate valuation of £300.

Left the cottage in Auldgirth at seven o'clock and headed home.

Till total £33.50
6 customers

MONDAY, 5 DECEMBER

Online orders: 0
Books found: 0

Callum arrived at 9 a.m. and began his morning ritual of hammering and drilling.

Granny in at 12.45 p.m. She was tidying up the art section and managed to drop a book on her foot. The ensuing barrage of cursing and swearing would have been enough to embarrass even the roughest of sailors. Unfortunately, one of the few customers in the shop at the time happened to be browsing in the archaeology section, which is next to the art section.

Called Midpark Hospital – the psychiatric unit – to make an appointment to see Pete.

Drove to Newton Stewart to pick up some screws for Callum. Noticed that the van is warning me that the engine is low on oil.

Came back to find a customer waiting at the counter with a three-volume set of J. G. Millais's *The Mammals of Great Britain and Ireland* (1904): 'Eeeh, this book is priced at £300. Can you do a deal on it?'

Yes, of course. How about £400 and you take me out to lunch?

Plugged my mobile phone in to charge after supper and noticed that it's not charging. Only 20 per cent power left.

Till total £12.50
2 customers

TUESDAY, 6 DECEMBER

Online orders: 0
Books found: 0

Email from an antique dealer in Dumfries with 2,000 books to sell. Photos attached – mainly Ian Rankin, Jeffrey Archer, Robert Ludlum paperbacks. I replied to say that we can't accommodate them.

Callum in at 9 a.m. This morning's symphony was largely a hammer drill with circular saw accompaniment.

Drove to Dumfries after lunch. Mary covered for the afternoon. She was clutching a large yellow teddy bear under her arm. She instantly spotted my look of concern and assured me that 'It's not for me, it's for the dog.'

Went to the post office in Dumfries to pay my vehicle tax. Long queue. The woman at the counter spotted my address on the form and said, 'Oh, I've been in your shop.' She then went on, at some length, to tell me about a holiday she'd spent in Bladnoch, much to the visible frustration of the ever-lengthening queue behind me.

From the post office I headed to Midpark Hospital to see Pete. Had to get through three sets of locked doors to get to Balcary, the secure ward, where I was left in a meeting room while they found him. The nurse told me that he would be with me shortly, once he'd finished his cigarette, which took about fifteen minutes. I'd forgotten to bring a book, as I hadn't antici- pated a wait, so I paced around looking for something to read. Found a cork board with lots of graphs on it containing informa- tion about the average length of stay in the ward, the number of violent incidents per week, that sort of thing. Curiously, there were some dramatic spikes in the latter, most of which had notes explaining that of the forty incidents that week, thirty-nine of them had been down to one dementia patient. I really wished that I'd brought a book.

Pete, sadly, was not as well as when I last saw him, in part because of his increased medication, but his mental health has certainly not improved either. He looked tense and frustrated. He told me that he has fallen in love with another patient but she has now been moved to a different ward. He also told me that he has an invisible daughter who he can't see but his girlfriend can. It breaks my heart, all of this.

Several years ago when he was sectioned, I remember talking to my mother about him. She told me that she was concerned at how terrible it was for his parents to have such a son. We had an argument. I asked her to imagine what it was like for Pete to be locked in a mind in which his reality was so vivid, so real and so clear, while everyone around him was telling him that he was in the throes of a psychotic delusion – that everything he thought and saw were no more than symptoms of an illness which he, of course, couldn't see. Then to be locked up in an institution and forced to take medication that he didn't want to take, and isolated in a room until a complete stranger had decided that he's well enough to be allowed back home. Yes, it must have been awful for his parents, and for everyone who cared about him, but nobody could possibly imagine how terrible it was – and is once more – for him.

Whenever he finds himself in trouble, I think of how few rods and cones – the visual receptors in our eyes – we have as human beings compared with other species, and wonder what they can see that we can't. Perhaps Pete, as Aldous Huxley suggested in *The Doors of Perception*, can see the world as 'if the doors of perception were cleansed', everything would appear to man as it is: Infinite. For man has closed himself up, till he sees all things thro' narrow chinks of his cavern.'

After I'd said goodbye, I went back into Dumfries and found a mobile phone repair shop. Gave the man my telephone and explained the problem. He told me to come back in twenty minutes, so I went to Debenhams and W. H. Smith and did some Christmas shopping. Twenty minutes later I returned to the shop to find my phone charging and working again, for the princely sum of £20. Apparently there was a bent pin in the charging dock, which he'd cleaned and repaired.

Home at 9 p.m.

Till total £25
3 customers

WEDNESDAY, 7 DECEMBER

Online orders: 0
Books found: 0

Callum in at 10 a.m. today. He had to pick up some timber from the sawmill.

By noon, the only person who had been in the shop was a young man carrying a backpack with a chainsaw sticking out of it, who didn't buy anything. I was tempted to ask him if he wanted to give Callum a hand.

Pete's father came to the shop at about eleven o'clock. We discussed his condition. Very difficult for him as his wife has dementia and he can't leave the house for long, so there's no way he can get to Dumfries to see his son.

Bob (blue eggs) dropped in at lunchtime and ordered two books as Christmas presents.

Sandy the tattooed pagan came in at noon. He brought a box of books, fairly good local history, but not valuable. Gave him £16 credit: 'Seamus, is that really the best you can do for your old pal Sandy?' Yes.

Man asked where our 'section on medieval Spanish cities' was, then wandered around the shop with his elbow bent, and forearm parallel to the ground, all fingers outstretched, as though he was about to execute a karate move. He spent £70 on books, mainly about Greek architecture.

Email from the woman in Canada who had asked me to put *The Complete Works of Gerrard Winstanley* aside for her last month until she could scrape the £158 together for it (I reduced it from £200 for her). Among other things, the email shared her opinions on Scottish independence, Brexit, the benefits of oats to the development of the brain and the fact that she owns neither a telephone nor a television (perhaps she has a problem with classical Greek prefixes). She also told me that in order to raise the money for the books she's had to forfeit Christmas and apply to the food bank for a hamper to see her to the end of the month.

Till total £261
4 customers

THURSDAY, 8 DECEMBER

Online orders: 2
Books found: 2

Callum in at 10 a.m. Anna appeared at eleven with a young bearded man – her new assistant, Harvey. He's a local man who grew up on a farm near Wigtown. It turns out that I crashed my first car into a drystane dyke just outside his farmhouse on my way to work on the gas pipeline in 1994. They had a meeting in the kitchen for an hour, then she left for Edinburgh, where she now lives, although she spends a great deal of time in Wigtown.

One of the orders today was for a copy of *La vida breve*, £100, sold to the Acquisitions Department of the National Library of Scotland. I'm not sure why, but I appear to have four copies of it, and it's a limited edition of 500. As I was taking it over to the post office, I walked across a bit of road which the council has decided to resurface even though there appeared to be nothing wrong with it. Six men were standing chatting in their fluorescent jackets and happily watched me walking over a bit of smoking tarmac over which a steamroller was casually passing back and forth. I noticed my feet getting considerably warmer. On the way back one of them redirected me, avoiding the smoking road. Got back to the shop and went upstairs to make a cup of tea. On the way back downstairs I noticed jet-black footprints on every step of the stairs.

In Lord Maclay's books I discovered a copy of *The Book of the Old Edinburgh Club*, volume XXVI, with a bookplate presenting it to the Secretary of State for Scotland in 1960. I thought I ought to find out who exactly held that office. It was Lord Maclay.

Two telephone orders for *The Birds of Wigtownshire*, both from Aberdeen. Must have been something in the newspaper up there. I'm astonished at how quickly the book has sold – Chris asked me to publish it under my Picto imprint, purely because I have ISBNs. He did all the hard work. We only published 500 copies, and they're almost all gone.

Till total £39
6 customers

FRIDAY, 9 DECEMBER

Online orders: 1
Books found: 1

Order for a book about Arthurian legend. In the locator code box on Monsoon, our database, Nicky's notes read, 'Ancient History, top shelf, where the Bibles should be kept.'

Callum in at 9 a.m.

First customer was a man with a beret, an open shirt and a big gold crucifix. He complained that we only have three Baedeker guides. These are guidebooks (usually red cloth covers, and pocket-sized) produced in the late nineteenth century. They were extremely collectable when I bought the shop, but seem to have gone slightly out of fashion.

My father called at 1 p.m. to tell me that my mother has been taken into hospital again, this time with a hernia. Apparently she's OK, but they're going to clear her system out then operate in the next few days.

Woman from Aberdeen came in and talked at considerable length about the charity she works for, which ships textbooks to developing countries. She wanted to know if we had any old textbooks that we could donate. I wonder quite how people think book businesses work: that we like to keep a stock of things which we can't sell, just in case a charity might chance to call by and take them off our hands? She brought in a bag of climbing books. Gave her £10 for them.

Isabel in at 3 p.m., with the customary berating of the state of my finances.

Till total £83
6 customers

Online orders: 2
Books found: 0

Sunny morning. Callum in at 9.15 a.m.

Opened the shop to find a massive, sloppy dogshit on the doorstep.

It was a quiet morning, but in the afternoon the shop filled with young women, who spent several hours picking over books and chatting. I think they may have been students from Stranraer Academy on a day out.

A man with a red woollen hat asked, 'Where do you keep your mindset books?' Despite considerable further interrogation, I was completely unaware of what he was looking for.

Two young Irish women bought books and prints and asked interesting questions about the history and architecture of the shop, so I showed them the upstairs. One of them is teaching at St Ninian's primary school in Newton Stewart; the other was her friend, who's visiting for the weekend. Whenever people show an interest in the history or architecture of the building, I give them a brief tour. It's one of the most interesting and attractive properties in the town. At least, I think it is.

At 4.10, as I was putting books out, a young man, probably about twenty-five years old, pointed from the stairs through the open door into the cellar and said, 'Hardy salmon reel, nice.' We spent the next ten minutes talking about fishing.

My father called at five o'clock to tell me that my mother is back home, and they've decided to give her some sort of truss to stop the hernia from causing problems again, but they didn't have any in the hospital, so they're going to send one out next week. He's not too happy with the situation. Apparently they're planning to operate in about five weeks.

Went to Christopher (Ciff) and Amy J-S (wine bar Amy), near Whithorn, for drinks after work; home at 11 p.m.

Till total £216.49
13 customers

MONDAY, 12 DECEMBER

Online orders: 2
Books found: 1

Callum in at 9 a.m. The delicate sound of thundering drilling followed shortly.

Customer spotted Captain and said, 'Bloody hell, that's a big cat!' Might be time for trench rations.

Out of nothing more than boredom, I made a Ghostbusters blackboard.

Cut back the buddleia in the garden yesterday. It took two trips to the dump in Newton Stewart to get rid of it. Dropped in on my parents after the second of them, but they weren't there, so I called my father to make sure that everything was OK.

My father telephoned at 9 p.m. to tell me that my mother has been admitted to hospital again – apparently the hernia ruptured again last night and she had to be taken to Dumfries by ambulance.

Finished James Robertson's *And the Land Lay Still* in front of the fire after I shut the shop. I fear that I am so pathetically impressionable that I adore every book I read, but I'm in no doubt that this is a fine book, and one to which I will return.

Till total £60
5 customers

TUESDAY, 13 DECEMBER

Online orders: 1
Books found: 1

Granny opened the shop, and I worked in the garden, clearing fallen leaves and tidying up the dead plants. The light was still fairly dim at 9 a.m., when Callum arrived. His opening arpeggio was the solitary wail of an angle grinder, whose name – I believe – is Makita.

At 10 a.m. my father telephoned to say that my mother is fine, and will be home in the afternoon. Called Lulu and Vix, my sisters, to let them know.

Jim McMaster, a bookseller I've known since I entered the business, appeared at one o'clock. We had our usual chat about the state of the second-hand book industry, and the rogues and others who inhabit it – who's died, who's still alive. He was about to leave empty-handed, so I showed him the four craft bindings which I'd bought from a house in Gatehouse earlier in the year – illustrated works of fiction from the early twentieth century which had been privately rebound in half-morocco with beautiful gilt tooling in limited editions of 1,000. He bought them all, along with a copy of *Leaves of Grass* in a similarly attractive binding for £150. They'll sell well at a book fair. Such things are hard to sell outside the trade as most customers don't appreciate the craft of binding.

Closed the shop, and Granny and I took the bus to Sorbie, where we had a delicious meal in The Pheasant. Swifty gave us a lift home in his taxi. I think Granny was keen to go there as a customer rather than a member of staff.

Till total £44.40
4 customers

WEDNESDAY, 14 DECEMBER

Online orders: 2
Books found: 1

Packed the Joseph Thomson book with the manuscript letters to Joseph Hooker and sent it to Lyon & Turnbull in Edinburgh for inclusion in their next sale.

Callum in at 9 a.m. Made us both a cup of tea and caught up before the first customer appeared at 11.35.

Telephone call from a woman looking for two copies of Jack Gordon's *Birds of Wigtownshire*. Apparently she is married to Gordon's grandson.

Spent the morning picking and listing books for Scot:Lands, an event that Eliot has organised in Edinburgh on New Year's Day, and which he's roped me into to represent the booksellers of Wigtown.

Ian Thin, who used to be the local vet, died recently. I had no idea until today when one of his children called in to see whether I wanted to buy his library. Told them that I would be interested.

Sandy the tattooed pagan and his friend Lizzie were in, as was James from the pub, with a young woman who I imagine is his girlfriend. James was in charge of the bar under French Ben and German Katie, and has continued now that Carl has taken over.

Delivery of a box of Italian food at 3 p.m. for Granny. She's threatened to cook tomorrow night. We went to a whisky cocktail evening at Craft after the shop closed. Granny managed to spill most of her cocktail on her skirt and blamed it on me for being a 'fucking bastard' even though I was about three seats away from her.

Till total £61
5 customers

THURSDAY, 15 DECEMBER

Online orders: 0
Books found: 0

Message on Facebook inquiring about a copy of Ivor Cutler's *Fremsley*, which we have priced at £20. I wonder whether Facebook is a good way of selling books, but I'm not entirely convinced that Zuckerberg has any more moral fibre than Bezos.

Decided to start a Spoonerism competition instead of making a Christmas video for the shop. I don't really have the time: started the ball rolling with West Bank.

Wrote to my graphic designer friend Luise to ask her to come up with some designs for merchandise. Not much else happening at this time of year.

Customer came to the shop with her husband; she came to the counter and slipped me a note which read, 'Do you have the 2014 edition of *Bradbury's Hallmarks*? It's a present for him.' We didn't, and it was a pretty long shot by any measure.

Carol-Ann appeared at 2.30 and told me that she'd left the key to the bothy in the office in Stranraer and won't be back there until next week, so I hunted around and found the spare among the enormous box of keys for which I know no door.

Giles, who sells garden plants and lives near by, dropped in to collect £45 for two boxes of books that he left here in November. He had a rant about Amazon and commented on Captain's enormous size, as did two other customers today.

Text from Eliot at four o'clock asking if he could stay tonight and tomorrow night.

Granny appeared at six o'clock. We did our back exercises, as we have done on a daily basis for months. Eliot arrived in the middle of them, laughed, kicked off his shoes and made a phone call before putting his shoes back on and going to the pub, from where he telephoned at 7.15 to ask what Granny was cooking for supper, clearly weighing up his options. In a singularly ill-advised decision, he decided to risk Granny's cooking. He came back at 7.30 and kicked his shoes off again. Granny promptly tripped over them, then wreaked her revenge by cooking a 'pizza' which appeared to consist of a dough made from cardboard, covered with the skins of vegetables which would probably take several years to compost.

Till total £31
5 customers

FRIDAY, 16 DECEMBER

Online orders: 1
Books found: 1

Awoke to the sound of doors slamming, and feet heavily pounding the creaking wooden floorboards downstairs, then remembered that Eliot was staying. Got up to find the bathroom occupied and the sound of the bath running. Resigned myself to brushing my teeth twenty minutes after opening the shop.

Callum in at 10 a.m. The sound of hammering, drilling and sawing was nothing when compared with Eliot's morning ritual.

Another telephone order for *Birds of Wigtownshire*, followed by a call from an elderly man who was in the shop about six months ago and found a copy of Surtees's *Handley Cross* in the equestrian section but didn't buy it, and has now decided that he wants it. Went and had a look, but couldn't see it, so called him back to say that it wasn't there any more and must have sold. I didn't remember selling it, so I decided to have another look. I was interrupted by the telephone ringing again. This time it was a woman looking for the same book – she explained that she'd been in the shop with a friend six months previously and he'd been looking at it. Her husband had died shortly before her visit, and the elderly friend had been a great comfort to her in her bereavement. She wanted to buy the book for him for Christmas as a way of thanking him. I took her number and promised to resume my search. Eventually found it, and called her back. Her excitement was almost contagious. She was clearly on the point of tears.

Anna arrived at 11 a.m. She's staying here for a few days to organise an event in January which she's called the Big Bang. It's about space. I have no doubt that it will be excellent. Not only is she well connected to NASA scientists, but she also has a sound understanding of, and a profound interest in, the subject.

William, my neighbour who lives above the shop next door, came into the shop at 3 p.m. and picked three books as a Christmas present from his sister, Michelle. I think Michelle admitted defeat when it comes to the subject of William's interests, which are – largely – military history. He's spent around thirty years travelling around the country recording the accounts of soldiers from Scottish regiments who served in conflicts. He probably has the most thorough and interesting audio archive of the last fifty years. I live in fear of it going up in smoke, or being stolen.

Woman brought in a box of maps, mainly OS and Bartholomews from the 1920s. Gave her £50 for them.

Isabel came in. I hid in the Scottish room when I saw her car driving towards the shop; I'm starting to feel that her visits remind me of being summoned to the headmaster's office, although I would struggle without her. She keeps the business on track. I told

Granny not to tell her that I was here. The moment she arrived, Granny told her that I was hiding in the Scottish room.

The woman who brought in the M. C. Beatons brought in a load of romantic fiction this morning. She looked pretty disappointed when I told her that I didn't want them. All my geriatric Mills & Boon readers are dead, and I can't sell romantic fiction these days.

Till total £108
7 customers

SATURDAY, 17 DECEMBER

Online orders: 0
Books found: 0

Eliot appeared at ten o'clock, Anna at eleven.

Lit the fire, expecting a busy day in the shop. I'm not quite sure why. By 12.30 we hadn't had a single customer.

Kate the postie delivered two parcels, both for Anna. I had four bills, one that had been repeatedly sent to the wrong address, and the sender of which was threatening to take me to court for late payment.

Letter accepting my offer on The Red Lion. Suddenly awash with a sense of regret. Now I have to do something with it, and find the money to do it.

Processed the last few days' orders and took them to Wilma at the post office. William was shuffling around in the background, complaining, like an ancient bear that had recently awoken from hibernation, only to be instantly stung on the arse by an angry wasp.

Eliot left at noon with a Christmas present for Arthur (his son and my godson). I'm the worst godparent of all time.

After lunch a customer who has been in a few times arrived with his wife and daughter. He's local, and quite friendly. The last time he was in he'd been looking at an old Bible which I had decided was destined for the recycling, so I gave it to him for nothing. As they were leaving, he gave me a box of Dreamies for Captain as a Christmas present, by way of a thank-you.

Inquiry online about a two-volume set of Baxter and Rintoul's *The Birds of Scotland* (£140). Customer in Germany wanted to know if it was a hardback or a paperback. It was the 1953 hardback edition, so I told her that she'd have to pay more than the ABE standard of £3 postage.

Just one customer today – a man who turned up at 3 p.m. and bought several John Buchan and Robert Louis Stevenson titles.

Till total £62.50
1 customer

MONDAY, 19 DECEMBER

Online orders: 0
Books found: 0

Granny opened the shop, and I drove to the Smurfit Kappa recycling plant in Glasgow with thirty-four boxes of books. The gruff forklift driver who usually (reluctantly) deals with me let me reverse the van into the vast warehouse and drop the books off near the shredder's conveyor belt. This is a departure from the norm. Usually he gets into his forklift and removes three huge plastic tubs from a pile, then puts them next to the van and makes me unload outside. Perhaps the festive spirit has finally got to him, and he let me unload the contents of the van inside because of the sleet and the wind.

Unusually, he struck up a conversation and began asking what I do for a living. When I told him where I was from, he visibly softened and began telling me about how he used to come to Galloway on holiday. Between the noise of the shredder and his strong accent, I only got about 30 per cent of what he was saying, but it was enough to maintain a dialogue without me asking him to repeat himself too often. It turns out that he used to go fishing from the rocks at Burrow Head – the promontory at the tip of the Machars peninsula. Once we got onto the subject of fishing the universal fishermen's bond kicked in, and he became friendly for the first time since I began taking boxes of books there to recycle three years ago. As I was about to drive off, he tapped on the window of the driver's door of the van. With some trepidation I wound it down. He wished me a happy Christmas. There's probably a word – or in Glasgow an expression – for the moment when someone who you thought disliked you shows you a disarming act of generosity.

Back in the shop by 2 p.m. Checked email and noticed that Luise had emailed me back with some graphics for merchandise, including a new logo for the shop and some material for mugs and bookmarks, including the sixteenth-century Spanish curse which I'd tinkered with:

> For him that stealeth this book, let it change into a serpent in his hand and rend him.
> Let him be struck with a palsy, and all his members blasted.
> Let him languish in pain crying aloud for mercy and let there be no surcease to his agony 'til he sink in dissolution.
> Let bookworms gnaw his entrails in token of the worm that dieth not, and when at last he goeth to his final punishment, let the flames of hell consume.

Customer came in at 4.50 p.m. as Janette was hoovering the railway room rug and complained about the noise of the hoover. Janette visibly stiffened, and I could see from her face that she recognised him and clearly didn't like him. He's an occasional visitor to the shop, about fifty-five years old, with thick glasses and an inability to pronounce the letter R. He always buys books about trains and is the archetypal trainspotter. He's far too familiar and always calls me by my first name, often several times in the same sentence. I have no idea how he even knows my name. I have no idea what his name is, and don't anything about him. Apart from his glasses and his rhotacism, he is the embodiment of average. There is nothing remarkable about him apart from his unremarkability. At 5.30 he was still bunkered down in the railway room, so I told him that we were closing. He scurried to the counter with two books about trains, gave me the money and thrust his business card, which proudly showed his website address. He pointed to it and told me, 'That should keep you busy for the evening.' Like a fool, I decided to see what the website was like, and instantly regretted it.

After he'd gone, Janette told me that she doesn't like him much. She once saw him with his father at the bus stop. His father, an elderly, frail man, was struggling to get onto the bus and, rather than helping him, the younger man was criticising and harassing him and eventually pushed the old man onto the bus.

Courier delivered another parcel for Granny. More food from Italy. You would think that would be a cause for celebration rather than concern, but what Granny can do with the most delicious of ingredients is quite terrible.

Till total £102.50
4 customers

TUESDAY, 20 DECEMBER

Online orders: 1
Books found: 1

Order for *Birds of Scotland* from the German customer. She reluctantly agreed to pay for the extra postage because it's a two-volume set.

The railway garden man came in again about a minute before lunchtime and asked if we had any books on the *Titanic*. I pretended that we didn't. As he left, he said, 'Thanks, Steve. See you again soon.'

Granny came in at noon, so I drove to Newton Stewart for a 1.30 meeting with Sharon, the bank manager. Set up a loan to buy the materials that will be required for the renovation of The Red Lion, the old pub down the street. My finances seem to be less parlous than usual. After the meeting with Sharon, I drove the 50 miles to Dumfries to look at a book collection that an ex-Forestry Commission employee was selling. By the time I got there it was getting dark (3.30 p.m. – shortest day tomorrow). He was friendly, and his house was full of interesting things. The books were largely about forestry and natural history, with a box of paperback fiction too. The most interesting thing was a New Naturalist mint first edition of their local title, *Galloway and the Borders*. The author, Derek Ratcliffe, sadly died before it made its way into print. Ratcliffe was one of the foremost conservationists of his generation and made the scientific link between agricultural pesticides and the decline in raptor populations, as well as the damage caused to peat bogs by planting non-native species of tree. Offered the man £50 for them but he wanted more, so I went up to £65, which he agreed to. Produced my chequebook which he took one look at and said that he wanted cash, so I walked to the nearest cashpoint in the cold rain and dark, and queued behind two old men who took an insufferably long time extracting their cash from the machine. I hadn't used a cashpoint for several years, as there's always cash in the till. I'm quite sure that the tutting teenager behind me thought that it was my first time using one.

Till total £130.50
7 customers

WEDNESDAY, 21 DECEMBER

Online orders: 2
Books found: 2

Winter solstice. This is the one day of the year to which I look forward with a masochistic glee – although it's the shortest day of the year, it is usually the harbinger of the coldest, wettest months ahead. Those I can tolerate, though, because even the two minutes and seven seconds more daylight every day is enough to pull me out of the slough of autumn, and the snowdrops will soon appear.

Alastair Dunn, the doctor's son, came in at 9.25. Within five minutes he was at the counter with a pile of Terry Pratchett novels. He told me that whenever he's back home visiting his parents he comes here because this is the only place he can find copies with the original cover illustrations. He doesn't like the more recent reprints because they don't have the classic fantasy novel cover styles of the earlier editions.

Customer came in at 11.30 and said, 'I'm trying to think of something memorable to say so that I get quoted on your Facebook page.' If that was the best he could do, then there's little hope for him.

One of today's orders was for *Lords and Men in Scotland*. It was sent to a Supreme Court judge.

Busy morning with customers, so I lit the fire in anticipation of a shop full of them for the rest of the day. From that moment on there wasn't another customer until the fire went out at 3 p.m., at which point there was another small rush of customers, who all complained that the fire had gone out.

Railway garden man came in again at four o'clock and asked for German books in an over-familiar way, and over-using my name (still Steve, apparently) several times in one sentence.

Email from Ben and Beth (Bookshop Band) to say that they're coming up for a couple of weeks in January, then going back south to pick up their stuff. They plan on moving up here – permanently hopefully – on 29th January.

Colin and Lara arrived at five o'clock and we had a drink in the kitchen – Carol-Ann and Granny appeared at six, then Colin drove us all to the Chinese restaurant in Newton Stewart. Lara's treat every time they're in the area.

Till total £147
7 customers

THURSDAY, 22 DECEMBER

Online orders: 0
Books found: 0

Sunny morning, after a wild, wet and windy night.

Father and four children came in at 9.05 a.m. Eldest daughter (about twelve) bought two books about fishing. Anticipating a busy day, I lit the fire.

Callum in at 9.15. Anna appeared at ten o'clock to help the festival company relocate their offices from the County Buildings, where they've been for ten years, to Number 11, a property far more visible, less municipal and much more suitable.

Matthew and Stephanie appeared with a Christmas card at 11.30 a.m. As Stephanie and I were gossiping, Matthew was browsing in the antiquarian section and found a book about punt gunning which he was reading enthusiastically – punt gunning is his latest obsession, so Stephanie bought it for him for Christmas as soon as his back was turned, and silently mouthed, 'Thank you,' to me.

Norrie came in at noon to cover the shop so I could go to the bank, then to the old railway line to cut some ivy for the Christmas window displays. Granny is busy working at The Pheasant. My Christmas window display is later than ever this year. No doubt there will be much tutting about my lack of enthusiasm from the other shops in the town.

Spent the rest of the daylight hours in the garden tidying up the last of the fallen leaves, although with a storm forecast for this weekend that may turn out to have been a fool's errand.

The miserable Welsh man who usually telephones for seventeenth-century theology called at 4.30 p.m. and asked if we had an Icelandic dictionary. To my astonishment, we did. I've finally made a sale to him after nearly twenty years.

Anna has decided that she's going to buy a house in Wigtown, despite having no money for a deposit, and not having spoken to the bank manager about how big or small a mortgage she can afford.

Granny cooked supper for me, Callum and Anna with the food she imported from Italy. While we were eating, Captain appeared with a live mouse in his mouth, which he promptly dropped under the kitchen table. It scurried away and hid in a corner as Granny and Anna leapt up onto their chairs shrieking. Callum and I debated whether to let the cat finish it off or throw it out of the window, while Granny protested that we should feed it and adopt it. The discussion terminated when Callum picked it up by the tail and threw it over the balcony, to shrieks of horror from both Anna and Granny. Granny's supper was surprisingly palatable, although it definitely tasted more of packaging than pizza. I was slightly disappointed that the cat didn't return with the mouse again to provide us with a mildly interesting topping.

Till total £135
10 customers

FRIDAY, 23 DECEMBER

Online orders: 2
Books found: 1

Callum in at 9.30 a.m.
        Hideous day, horizontal rain and powerful westerly wind.
        Young woman came in for a copy of *300 Farmers of Scotland*. Of the ten that I bought, only two remain. This is probably the best-selling book in the shop at the moment, and is clearly being given as a Christmas present in the local farming community.
        Anna left for London at noon. She's spending Christmas there with her friend Diana and her family.
        Telephone order for *The Birds of Wigtownshire*, this time to a customer in Florida. That leaves us with just three copies.
        Couple in from Ireland; the man bought £75 worth of books on falconry. As they left, a group of five people came in; three women in their twenties and an older couple who I assumed were their parents. An hour after they arrived (1.30 p.m.) the place was plunged into darkness, as was the entire town. I went upstairs and found a candelabra and lit the candles. They browsed by candle-light for a few more minutes. One of the daughters bought *Marabou Stork Nightmares*, by Irvine Welsh.
        Callum, unable to work on the boiler room in darkness, went to the pub. Told him that I'd join him there if the power wasn't back on by 2.30. At 2.15 the lights came back on, just at the moment when Colin and Lara appeared with some friends and I

was putting on my coat to walk down to the Bladnoch Inn for a pint with Callum.

Till total £214
12 customers

SATURDAY, 24 DECEMBER

Online orders: 2
Books found: 1

Ancient Yorkshireman spent an hour poring over the aviation section. He came to the counter with a book and asked, 'Where's your Biggles?' When I told him that Biggles books are in the children's section, he replied indignantly, 'Children's? Children's?' as though I'd put them there deliberately as some sort of personal insult directed towards him. He then proceeded to tell me at considerable length that W. E. Johns was never a captain. I can't think of a bookseller who is unaware of this fact.

Telephone order for three copies of *The Birds of Wigtownshire* to a customer in Leeds. Late (too late) Christmas presents. That's the last of them gone.

Ken and Gail dropped in with their baby, Angus. They're down for Christmas. They came to Wigtown today for lunch, but everywhere is closed. Gail and I have known one another for years, and worked together on several gas pipeline construction projects in a previous life. Her parents have a farm near Wigtown, and she's one of nine (I think) children.

Peter, Heather and Zoe came in and sang 'We Wish you a Merry Christmas' in the full knowledge that it would enrage rather than delight me.

Till total £126.50
8 customers

SUNDAY, 25 DECEMBER

Shop closed.

MONDAY, 26 DECEMBER

CLOSED.

TUESDAY, 27 DECEMBER

Online orders: o
Books found: o

Opened at 10 a.m. At 11 a.m. an Australian woman came in. She's writing a piece for a travel magazine and wanted to talk about Wigtown. Showed her around the shop and the house.

Granny came in just after noon. As she was removing her 'trench' a man called Pete Swan from the RSPB (nominative determinism) came round to see how many copies of the RSPB book about birds in Dumfries and Galloway had sold. This is not *Birds of Wigtownshire* but a far duller book which only twitchers could possibly get excited over. Of the six he dropped off last year, four remain. He wrote me an invoice with a carbon paper copy: a document so detailed and wasting so much time that only an employee of a wealthy and inefficient organisation could possibly have produced it.

For most of the morning there were more dogs than people in the shop.

At 2.30 I took my new drone out to fly it at the stone circle for the first time. Just as I arrived, a white car whizzed past, honked the horn, then reversed into the car park. It was Tom and Willeke, who were heading to Wigtown to go for a walk. They stopped and watched the drone's inaugural flight, which was a circuit of the standing stones. After I'd landed the drone we all agreed that, rather than a walk, we should go for a beer, so we headed to Bladnoch and had a couple of pints.

The week between Christmas and New Year is usually the only week in the winter during which we make any money and have customers. If today is anything to go by, that looks pretty unlikely this year.

Till total £92.98
3 customers

WEDNESDAY, 28 DECEMBER

Online orders: 1
Books found: 1

Late opening the shop this morning – forgot to set the alarm.

Busy afternoon. An American couple bought some books and wanted to pay by card. At that moment the card machine stopped working. I tried three or four times, then attempted to blame the customer, explaining to the man that the machine didn't like his card, at which point he patronisingly suggested that I 'push it in all the way' as if this thought hadn't previously occurred to me. It didn't work, and eventually he paid cash. Five minutes later another customer tried to pay with a card and the same thing happened, so I restarted the machine and it worked fine again.

Local retired dentist came to the shop and bored me for an hour with tales of his Amazon Fire tablet and how he has cleverly circumvented Amazon's block on Google Play and now has access to lots of free apps, including one which remotely controls his son-in-law's digital SLR so that he can instruct him to put it on a tripod and watch gannets in Fair Isle (where his son-in-law lives) from the comfort of his bungalow in Wigtown. I shudder to think what his son-in-law thinks of a remote dentist having control over his camera.

Email appears to have stopped working.

Till total £162.94
15 customers

THURSDAY, 29 DECEMBER

Online orders: 0
Books found: 0

Callum in at 10.30. He borrowed the van yesterday and turned up with several sheets of plasterboard, which we unloaded for the boiler room.

Customer and his wife came in at 11 a.m.

> 'Let's ask the lady about that book.' (I turn around.) 'Oh, you're not a lady.'
>
> Me: 'No, I'm not.'
>
> 'Never mind. Where are your military books?'
>
> Me: 'They're behind you.'
>
> 'Where?'
>
> Me: 'Behind you. Turn around.'

Customer turned around to face eight shelves, every one of which has a large label saying 'MILITARY'.

'Where?'

The 'mistaken for a lady' thing might seem like a languid trope, but it isn't. It happens with depressing regularity.

He was interested in the Zulu war, and kept talking over me every time I attempted to answer any of his questions. He demanded a business card and told me that 'of course, all your stock will be listed on your website', then looked gobsmacked when I told him that it wasn't. And he kept calling me 'boss'. Apparently his grandfather was 'a very famous Scotsman, much decorated in the First World War'. He paid with a credit card and insisted on grabbing the machine and attempting to stuff the card in in various incorrect ways before he finally got it right. As he left, he complimented me on the new boiler, going into raptures about how well fitted it is. The only other customer in the shop gave me a very bemused look and then, as he paid for his small pile of naval history books, commented that 'It's not every day you get complimented on your boiler.'

Sandy the tattooed pagan came in at 11 a.m. and bought four books. While we were chatting about our blood pressure, a young woman came to the counter and handed me her telephone. On it she had written the following message: 'Hi, I'm Lindsey and I'm working in The Open Book this week. Earlier this week a bunch of kids came in and stole some books, so keep a lookout.' I suppose she was being discreet. To be honest, if they'd stolen books from The Open Book, they'd probably done her a favour by freeing up shelf space.

Eventually got the email working again, lots of new RBC subscribers, as happens at this time of year.

Man came to the counter with three books, total £8.50. He gave me a credit card and I reluctantly put it into the card machine, at which point the machine produced an error message. After several subsequent attempts and a restart, it still wouldn't work, so he produced a £10 note and paid with that instead. Called the number on the side of the card machine to be put on hold and told that I was the eleventh in the queue. An hour later I was still the eleventh in the queue so I hung up.

Parents appeared at two o'clock, mother complaining about feeling constantly tired. Hardly surprising after several trips to the hospital.

Granny came to the shop at four o'clock complaining about having a cold. She spotted some puff pastry in the fridge which I'd planned to use for a chicken pie, and asked, 'It is OK that I take the puffy paste for my dinner?'

Busy day in the shop until about 3 p.m., after which nobody other than Janette and Granny came in.

Went to the pub with Callum, Tom and Willeke, and Granny. Intended to stay for one pint, but Carol-Ann came along with her friends Gillian, Bug and Debs, so we ended up staying for quite a few more. Carol-Ann and the others came back here for a drink afterwards, then we ended up playing Cards Against Humanity

– a card game that pushes the boundaries of taste to their limits – in the bothy until 2 a.m.

Till total £86.50
9 customers

FRIDAY, 30 DECEMBER

Online orders: 3
Books found: 3

Late opening the shop – woke up to the sound of Carol-Ann shouting my name from the kitchen and telling me that it was 10.30 and I needed to get my 'lazy arse out of bed'.

Kate the postie delivered a bill for me, and a parcel for Ben and Beth, the Bookshop Band, who are planning to move to Wigtown at the end of January.

Callum in at 11 a.m., finished at noon. Carol-Ann and the others went off mountain-biking in Kirroughtree. I don't know where they find the energy.

Old man with a beard and beret and very clipped RP accent marched to the till and barked, 'Can you help me?' as though it was an order to one of the lower-ranking members of his battalion rather than a request for assistance. He then asked where the foreign language section was and asked, 'Have you got any Tantan books, or Tintin, if you insist on calling them that? They have to be in French, though. It's pronounced Tantan. You do know that, don't you? You booksellers usually pronounce it "Tintin", which is completely wrong, of course.'

No, I didn't know that, but I expect that you are more than familiar with the correct way to pronounce 'Dickhead'.

Small boy, probably about eight years old, bought a biography of Amy Winehouse.

Finn and Ella's friends Elke and Florian appeared at four o'clock and we discussed the various merits of Facebook and Instagram as marketing tools. They came to stay in one of the cottages, and became good friends with Finn and Ella. Elke has mastered Instagram in a way that I haven't really mastered anything.

Till total £226.98
16 customers

SATURDAY, 31 DECEMBER

Online orders: 1
Books found: 1

Lit the fire moments after I opened the shop, shortly after which Granny appeared and complained that it was far too cold.

Another parcel arrived for Ben and Beth – it looks as though they're serious about moving to Wigtown.

An old man wearing trousers that were hideously tight around the crotch spent a couple of minutes whistling what I imagine was 'Rule Britannia' while he was reading the Bookseller's Code, the first rule of which is 'No Whistling'.

Norrie came in at noon and I drove to Lockerbie at 12.30 to catch the 2.30 train to Edinburgh for the Wig:Land – Wigtown comes to Edinburgh – event which Eliot had organised as part of the Scot:Lands New Year festival. When I tried to get my tickets, I realised that I'd accidentally booked onto the 4.30 p.m. train, so I bought another ticket and got to Waverley at 3.45 p.m. Met up with Charlotte in a pub just off Princes Street, the Guildford Arms, and had a drink with her. Eliot appeared at 4.30 (half an hour late) and we made plans for the evening. Charlotte, who is well connected in Edinburgh, gave us Access-All-Areas passes for the Hogmanay celebrations. She is chaperoning a group of six Chinese bloggers, and every few seconds her phone came alive, the screen filled with Chinese characters.

Left the pub at 5 p.m. for my sister's flat. She'd given me strict instructions about disabling and setting the alarm. I'm not accustomed to using alarms, so the combination of nerves that I might set the damned thing off for the entire night of Hogmanay combined with a couple of pints of St Mungo meant that by the time I got there I was desperate for a pee, so I raced down the steps into the courtyard below road level where the door to the flat was, and relieved myself into a plant pot, after which I attempted to open the door. The key didn't fit in the lock. After a few seconds I looked up and realised that I was at wrong house, so quickly scampered up the stone stairs back onto street level then down to the entrance to the correct house. Managed to disable the alarm in a minor panic.

Left the house (alarmed) at 6.30 after a quick shower and headed up Lothian Road to meet Ben and Beth (Bookshop Band) and Eliot for supper in a Thai restaurant. Superb food, and lots of it. Afterwards we wandered up to the castle and sat in pubs until the fireworks were finished, after which I went back to Lulu's flat and performed an exact repeat of what I'd done earlier that evening, down to the last detail of urinating in the same neighbour's plant pot.

Sent Granny a text at 12.30 a.m. to wish her a happy new year. She replied that I'd woken her up – she'd fallen asleep in the snug with the cat.

Bed at 1 a.m.

Till total £245
10 customers

JANUARY

Old books in general do not increase in value, certainly they increase in weight, and when the dust of ages settles on them one's chief desire is to get rid of them. The popular idea that if a book is over a hundred years of age it must be of value is a fallacy.

Age alone is no criterion of value. A copy of 'Waverley' by Sir Walter Scott, 3 vols. boards, published 1814 was sold in London in 1892 for £162. At the Gibson Craig library sale in 1888, an uncut copy of the same book brought only 10 guineas.

R. M. Williamson, *Bits from an Old Bookshop*

It's remarkable how often the telephone in the shop rings and someone tells me that they are clearing a great-aunt's house which is full of 'very old' books. Perhaps it's just because I've been in the trade for sixteen years and have encountered this so often that I know that the reply to my question 'How old are they?' will almost inevitably be met with 'Oh, very old. There's one from 1950.' It's unfair to dismiss anyone who thinks that a book published in 1950 is 'very old' – after all, anyone who was born in 1950 would probably be considered as fairly old – I was born in 1970 and am starting to think of myself as falling into that category, but in the history of publishing a book that was born in that decade is a mere infant. And even books that have been around for several generations don't necessarily, as Williamson points out, have any intrinsic value unless someone wants to buy them. It really is a simple question of supply and demand.

The *Waverley* set that he describes is a 'three-decker' or 'triple-decker', a format that came into existence in the early nineteenth century. Arguments over whether it allowed writers the luxury of time to produce work or whether it was a publishing wheeze to allow circulating libraries to charge readers three times to read a book that could easily have been published in one volume still abound, but it was the fashionable format for fiction for most of that century. By the 1880s it had almost died out, as have collectors of triple-deckers. When I bought the shop, there were regular customers in search of the three-volume sets of Dickens, Thackeray and George Eliot. Now there are none.

SUNDAY, I JANUARY

Shop closed.

Up at 9.30 a.m. and headed to the Royal Mile (house alarm set) to the Signet Library, where Eliot had organised about twenty of us to create Wig:Land, a taste of Wigtown in Edinburgh. It's part of an event called Scot:Lands, the concept of which is that cultural corners of rural Scotland can bring a flavour of their place to a beautiful venue in central Edinburgh for 1 January. The event is ticketed, and tickets sold out weeks ago. We spent the morning setting up on the ground floor of the Signet Library. Lee Randall and I set up the bookshop, Anna set up the kist – a shop selling produce from Galloway, from pickles to candles. Christian set up his book bindery, Astrid set up her Windows of Wigtown display around the edges, and in the middle of it all was a huge table covered in packages, each of which had been hand-wrapped in brown paper and tied with a string, and onto each of which Lee and Charlotte had written a description of the book inside, and a price, but no title or author.

As 1 p.m. (opening time) approached, things looked chaotic, but by the time the doors opened, all was fine and organised, and we assumed our positions. The upstairs was a live music venue with local folk musician Robyn Stapleton and her band alternating sets with Ben and Beth (the Bookshop Band). Charlotte and I staffed the bookshop; Anna and others took turns at the kist. I expected a slow dribble of people, and possibly a handful of sales of the random books (of which there were 240), with each bookshop in Wigtown having supplied forty books. I could not have been more wrong – by the time we opened there was a huge crowd outside, and it didn't let up until five o'clock, when the event ended. Lee and Debbi Gliori took turns being The Book Doctor, advising people what to read, Christian demonstrated bookbinding techniques and I sold books while the musicians entertained everyone upstairs. Visitors were encouraged to experience everything, and over the course of the day there were around 3,000 of them. Considerably more than we had expected. Of the 260 secret, random books we brought up, only eleven remained unsold.

Another part of the experience was what Eliot called 'The

Human Book': a chance to have a one-on-one conversation with an author. Despite having nothing in print, I was wheeled out as one of these exhibits. The whole event went like clockwork. The take-down was frantic and fast, everything boxed and packed in under an hour. Kenny managed to park the van (which he'd driven up at 6 a.m.) next to the entrance. He packed it while I ferried the boxes and props from the hall and passed them to him. We were out by 6.30 and all headed to the Jolly Judge for a drink, then up to somewhere off Teviot Place for supper. Bed at midnight, this time without urinating in Lulu's neighbour's garden.

Called Granny to see how things are in Wigtown. She was asleep in the snug again.

MONDAY, 2 JANUARY

Online orders: 1
Books found: 1

Woke up feeling a bit rough, had a cup of tea then left Lulu's flat – posted the key through the letterbox, but not before arming the alarm and waiting for the happy jingle that confirms everything is fine. Walked to Waverley station and bought a bacon and brie baguette and another cup of tea, then caught the train to Lockerbie. Drove from Lockerbie to Wigtown. Back home at 5 p.m. to discover that Granny had opened the shop at 10 a.m. and was just closing up. Asked her how her Hogmanay had been. She replied, ''Orrible.' Poor Granny brought in the New Year with just the cat for company.

Anna messaged me to say that she would be back by 7 p.m., so I had a drink with Granny before she left, and Anna arrived.

Till total £72
5 customers

TUESDAY, 3 JANUARY

Online orders: 3
Books found: 3

Opened at 10 a.m. (still on Christmas hours). First customers were a middle-aged German couple looking for a biography of James Clerk Maxwell, a Galloway man whose work Einstein credited as being the 'most profound and the most fruitful that physics has experienced since the time of Newton'.

Lit the fire, which promptly went out, so I lit it again. It went out again. Gave up. There won't be any customers anyway.

Woman brought in a pile of books at 11.30 and asked if I wanted to buy them. Sorted them into two piles and offered her £5 for the pile I wanted. She seemed unduly confused that I wanted some but not all of them, then brought in more, in bundles of three or four, until the table was covered in them. She was completely incapable of understanding that I didn't want them all, and kept pointing at the piles that I'd rejected and asking, 'But what about these ones?' Eventually she and her friends decided to leave them with me while they went for lunch in Whithorn. They came back three hours later and – completely baffled by the idea that I only wanted some of the books but not all – decided to take them all away. I could scarcely have been more relieved.

The boiler appears to have stopped working again. I checked the hopper and it seems to have an empty space around the hose which sucks the pellets into the boiler, so I changed into what I would now describe as my 'boiler suit' (old shorts and a T-shirt), climbed in and shovelled a pile of pellets back over the suction hose.

Granny came in at three o'clock and excitedly told me that 'The charity shop are 'aving a sale!'

Till total £110.48
9 customers

Online orders: 3
Books found: 3

Back to opening the shop at 9 a.m. once again after what doesn't exactly feel like a holiday. We open at 10 a.m. between Christmas and New Year. Granny was standing at the bus stop opposite the front door with her ear warmers on, smoking a roll-up with one hand and with the middle finger of the other hand extended in my direction in the universal gesture of contempt which we have come to recognise as our morning greeting.

Orders this morning were for *Protestant Theology and the Making of the Modern German University*, *The British Duelling Pistol* and *The Trinity Foot Beagles, 1862–1912*.

Sunny day. The warming crawl of spring begins.

Met Fred, the new resident of The Open Book, an American book dealer. He came in and introduced himself. He has a bookshop in a town in Appalachia. Apparently the people of the town were so grateful that he opened that he has a stream of regular customers who are determined to make his business a success. Lucky bastard.

Sandy in at 3 p.m. with his usual cohort of women. He was armed with a box full of copies of his latest pamphlet – a series of short stories called *Bragword & Gowk Spittle*. He's a very articulate and erudite man and occasionally produces works of either poetry or folklore.

A couple, slightly older than I am, came in at about two o'clock and bought a pile of gardening books. It turns out that their neighbour in England is Catriona, who used to work for the Galloway Fisheries Trust and who I've known (but not seen) for years.

In the afternoon I cleaned the filters on the air source heat exchangers. They always work significantly better once they've been cleaned. In the evening I went to Finn and Ella's with Ben, Beth and Anna for a film night: *Vertigo*.

Till total £116.49
12 customers

THURSDAY, 5 JANUARY

Online orders: 1
Books found: 0

Clear blue sky, frosty morning. Granny was waiting at the bus stop, as usual, cigarette in one hand, middle finger of the other extended in my direction as I opened the door at 9 a.m. To my enormous delight she had a coughing fit and had to sit down.

Email this morning from an American ABE customer who had repeatedly emailed throughout the Christmas period protesting that his book order for a biography of James Cook hadn't arrived. Eventually, exhausted by his war of email attrition, I refunded him, despite the fact that I remember posting the book and that it was still within the allotted time period for delivery. He told me that he'd ordered the book from another bookseller, and ten minutes later our copy had arrived. It wasn't an expensive book, so I told him to keep it.

Article in the *Guardian* about a 'bookseller from hell' who charges customers an entry fee of 50p and is spectacularly rude to them. I need to learn from this man. At least a dozen people emailed the link to me.

Text message from Granny asking if I still want to do my back exercises with her at six o'clock: 'Is it OK at six? Duncan played with my bag. Tobacco everywhere.'

Anna had a meeting in the kitchen with Ben and Beth and her new assistant, Harvey. Harvey seems lovely – he's quite short and youthful. His bushy beard may, I suspect, be an attempt to make himself look less like a boy.

Took the Christmas decorations out of the windows, an exercise that took less than a minute.

Courier delivered another parcel for Granny, who came over at six to do back exercises and drink my gin. Today in Italy is Befana day. Apparently Epiphany is like a second Christmas, on the eve of which (today) a witch-like creature delivers either sweets or coal to children, depending on whether they've been good or bad. Granny has decided that she is Befana. She will be busy tonight.

Spent the evening painting the ceiling in the boiler room,

which Callum has nearly finished. Anna invited Carol-Ann and her friend Gillian over for supper, which I had to cook. Made a sausage casserole.

Till total £90
7 customers

FRIDAY, 6 JANUARY

Online orders: 2
Books found: 2

Dreich day, the sort that, as my friend Nick says, is so damp that somehow moisture can get through even the most waterproof of jackets. Granny was at the bus stop when I opened up, this time with an umbrella in the hand that she usually uses to insult me. As soon as she spotted me she managed to execute a new manoeuvre

– holding her cigarette and the umbrella in the same hand while she extended the middle finger of her other hand in my direction.

One of today's orders was for the splendidly titled *Britannia Waives the Rules*, by A. T. Culwick. It's a searing indictment of British colonial foreign policy.

Kate the postie delivered the mail: just a single letter, this time for Anna. I'm starting to feel that my house is a combination of a Royal Mail sorting office and women's refuge.

Jack from the butcher's dropped Granny's loaf of bread off at 12.30. A few months ago she discovered that the butcher bakes a particularly nice loaf of bread, and has been going there every Friday to buy it. When she doesn't turn up, Jack drops one into the shop for her. This is particularly annoying as it means I end up paying for it, a result that delights Granny enormously, although she always leaves the money in the till when I'm not there, and thinks that I don't know that she does it.

Callum telephoned to ask whether I'm going to manage to go on the GR7 walk in Spain with him next week. He goes to Spain every January and spends a few weeks walking on trails. I usually join him, but only for a few days. It's the perfect time to get away to a place where there's a bit of sun and some warmth in the air.

Went to the pub after closing the shop with Ben, Beth, Granny, Anna, Willeke and the people from The Open Book, Fred and his wife, Cathy. I don't think they'd had a single customer all day. I suspect the experience is making Fred appreciate his business in the USA.

Till total £10
1 customer

SATURDAY, 7 JANUARY

Online orders: 0
Books found: 0

Another dreich day. Granny in her customary position when I opened the shop for the 9 a.m. salute.

Anna and Ben set off to distribute Big Bang fliers around businesses in the Stewartry at lunchtime (the Stewartry of Kirkcudbright is our neighbouring county, and far more wealthy than its poor cousin, Wigtownshire, as people from the Stewartry rarely hesitate to remind us).

Customer bought a copy of *Travels in Galloway*, by Donald MacIntosh. In his introduction Donald quotes an old Galloway shepherd he'd met in the pub. They got to chatting and Donald told him that he'd written a book. The shepherd, profoundly unimpressed, replied, 'Any fool can write a book, but it takes a man to herd the Merrick.' (Merrick is the highest hill in Galloway.) Our copy had belonged to a man called Farquhar Macintosh, who had grown up in Skye and had become a highly respected figure in the world of Scottish education, and a champion of the Gaelic language. I often wonder how close the MacIntoshes are. I know that Donald was a native Gaelic-speaker from one of the Western Isles. He once told me that his publisher, with whom he had fallen out, had bought a boat, and wanted to give it a Gaelic name. He'd asked Donald what the word for 'breath of wind' was. Donald obligingly gave him the Gaelic word for 'big fart', which, as far as I know, is still what the boat is called, and his publisher is still none the wiser.

I had a maths teacher called Major MacIntosh. He was a pilot, shot down over north Africa in the war. He was taken in by a nomadic tribe who hid him in a cave. His wounded arm became gangrenous, and they put maggots on the rotting flesh to save him. He also had a cigarette case which had stopped a bullet. At the end of every Christmas term he'd produce the dented cigarette case and roll up his sleeve to show us his arm. It was the highlight of the year.

Anna returned from her distribution of Big Bang propaganda at 4 p.m. and decided to bake a cake.

An American woman and her daughter bought an antiquarian medical book for £150.

Customer bought seven books on marine engineering. He owns the boatyard in Lamlash.

As I edit this I've discovered this diary entry, which has clearly been planted by Granny when she had access to the computer: 'Granny cooked an amazing supper. She cooks always good food, full of fat. Delicious.'

Till total £328.97
10 customers

MONDAY, 9 JANUARY

Online orders: 6
Books found: 4

Email from (Bookshop Band) Ben's father about a property next to the Old Bank in Wigtown which he's interested in buying. He still insists on calling the place Wigton in his correspondence.

Isabel turned up at 11 a.m. They're getting ready for the start of lambing. The farm is close to sea level, so they can start earlier than the higher hill farms. They also breed Texels, which they lamb indoors, rather than in the fields.

Granny in at noon. Just spotted another planted diary entry: 'The beautiful and clever Granny is not so blind, today she saw two books that I didn't find this morning because I'm becoming a blind Lord. She found also my cheque book that was in front of my horrible face.'

Went to Newton Stewart after lunch to lodge takings at the bank and drop off empty boxes at Mary's. She's always after small boxes – she sells antiques online and they are obviously useful.

One of the remits of the festival company is to expand the cultural content of the region. Eliot has commissioned Ben and Beth to see whether a music festival is viable, so they were in the drawing room all day planning – Anna left at 3 p.m. for Edinburgh.

Cooked a stir-fry for Granny, Ben and Beth, then we watched *Elevator to the Gallows* (again).

Till total £46
2 customers

TUESDAY, 10 JANUARY

Online orders: 1
Books found: 1

Miserable morning. Granny arrived in the shop at 11.56. I've thought of a title for her autobiography, if she ever chooses to write one: *Fifty Shades of Granny*.

Another Granny planted entry in the diary: 'Tomorrow I will say "See you soon, Wigtown and fucking people", I am on holiday, woo woo!'

Two customers came in this afternoon looking for old maps of Scotland. One of them spent more than £60 and didn't complain or ask for a discount. I think I've seen this pair before: there aren't many collectors left, particularly of OS maps.

Nicky appeared at about noon to collect the antique fire screen that she'd asked me to sell for her last year. As I was loading it into her van I told her how happy I was to see her again. My words were met with a stony silence, broken only by a very reluctant 'thank you' for helping her. She gave me four boxes of books. I'm not sure what I've done, but she's clearly annoyed with me about something.

Left Granny in charge of the shop and drove to Glasgow airport in the afternoon where I spent the night in a hotel. I'm going walking with Callum in Spain for a few days.

Till total £97.99
3 customers

WEDNESDAY, 11 JANUARY

Online orders: 2
Books found: 0

Norrie covered the shop. Granny had to work in The Pheasant, but she's staying here at night to feed the cat and keep him company. They have a similar IQ and grasp of English.

Flew from Glasgow to Málaga at 11 a.m. Started reading *Death at Intervals*. Landed a few hours later and caught the train to El Chorro, where I met up with Callum and Sammi, Callum's Finnish friend, who were drinking beer at the station bar when I arrived. We had some beers, then a delicious meal in the hotel they'd booked, three of us sharing a room. The stench was atrocious – stinking feet and unwashed clothes. It took me straight back to being a teenager.

THURSDAY, 12 JANUARY

Online orders: 1
Books found: 1

Norrie in the shop.

Up at 8 a.m., Sammi, Callum and I walked the stunning Caminito del Rey at 10 a.m. then Callum and I said goodbye to Sammi and set off up a hill. The walk to the next town was supposed to be 10 km, but after a few wrong turns it turned out to be nearer 30 km. We arrived at Valle de Abdalajís at 6 p.m. and found a hostel, ditched our bags and went to a bar for something to drink, then back to the hostel for a shower and into our 'evening wear' (socks, pants and shirts that weren't worn during the day, and consequently stinking) and out for food, a greasy burger in what looked like a school canteen. Bed at midnight.

Till total £10
1 customer

FRIDAY, 13 JANUARY

Online orders: 3
Books found: 2

Norrie in the shop.

Up at 8 a.m. and straight to the pharmacy for some Compeed plasters for my blisters. Legs aching after yesterday but feet in agony. Set off from Valle de Abdalajís for Antequera as the mist came down and the wind picked up.

Till total £40.50
4 customers

SATURDAY, 14 JANUARY

Online orders: 3
Books found: 1

Email from Granny with a photo of her foot. The puppy in her new home has clearly identified her as its arch-enemy, and her left foot in particular. Apparently it attacks viciously at every opportunity. Her foot was completely covered in bite marks and bruises.

Caught the train back to Málaga and found a cheap hotel for the night.

Till total £165
6 customers

SUNDAY, 15 JANUARY

Shop closed.

Flight left Málaga at 11.55 a.m. On the way home, driving

through Ayr, I spotted several large posters of a missing Jack Russell whose owners were offering a £1,000 reward to whoever finds it. That could have paid for the Spain trip and left me with a good bit to spare. I wonder if I can stick a few bits of carpet on Captain and see if I can pass him off as the missing dog.

On the road home I chose to take the single-track road via the Nick of the Balloch. It's the shortest route, and climbs high as it winds through the Galloway Hills, but it is beautiful and dramatic in places, particularly at the Nick of the Balloch – a pass cut into a steep hillside. As I was nearing it (roughly 10 miles from the main road), I encountered the only other vehicle I'd seen since Maybole. As always when meeting another vehicle on this road, we both edged to the roadside and into the verge. When we were parallel, the driver of the other vehicle (a Land Rover) indicated for me to wind down my window. He told me that the Nick of the Balloch was impassable, and that there was a massive snowdrift across it. It's not a road that is ever gritted, or which the snowplough ever visits. Undoubtedly foolishly, and just a mile away from it, I decided that I'd give it a shot, so I drove on. Sure enough, the snow was as high as my windscreen, but I decided that with enough momentum I might have a chance of blasting through it. I didn't want to drive all the way back, so I hit the accelerator and went for it. I made it through the first drift reasonably comfortably, but lost a lot of speed and momentum as the snow piled up in front of the van. There was a small patch of road which hadn't been covered by snow and on which I managed to finally gain purchase, enough to floor it and hit the second drift at some speed. As I ploughed into it I was starting to doubt the wisdom of my decision, but the momentum of the van was enough to push through it, wheels spinning frantically. As I inched through the last few feet of snow towards the next patch of clear road, it dawned on me – far too late – that if I hadn't made it through the next section there was every chance that I'd have been stuck there until the morning, or possibly the following morning.

Made it home at 4 p.m. expecting to find Granny in the house, but there was no sign of her. Texted her to find that she was on the bus from Sorbie (she'd been working at The Pheasant) and would be back in twenty minutes.

In the enormous pile of post which has accumulated during my brief absence there were two magazines from The Time Traveller's Bookshop in Kinsale and a letter from a solicitor in Kirkcudbright who has been charged with disposing of a deceased estate near Castle Douglas and has invited me to view the books with the option of buying them.

MONDAY, 16 JANUARY

Online orders: 2
Books found: 1

Email from a customer this morning about a book called *Wragg's Improved Flute Preceptor*, dated 1818: 'Are there fingering charts included (and if so, how many?)?'

Message from Granny at 10.41 a.m. saying, 'Uh, I didn't hear the alarm clock, I put in order my face and I come to the shop.'

Ben and Beth arrived at about eleven this morning. Made up the bed in the spare room, but it's a bit chilly. Moved a small heater there.

Baird Matthews, retired local solicitor, came in and dropped off a bag of books. Lisa, the doctor's wife, dropped off three bags of her son Angus's DVDs.

Granny in at noon. Drove to Tarff Valley to get cat food and washing powder, then to Scott Stores, the builders' merchant, to ask about hiring a garden shredder. They don't supply them any more, which means all the rubbish from the shrubs I cut back in the garden will have to go to the dump.

Cooked steak with grated potatoes for supper. Granny left at about midnight.

Till total £46
5 customers

TUESDAY, 17 JANUARY

Online orders: 1
Books found: 1

Callum in at 10 a.m. He's back from Spain.

A very small woman from Kirkcowan brought in a pile of art books; gave her £10. She's been bringing bags of books in for years, but it's a while since I last saw her.

Called the solicitor who sent the letter about the deceased estate near Castle Douglas. While I was on the phone arranging a date to view the books, a tall, gaunt man in a trench coat carrying a bag of books appeared and stood silently in front of the counter. He looked familiar – in the way that someone you vaguely remember but instinctively want to forget looks familiar. Once I'd arranged a time and date with the solicitor he began producing books from his canvas bag, and telling me that he's a 'local author' – words guaranteed to bring a scowl to my face. I've stocked his books before – lightweight Christianity; semi-autobiographical. They didn't sell before, and after listening to him droning on about how they've got 95 per cent positive feedback on Amazon (clearly planted by him and his friends) I reluctantly bought two copies of each of his three books just to get him out of the shop.

Granny appeared at noon, coughing and swearing about the weather and my shoes. I have no idea why she took such exception to them, but they clearly caused her some considerable irritation.

Till total £74.50
6 customers

WEDNESDAY, 18 JANUARY

Online orders: 1
Books found: 1

Opened at 9.05 a.m., Granny outside at the bus. She was having a cigarette with Callum, who had clearly been waiting to get in to work in the boiler room.

Went through four boxes of books that had been dropped off while I was in Spain. Not much of interest apart from twenty-six books about tractors. Telephoned the woman who had left them. Not greatly surprised to discover that the books had belonged to her father – a farmer.

American woman came to the counter and said, 'Art books. Where?'

Shortly before closing time a fat, breathless man (regular customer) bought £46 worth of railway books.

Anna telephoned at 8 p.m. to ask if she can come and stay for a few days from tomorrow. I wonder when I'll next have the house to myself. And Captain.

The shop computer performed an automatic reboot at 5.30, just as I was in the middle of filling in an online form for landlord registration. I'd spent over an hour on the damned thing.

Beth's early birthday party in the pub. She and Ben cooked supper for me and Granny.

Till total £154.50
16 customers

THURSDAY, 19 JANUARY

Online orders: 6
Books found: 6

I was late opening the shop this morning: 9.10 a.m. Cold day, so I lit the fire in the shop.

Ben and Beth loaded their instruments into their car at 10 a.m., freeing up the big room which had been full of cellos, guitars and accordions since they arrived. I'm amazed that they managed to fit so many instruments into such a small vehicle.

Six orders this morning, an unusually high number. I wonder

whether the reboot may have resulted in our online stock refreshing and consequently coming up higher on ABE searches.

Callum in at 9.20. He's not that happy to be back in a wet and cold Galloway after his time in Spain.

The woman who brought the tractor books in came back to pick up the boxes of books that I didn't want. She asked me my surname, so I told her. She then asked me if I was related to Rosemary Bythell. I told her that she's my mother, at which point her face lit up and she explained that she works for Stena Line, the ferry service that runs from Stranraer to Belfast, and that my mother always charms her into giving her a reduced fare when she visits her family in Ireland – 'I always try to look after her. Please tell her I was asking after her.'

Packed the orders and processed them on the Royal Mail website and took them over to Wilma, who was busy trying to reconcile the till.

Message from Granny: 'Today Duncan used me like a dog. He threw away the stick and asked me to bring it back. Five times.' Duncan is probably three years old now.

Tall, stooped old man with the hat came in at 1.15, this time wearing a tweed cap instead of his usual Crocodile Dundee number. As always he was obsequiously friendly and headed for the anti-quarian section, where (again, as always) he made great play of thumbing through the most expensive books before shuffling off to the erotica section for a couple of hours.

Parents came round at 4.30, when Anna, Carol-Ann and Harvey were here for a meeting in the kitchen about how we can promote Wigtown outside of the festival season. My mother gave me a hideous Picasso print which she no longer wanted. The fact that I didn't want it either didn't deter her from leaving it with a flourish: 'You can sell it for £10 in the shop.'

Till total £58
5 customers

FRIDAY, 20 JANUARY

Online orders: 1
Books found: 0

Callum in at 9.20 a.m. He's thinking of moving to Spain.

Tracy appeared at ten o'clock. She's got a job working for Matthew Clark, the drinks distributor in Dumfries. It has been frustrating watching her trying to find work. She's capable and bright, but has struggled to find a job that she likes. This area is largely composed of people who are self-employed, so opportunities are scarce, even for someone like her.

Jack from the butcher's dropped off Granny's weekly loaf of bread. As usual, I paid for it.

Pete telephoned. He thinks he'll be out of the psychiatric unit in two weeks. I very much hope that he's right but, having spoken to him and his nurses, I have grave doubts.

An elderly man brought in two books illustrated by Arthur Rackham which he'd bought here last year for £100 each. I offered him £120 for the pair. He seemed quite pleased. When I asked him why he was selling them so soon after buying them, he told me that he'd been given a month to live, and was selling things which he knew were of value and wanted to enjoy his final few weeks travelling, eating well and staying in decent hotels. Hats off.

Till total £86
8 customers

SATURDAY, 21 JANUARY

Online orders: 1
Books found: 1

Shop open at 8.50 a.m.

Email from Sara Maitland, who is organising an event about

her book *Gossip from the Forest* in Wigtown and struggling to get numbers up. It's a hard time of year to organise events, even if you're Sara. She once told me that she'd dropped the 'h' at the end of Sarah as teenager because she'd read that one of the Romantic poets – Shelley, I think – had written that he thought it was a redundant consonant, and she'd been so impressionable that she decided to dispense with it.

Spent the day putting labels on the parcels for the Random Book Club, and sorting them into the categories required by the Royal Mail before bagging them, and processing them on the Royal Mail website. We have 166 members currently.

French wildfowlers came in at 10 a.m. They used to stay in one of my parents' holiday cottages when they had the farm. They don't speak a word of English between them. It took a while, but my rusty French was just about good enough to explain to them that my mother had been ill, and what had happened. They left a letter for her. They'd shot ten geese during the week. I have mixed feelings about wildfowling: my grandfather was a keen shot on the marsh, and the local economy benefits enormously from it, but – and I'm starting to feel this way about salmon – creatures that survive terrible odds and travel almost unimaginable distances probably deserve a little clemency.

Drove with Granny and Anna to Tom and Willeke's for supper and a film, *Argo*.

Till total £119.49
10 customers

MONDAY, 23 JANUARY

Online orders: 2
Books found: 1

I was a bit late opening the shop again, 9.20 a.m. today. Not that it matters hugely when there are barely any customers.

Granny wasn't in today, nor was she waiting at the bus stop with her morning salute. She's taken two days off to go and explore Glasgow.

Anna has been staying for a couple of nights, and came down to the kitchen at 10 a.m. She made a breakfast of various pulses and things which would normally only be used in a stew.

Callum in at eleven o'clock. His roof was leaking, so he spent a few hours trying to fix it, then gave up. I'm starting to think the same about my house. It never seems to end. Callum and I have more or less agreed that the solution is not tradesmen, slates and scaffolding but buckets and strategically placed saucepans.

Parents dropped by at 3 p.m. Apparently they're having pheasant casserole for supper. I would bore you with all the ingredients, which my mother insisted on telling me, but I've managed to forget them. Juniper berries were repeated several times, though. Enough to stick in my mind, probably for several weeks.

Found a woman with a baby strapped to her chest in the drawing room after I'd briefly left the 'PRIVATE' barrier up while making a cup of tea. She was apologetic and exhausted-looking.

Clive of Bladnoch came in and wandered around before coming to the counter to inform me that he had no intention of buying any more books, because he already has 500 of them. I'm going to start charging him for oxygen consumption.

Postman picked up the random books just before 5.

Anna bought a vegetarian pizza from the Co-op and managed to burn it. She's here for the Big Bang weekend, one of the projects she has devised in her role as Cultural Tourism Developer, and which she is uniquely positioned to organise, with her NASA background.

Till total £81.49
4 customers

Online orders: 2
Books found: 1

Opened the shop to the sight of geese flying overhead, and the sound of a Skoda backfiring as it passed the front of the shop, startling the cat, who almost knocked me over when he bolted through the door in terror.

Elderly couple brought in two boxes of books, mostly material that is almost impossible to sell – Churchill's five-volume history of the Second World War, lacking jackets. A good set of this used to sell regularly for £50 fifteen years ago; now they occupy shelf space that could be better occupied. I haven't sold a set for nearly ten years. Most of the other books were turgid Victorian moralistic novels; again unsellable. Picked out a few Enid Blytons and a book about Devorgilla, and gave them £12.

Three people came in at about 11 a.m., including an American man with a goatee beard. He spotted Anna's banjo, which she'd left at the bottom of the stairs, and asked if he could have a look at it. His name is Joe Newberry, and apparently he's a famous musician. Anna appeared as he was playing a song on her banjo, and they chatted for over an hour. He's on tour, and was in Dundee last night, is doing a gig in Moniaive tonight and Celtic Connections later in the week.

Clive of Bladnoch came in again today, at 3.30, and wandered around, muttering and singing tunelessly. For once he actually bought a book – *Ars Erotica*. He then proceeded to describe in detail every action he was taking as he paid for it: 'I'm going to open my wallet. I'm opening my wallet. Look, there's a £10 note, I'm going to take it out and give it to you. I'm taking it out now. There, I'm putting it in your hand.'

Anna was fairly flustered today because ticket sales for the Big Bang weekend are poor. I'm sure they'll pick up.

As I was going through boxes of books I came across an early Edwardian photo album with about half the spaces empty and the other half full of portraits. I wonder what might have happened to the missing photographs: who the subjects were, and where the photographs went. Was someone performing a Stalinist purge on family history?

Telephone rang at three o'clock.

Me: 'Good afternoon, The Bookshop.'
Elderly woman: 'Is that you, Barbara?'

At four o'clock Bob dropped round with a tray of blue eggs. His hens are under lockdown as apparently there's been a case of avian flu reported in the area.

Till total £42.50
3 customers

WEDNESDAY, 25 JANUARY

Online orders: 2
Books found: 1

Twenty minutes late opening the shop. Came into the kitchen to find Granny in the kitchen eating a slice of toast. 'Where you been, lazy bastard.'

Anna appeared at 10 a.m.

An old man – a regular customer whose son Ian puts the market stalls up in the summer – came in at noon and asked for a copy of Pascal's *Pensées*, clearly convinced that we wouldn't have one. We had two copies in the Penguin Classics edition. He bought both. He left a very happy man.

Spent the morning writing up the AWB minutes, and sent them out.

Burns Night, so after work I went to the Co-op to buy some haggis, only to be told that they don't stock haggis any more, so I made Cullen skink for Anna and Granny. Every Burns night I tell people who are unfamiliar with the bard about a poem called 'Cock up your Beaver'. Nobody believes that it exists, but here it is:

When first my brave Johnie lad came to this town,

He had a blue bonnet that wanted the crown;
But now he has gotten a hat and a feather,
Hey, brave Johnie lad, cock up your beaver!

Cock up your beaver, and cock it fu' sprush,
We'll over the border, and gie them a brush;
There's somebody there we'll teach better behaviour,
Hey, brave Johnie lad, cock up your beaver!

Till total £79
14 customers

THURSDAY, 26 JANUARY

Online orders: 2
Books found: 2

Anna left at 6 a.m. to drive to Glasgow and pick up her friends who are flying in from America to attend the Big Bang weekend. I'm not sure the Honda Jazz is up to the task, but she's determined.

The days are starting to lengthen noticeably, but at 6 a.m. it's still dark. Even at seven there's barely the slightest sign of light. The crows begin their raucous cacophony at about 7.30. Sometimes the geese beat them to it; sometimes the crows beat the geese. I have no idea what drives these early movements.

Isabel in at 11 a.m. Lambing hasn't started yet, but soon will be upon us.

Anna came back at 1 p.m. with her friends Dana Bachman and Amy, two scientists here for the Big Bang weekend. Anna has always raved about Dana since I've known her. He fired her interest in astronomy and astrophysics and, in a wonderfully American way, told her that a lack of knowledge of maths and physics was no barrier to a successful career in the subject. Einstein would have agreed.

Woman with a very unusual accent – a sort of combination of Cornish and Irish – brought in a bag of military history books, very recent and clearly unread. They'd belonged to her late husband. Gave her £25 for them.

After lunch a man came in and asked for 'wayway books'. Initially I thought he was asking for books about Ai Weiwei, the Chinese artist, so I showed him to the art section, at which point he became quite agitated and kept repeating 'wayway' until I worked out he was interested in railways, but afflicted by rhotacism.

Janette made up the bed in the snug for JFW and his wife, Pauline, friends who arrive tomorrow. I bought his late father's books earlier this year from a house in Perth, and like him a great deal. They're here for the Big Bang weekend.

Changed a bulb on one of the chandeliers in the front of the shop. There are two six-branch chandeliers in the front room, and they're on for a minimum of eight hours every day. In the fourteen years since I fitted them, that's the first bulb that has died. In an odd coincidence Anna told me that the standard lamp in her room has started making a strange noise when she turns it on. It sounds like it's probably a loose connection. Will look at it later.

Went to the Co-op to pick up food to cook a chilli for the house guests. There were no red peppers, but helpfully there was a sign next to the empty shelf explaining that there was a shortage because of a heavy snowfall in Spain.

Till total £75.50
5 customers

FRIDAY, 27 JANUARY

Online orders: 1
Books found: 0

Awoke and went downstairs to find Dana and Amy, two of Anna's Big Bang speakers, in the kitchen. Anna appeared and took them to Wigtown primary school, the place where I spent the first years of my education, to give a talk to the children.

Callum in at 1 p.m. He was caught in a hailstorm on the way over from his house, which appears to have convinced him more than ever that a move to Spain is a good idea. He's ordered more material from the sawmill to finish the boiler room.

Ran out of Lady Grey tea at 2 p.m. As bourgeois complaints go, this may be my finest.

Callum left at 2.30, tired of waiting for the timber delivery. Five minutes later it arrived.

Stuart Kelly arrived at three o'clock with a box of books from one of his elderly neighbours. He's chairing one of Anna's events at the Big Bang weekend, and staying in one of the spare rooms.

JFW and Pauline, his wife, arrived at 4.45. We opened a bottle of wine, then went to a talk about women in science in the County Buildings, chaired by Stuart and with contributions from Amy, Pippa Goldschmidt and Maya Tolstoy. All went to Craft for a meal afterwards, then Willeke, Callum, JFW, Pauline, Stuart, Granny, Anna and I came back here for more drinks. Bed at 2 a.m.

Till total £26.50
5 customers

SATURDAY, 28 JANUARY

Online orders: 0
Books found: 0

Half an hour late opening the shop. JFW and Pauline were in the kitchen having breakfast when I staggered downstairs.

Telephone call from a man who has some Andrew Lang Fairy Books to sell. He's going to bring them in on Monday.

Granny slept on the sofa in the drawing room last night, and appeared at 10.30 looking bleary-eyed. As she made herself a cup of coffee which smelled so strong that it could have awoken a kraken, she explained that she'd slept in and was late for work at the restaurant. She'd been to the butcher and was clutching a sausage roll, or 'shaushage roll', as she insists on calling it, much to their initial bewilderment, and now delight. The moment she appears, they ask her if she wants a shaushage roll.

My sister Lulu, Scott and the children appeared at three o'clock, after a visit to my parents. More wine.

Big Bang pub quiz at 8 p.m. chaired by Finn, and all related to the cosmos. Our team comprised JFW, Pauline, Pippa, Granny and me, and to our stellar amazement we won.

All came back here to celebrate.

Bed at 4 a.m.

Till total £103.60

14 customers

SUNDAY, 29 JANUARY

Online orders: 0

Books found: 0

Late up once again. Came downstairs to find everyone in the kitchen drinking tea and chatting. Opened the shop, but the stomach cramps kicked in with a vengeance shortly afterwards, so I asked Granny if she'd mind taking over at eleven o'clock, which she kindly did.

JFW and Pauline left at lunchtime. I think they enjoyed themselves, and hopefully it was worth the journey down from Perth. I went to bed after they'd left. Emerged at about 3 p.m.

Stomach pain was temporarily relieved with the administration of wine with Stuart in the evening.

Slept very badly.

Till total £16.99

2 customers

MONDAY, 30 JANUARY

Online orders: 1
Books found: 1

Up at 8 a.m. to find Stuart in the kitchen making an omelette for breakfast. Opened the shop and let the cat in. He was soaking wet, and clearly very annoyed that he'd had to spend time outside. I think he's forgotten where the cat flap is.

Young man with four Andrew Lang Fairy Books turned up with his partner and a baby at 11.30. I gave him £120 for them. The Fairy Book series was produced between 1889 and 1913, and each is a different colour, all with spectacularly gilt-illustrated front boards and spines. It is many a bookseller's dream to come across a complete set (twelve volumes) in fine condition, but this has only happened to me once, in 2003, when another dealer – urgently needing to pay off a few debts – sold me a set. I took them to a book fair in Lancaster University (along with many other things), and another dealer spotted them as I was setting up and offered me £600 for them, which I gladly took. That was the first and last book fair I went to, and the only complete set of Fairy Books I've ever seen.

Stuart left at noon, so I went back to bed again for a couple of hours, and left Granny in charge. I've been feeling ill for a while, but it's hard to disappear to bed when you have guests.

Anna went to Rigg Bay for a walk, then picked up a Chinese takeaway from the Chinese restaurant, the Unicorn in Newton Stewart for supper, which we ate at the kitchen table. Funny how the smell of takeaway food can cure a sore stomach.

Till total £63
6 customers

TUESDAY, 31 JANUARY

Online orders: 1
Books found: 1

Horrible, wet and windy day. Granny in at 9, Callum soon after.

Couldn't find today's order for a book about Latvian art, so I asked Granny to look for it. She found it in the mountaineering section. I have no idea what possessed her to look there.

Photographed the *Green Fairy Book* and posted the picture on Facebook. Listed the others on Monsoon.

Left for a book deal at 3 p.m. in Crossmichael – a deceased estate belonging to someone called Shapeero. Bungalow in the middle of nowhere. I was met by the lawyer, Neil, and his wife, Margaret, whose name I recognised from the Random Book Club. The house was modern and light, despite the greyness of the day. Some interesting books on architecture. She had been a seamstress and he'd been an architect. They'd died without issue and had left the books in the hands of the solicitor, the books to be sold and the money divided between three charities. Neil said that dealing with three charities is far worse than dealing with three children as far as inheritance is concerned.

Home just after five. There's still a little light in the sky now, at that time of day. Granny was in a foul mood for some reason. I think it's her knees. Or her elbow.

Till total £63
6 customers

FEBRUARY

We may expect to see American book stores opened in all our chief
centres and their windows filled with an array of books on every
subject offered to the British public at the uniform factory price of,
say, one and elevenpence and a halfpenny per volume.

Authors, publishers and booksellers of the old school would be
extinct within a year if the factory idea could be carried out.

R. M. Williamson, *Bits from an Old Bookshop*

I don't really think an explanation of where this is going is required
– nor need I probably say any more than Williamson did in 1904
when it comes to monopolistic American booksellers driving the
rest of us to penury. Although Williamson could scarcely have
imagined that an online bookseller would make so much money
(and pay so little tax) that he could be fired above the Kármán line,
and technically into space, sadly to return.

The extract is from Williamson's final chapter, which is titled
'THE PAINS AND PLEASURES OF BEING AN AUTHOR'.
Earlier in the book, he refers to a spat between Samuel Richardson
and Henry Fielding: 'Fielding, the author of *Joseph Andrews*,
ridiculed the "puny Cockney bookseller pouring out endless
volumes of sentimental twaddle" and called him "a moll-coddle
and a milksop". Richardson retorted by – "Had he not known
Fielding, he would have believed the author of *Joseph Andrews*
to have been an ostler."' If you dare to put your head above the
parapet of print, you can reasonably expect a few slings and arrows,
but whereas Richardson and Fielding's disagreement was reasonably intelligent and entertaining, the online 'American book stores'
afford their customers the luxury of unfettered critical invective.
And while historical criticism seems to have been between authors,
now everyone's a critic. Two of the most unintentionally hilarious
reviews of my literary efforts have come from fellow booksellers,
one from Hay-on-Wye (he had a very slender grasp of punctua-
tion) and another whose one-star review reads:

> I have been looking forward to reading this book for some time
> – I don't like hardbacks, so I waited for the paperback. What a

letdown!! I was expecting Adam Kay's 'This is going to hurt' in bookshop format, and was severely disappointed. This is literally what it says on the cover – a diary. As a bookseller myself, we have some pearlers in during the day, not just the customer requests, but moments with other staff, hiccups in deliveries and just general issues coming from working in retail – just one of my days at work is more interesting than this book! I feel that this could have really been something special, but instead was just one man who wanted to share his dull life with others!

Well, reviewer, you didn't write a book, but it's not too late to hear about your pearlers, your moments with other staff and your general issues. They sound side-splitting – the hiccups in deliveries, particularly. Please, let's hear about one of your days at work. If James Joyce could make 265,000 words out of a book whose narrative spans just a single day, I'm sure you can do better.

WEDNESDAY, I FEBRUARY

Online orders: 2
Books found: 2

Two orders to the same customer: the Andrew Lang Fairy Books which came in on Monday and which I'd listed on Monsoon yesterday.

Quiet day in the shop until a man came in at 4 p.m. and bought £70 worth of architecture books, all Pevsners. Nikolaus Pevsner was born just two years before Williamson's book was published – in 1902. He wrote a forty-six-volume set of highly regarded architectural histories called *The Buildings of England*. They've been reprinted numerous times, and are still collected.

The two women who are running The Open Book came in at 4 p.m. and introduced themselves as Fern and Heather, which could pass for a description of the flora of most of upland Scotland.

Till total £152
7 customers

THURSDAY, 2 FEBRUARY

Online orders: 1
Books found: 0

Grey, windy day. There was a cold draught whistling through the shop, so I lit the fire.

A friend of my parents (resident of Bladnoch, which he, along with most English people, pronounces as 'Bladnock') came in with two gardening books to sell. They weren't worth anything. Bladnoch, which is only a mile from Wigtown, is almost entirely populated by English people, mostly retired. Callum has a theory, which I think is probably correct, that there aren't many languages in which the 'ch', so common in Scottish words, is pronounced as a sound which comes from the back of the throat. It's common in Dutch, and a few Scandinavian languages, but doesn't appear to exist south of the border. We spent half an hour talking about salmon fishing. He's a thoroughly charming man, and wants to take a rod on the River Minnoch.

At two o'clock a woman came in to sell copies of a children's book that she has just written and self-published. Reluctantly took two copies.

At 2.30 a man came in and told me that he has 'wheelbarrows full of books' that he inherited from his great-aunt. He's moved to Wigtown and has bought Barbados Villa, a grand old merchant's house whose name was changed to Dunure a few decades ago in an attempt to disguise the fact that it was built from money made on the back of the slave trade.

Granny took a telephone call from someone called Neil Armstrong. She immediately assumed it was a crank call, but thankfully gave him the benefit of the doubt. He turned out to be a journalist writing a piece about Britain's best bookshops. I spoke with him for a few minutes, then agreed to email him a photo of the oldest book in the shop at the moment, which is *Historia Ecclesiastica de Martyrio Fratrum Ordinis Minorum Divi Francisci*, published in 1583. Neil Armstrong isn't an unusual name in Scotland. There's a local farmer with the same name. His nickname is Space.

Sudden flurry of activity at about three o'clock when a dozen or so people came into the shop within five minutes. None of them bought anything.

Power cut at 3.30, just as a man came in with two boxes of books from a local house. They were mainly books about the Lake District. He wandered around the shop in the dark while I went through them by candlelight. Gave him £40 for what I wanted from them. Locked up as soon as he'd gone at four o'clock. Power came back on at 4.50, but there was no point in opening up again.

Till total £28.50
5 customers

FRIDAY, 3 FEBRUARY

Online orders: 1
Books found: 1

Beautiful sunny day – cold and crisp, the way that I remember the winters of my childhood. I'm sure they are false memories, though, and the winters of the 1970s were probably just as damp and grey as they are today.

At 10 a.m. Bob dropped off a tray of blue eggs.

Sheila came in at 10.30 to see if we had any international mail. We didn't.

Sandy the tattooed pagan came round at about two o'clock and spent an hour chatting to the only other customer in the shop about the role of ceremony in religion.

Found a copy of *The Modern Gasoline Automobile*, up-to-date 1916 edition.

Closed the shop and went for supper with friends who live near Whithorn, about twenty minutes away, with Tom and Willeke (Tom drove). Home just before midnight.

Till total £69
7 customers

SATURDAY, 4 FEBRUARY

Online orders: 0
Books found: 0

Wet start to the day, but it brightened up at eleven o'clock. There was no sign of Granny at the bus stop when I opened the shop.

Kate the postie came in with a pile of bills at 10 a.m., and with it the news that the post office is closed today because William's mother seems to be close to death in the palliative care unit of Newton Stewart hospital, and Wilma's mother has had a stroke and is unconscious, leaving nobody qualified to run the post office. Despite William's almost complete lack of charm, his mother is a lovely woman – kind, friendly and interested in her customers. I'm sorry to hear that she is ill. The news of her condition didn't stop several people coming into the shop and complaining bitterly that they'd driven in from Garlieston, which is 8 miles away. As Kate pointed out, it's only a further 7 miles to Newton Stewart where there is another post office.

A man with combat trousers and a grey ponytail came in at 11.30 and asked if I knew every book I had in stock. I told him that I didn't and asked what he was looking for. He told me it was

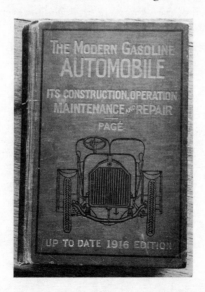

a book called *The Family*. When I asked him what sort of book it was, he became extremely cagey and eventually said, 'It's about Charles Manson.' I told him that if we have a copy it will be in the crime section. Five minutes later a woman who was identically dressed, down to the ponytail, came in and stood in front of the counter looking confused. There were three other people in the shop, but it was so obvious that they were together that I coughed to attract her attention and told her that she'd find him in the crime section. A minute later they left the shop together. On their way out of the shop he told me that we didn't have a copy. I'm glad. He looked as though he might have been looking for it as a template for how to start a cult.

There was nobody in the shop at 4.30, so I closed up. The street was empty too, and it had begun to rain. The only other living creature I could see was a dog, tied to a lamp post, barking.

Till total £136
15 customers

EPILOGUE

A few years have passed since I wrote this diary in 2016. I'm now married and have a daughter, and another child on the way. I've since turned fifty, as have most of my friends. Everyone seems to have married: Tracy and Chris, and Granny, who I'm now obliged to refer to as Manu and who is now married to Callum. Pete is back home. Others have parted company.

The years between 2019 and 2022, especially, have been curious, and I have no doubt that everyone is completely fed up of reading about how miserable the pandemic was. I feel slightly ashamed to admit that I absolutely adored it. I was forced to shut the shop. The first lockdown from March 2020 was like a three-month holiday in the place I love the most in the world, with the people I love most, during the finest spring I can ever remember. The 5-mile travel limit imposed by the government – while it didn't reach as far as Barnard Castle – still allowed us to visit beaches, lochs, rivers and bluebell woods, to pick wild garlic and to shout across garden fences to friends and neighbours while we barbecued one another's pets.

Captain is still alive. Global hysteria has not dented his appetite, nor has it dented the public's appetite for books. If anything, it has had the opposite effect. The shop has never been so busy.

The sun still rises in the east, and sets in the west. The shop is still here.